Sammy Addy's Canon EOS R10 Guide to Smart Photography & Videography

Sammy Addy

Disclaimer

This book, *Sammy Addy's Canon EOS R10 Guide to Smart Photography & Videography*, is an **independent educational guide** created to help users understand and operate the Canon EOS R6 Mark III camera.

This book is **not affiliated with, endorsed by, sponsored by, or approved by Canon Inc.** or any of its subsidiaries. Canon®, EOS®, and all related names, logos, and trademarks are the property of their respective owners and are used in this book **solely for identification and instructional purposes**.

The information provided in this book is based on practical use, research, and user experience. While every effort has been made to ensure accuracy and clarity, camera firmware updates, settings options, or operational behavior may change over time. The author and publisher **do not guarantee that all information will remain current or error-free**.

This book is intended for **educational purposes only**. The author and publisher shall not be held responsible for any damage to equipment, data loss, personal injury, or other issues resulting from the use or misuse of information contained in this book. Readers are encouraged to follow official safety instructions provided by the manufacturer and to use the camera responsibly.

By using this book, the reader acknowledges that **all camera operation decisions are made at their own discretion and risk**.

Introduction

PART 1 — Getting to Know Your Canon EOS R10

1.1 What Is in the Box

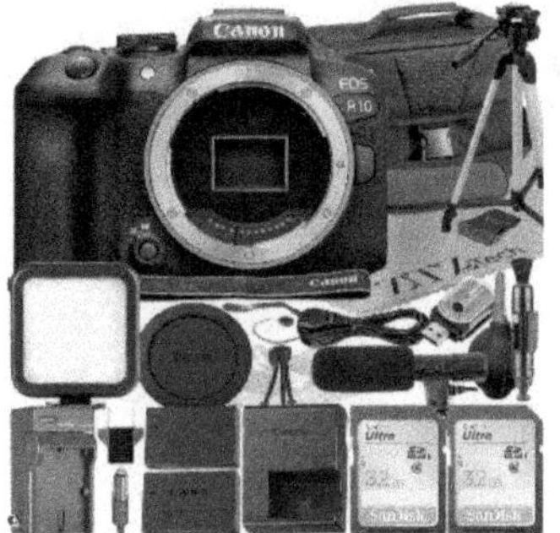

When you open your Canon EOS R10 box for the first time, you will find the following items. Take everything out carefully and lay them on a flat surface so you can identify each one before you begin.

Canon EOS R10 Camera Body

This is the main camera. It is a compact mirrorless camera with a black body, a grip on the right side for your hand, and a large circular opening at the front called the lens mount. The camera does not come with a lens attached — the lens mount will have a white plastic protective cap covering it called the body cap. Do not remove this cap until you are ready to attach a lens.

Battery LP-E17 (Rechargeable Lithium-Ion)

This is a small, flat, black rectangular battery. You will find the model name **LP-E17** printed on its surface. This battery powers the camera. It is not pre-charged from the factory, so you must charge it fully before your first use. Do not use any battery other than the LP-E17 in this camera — other batteries can damage the camera or cause safety issues.

How to identify it: It has a grey plastic sliding cover over its gold contact pins. Slide this cover off before inserting the battery into the charger or camera.

Battery Charger LC-E17 or LC-E17E

This is the device used to charge the LP-E17 battery. Depending on your region, you may receive the **LC-E17** (which has fold-out plug prongs built directly into the charger body) or the **LC-E17E** (which has a detachable power cord instead of built-in prongs).

How to use it:

1. Slide the battery into the charger with the orange-marked end inserted first, facing the charger's contact pins.
2. Push the battery in until it clicks and locks.
3. Plug the charger into a standard wall power outlet.
4. A small indicator lamp on the charger will glow **orange** while the battery is charging.
5. The lamp turns **green** when charging is complete — this takes approximately 2 hours for a fully depleted battery.

Important: Remove the battery from the charger once it is fully charged. Do not leave it plugged in indefinitely.

Interface Cable IFC-600PCU (USB-C)

This is a cable with a **USB-C connector** on one end and a **standard USB-A connector** on the other end. It is used to connect the camera directly to a computer for transferring images and videos, or for charging the camera battery inside the camera using a compatible USB power adapter.

How to identify it: It is relatively short (approximately 80 cm / 31 inches), with the smaller oval USB-C plug going into the camera and the larger rectangular USB-A plug going into your computer or charger.

Where to plug it in: The USB-C port is located on the **left side of the camera**, behind a rubber protective flap. Open the flap gently by pulling it toward you to access the port.

Eyecup ER-h (Viewfinder Cushion)

This is a small soft rubber cup that fits around the electronic viewfinder eyepiece at the back of the camera. Its purpose is to provide a comfortable seal around your eye when you look through the viewfinder, which also helps block out surrounding light for a clearer view.

How to check it: The eyecup is already attached to the camera when it ships. If it ever becomes detached or worn out, you can purchase a replacement ER-h from Canon or a camera retailer.

To remove it: Grip the eyecup and slide it upward firmly — it slides off the top of the viewfinder housing.

To reattach it: Align the bottom clips with the viewfinder housing and slide it back down until it locks.

Neck Strap EM-200DB

This is a fabric camera strap that attaches to the two strap lugs on the left and right sides of the camera body. It allows you to carry the camera around your neck or over your shoulder safely.

How to attach it:

1. Thread one end of the strap through the strap lug on one side of the camera (the small metal triangle fixed to the camera body).
2. Feed the strap end through the plastic buckle, then back through the strap keeper loop.
3. Pull firmly to tighten and secure.
4. Repeat on the opposite side of the camera.
5. Tug both ends to confirm the strap is secure before hanging the camera from it.

Important: Always attach both ends of the strap before using it to carry the camera. Never carry the camera by a single attached end.

Camera Cover R-F-4 (Body Cap)

This is the circular white plastic cap that covers the lens mount on the front of the camera when no lens is attached. Its purpose is to keep dust, moisture, and debris out of the camera body and away from the sensor.

How to remove it (when attaching a lens):

1. Hold the camera in front of you with the lens mount facing you.
2. Press the **Lens Release Button** — the small silver button located to the left of the lens mount at the front of the camera.
3. While holding the release button, rotate the body cap **counter-clockwise** until it comes free.
4. Set it aside in a safe place.

How to reattach it (when removing a lens):

1. Align the white dot on the body cap with the white dot on the camera's lens mount.
2. Insert the cap and rotate it **clockwise** until it clicks and locks.

Keep this cap: Always place this cap back on the camera whenever a lens is not attached. Even a few minutes of exposure can allow dust to settle on the sensor.

Instruction Manual and Warranty Card

The box includes a printed **Quick Reference Guide** (a small folded booklet) and a **Warranty Card** specific to your region.

About the manual: The quick guide covers only the most basic operations. Canon provides the full, detailed instruction manual as a **PDF download** from their official website. To find it:

1. Go to **canon.com** in your web browser.
2. Search for **EOS R10 instruction manual**.
3. Download the PDF — it is over 500 pages and covers every feature in Canon's own technical language.

This user guide you are reading now is designed to replace that dense technical document with plain-English, step-by-step directions.

The Warranty Card: Fill in your purchase date and retailer name and keep it in a safe place. Register your camera on Canon's website for full warranty coverage and access to firmware update notifications.

✎ **NOTE — What Is NOT in the Box:** Two essential items are **not included** and must be purchased separately before you can use the camera:

1. A Memory Card The Canon EOS R10 uses **SD, SDHC, or SDXC** memory cards. For best performance — especially for video recording and burst photography — choose a card rated **UHS Speed Class 3 (marked U3)** or **Video Speed Class 30 (marked V30)** or higher. A capacity of **64GB or 128GB** is recommended for most users.

2. A Lens The R10 uses **Canon RF mount** lenses natively. If you own older Canon EF or EF-S lenses, you can use them with a **Canon Mount Adapter EF-**

EOS R (sold separately). Without a lens attached, the camera cannot take photographs.

1.2 Full Camera Body Tour

Before you start using the Canon EOS R10, take a few minutes to become familiar with where everything is physically located on the camera. This section walks you through every part of the camera body, face by face, so that whenever a step later in this guide says "press the MENU button" or "rotate the Main Dial," you will know exactly where to look and what to touch without any confusion.

Pick up your camera now and hold it naturally in your right hand, with your fingers curled around the grip and your thumb resting on the back. Keep it in front of you as you read through each part below.

Front of the Camera

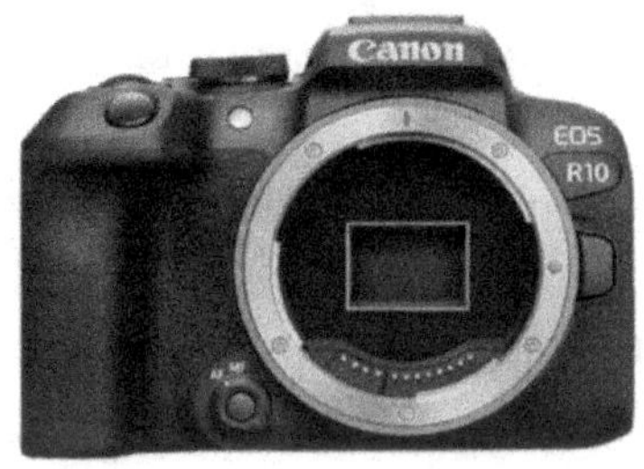

Hold the camera so the lens mount is facing you. This is the front face of the camera.

Lens Mount (RF Mount)

This is the large, circular, silver-rimmed opening at the centre of the front face. This is where your lens attaches. Inside the mount you will see the camera's sensor behind a thin curtain — do not touch this area with your fingers. Around the inner edge of the mount you will notice a row of electrical contacts. These small gold pins allow the camera and lens to communicate with each other, transmitting focus commands, aperture settings, and stabilisation data. On the very inside of the mount rim you will also see a small white dot. This white dot is your lens alignment marker — you will use it every time you attach a lens.

Lens Release Button

Look to the left of the lens mount as you face the front of the camera. You will see a small, oval-shaped silver button sitting flush against the camera body. This is the Lens Release Button. Its only purpose is to unlock the lens so you can remove it. To remove a lens, you press and hold this button while rotating the lens counter-clockwise until it comes free. You will learn the full process in

Section 2.4. Never try to pull or twist a lens off without pressing this button first — doing so can damage both the lens and the camera mount.

No Built-In Flash

Unlike many entry-level cameras, the Canon EOS R10 does not have a built-in pop-up flash. There is no flash window on the front of this camera and no flash that rises from the top. If you want to use flash, you will need to attach an external Speedlite to the hot shoe on top of the camera (covered in Section 10). Some photographers see this as a limitation, but it also means the camera body is more compact and the top panel stays clean and uninterrupted.

AF-Assist Beam and Self-Timer Lamp

Near the upper-left area of the front face, you will see a small rectangular window — it looks like a tiny dark orange or red lens set into the body. This window serves two functions depending on the situation.

Its first function is the AF-Assist Beam. When you are trying to focus in a dark environment and the camera cannot lock focus on its own, it emits a brief pattern of light from this window to illuminate the subject just enough for the autofocus system to find contrast and lock on. This happens automatically — you do not need to activate it manually. It only fires when needed during a half-press of the shutter button.

Its second function is the Self-Timer Lamp. When you are using any of the self-timer drive modes (where the camera counts down before taking a photo), this same window blinks red during the countdown and glows solid red in the final two seconds before the shutter fires. This lets you and others in the scene know that the photo is about to be taken.

Grip

On the right side of the front face there is a raised, contoured section covered in a textured rubber material. This is the grip. It is shaped to fit the natural curve of your right hand when you hold the camera. Your middle finger, ring finger, and little finger curl around the front of the grip, your index finger rests on top near the shutter button, and your thumb rests on the back of the camera. The grip is deep enough to hold the camera securely with one hand, though you should always support the lens from below with your left hand when shooting.

Stereo Microphone (Front)

On the front face of the camera, near the top edge on the left side, you will see two very small holes side by side. These are the front-facing stereo microphone inlets. They capture ambient sound when you are recording video. Because they are on the front of the camera, they pick up sound from the direction the lens is pointing, which is generally what you want for video. However, they also pick up any mechanical noise from the camera itself — autofocus motor sounds, button presses, and handling noise. For serious video work, connecting an external microphone (see the Left Side section below) is strongly recommended.

Top of the Camera

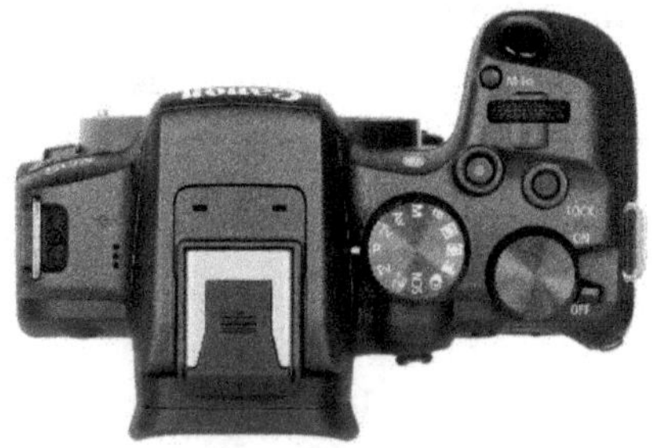

Now tilt the camera so you are looking down at the top surface. You will find most of your primary shooting controls here.

ON/OFF Switch

Surrounding the base of the shutter button you will see a two-position rotating collar. This is the ON/OFF switch. Rotate it clockwise to the ON position to power the camera on — the rear LCD screen or electronic viewfinder will activate. Rotate it back counter-clockwise to the OFF position to power the camera down. When you power the camera off, it saves your current settings before shutting down, so your preferences are always retained between sessions.

Shutter Button

This is the large, round, slightly concave button at the top-right of the camera, sitting inside the ON/OFF collar. The shutter button has two distinct stages of pressure and you need to learn both.

Half-press means pressing the button down gently, about halfway, until you feel a soft resistance. When you half-press, the camera activates autofocus and takes an exposure reading. A confirmation signal — either a green dot or a beep — tells you the camera has locked focus. You should always half-press first before taking any photo.

Full-press means continuing to press the button all the way down until the photo is taken. The shutter fires and the image is saved to your memory card. The entire motion from half-press to full-press should be smooth and deliberate — jabbing the button down quickly without the half-press stage is one of the most common causes of blurry or out-of-focus photos.

Main Dial

Directly behind the shutter button — positioned so that your right index finger can reach it without moving your hand — is a small, textured rotating wheel. This is the Main Dial. You rotate it with the pad of your index finger. What it controls depends on which shooting mode you are in. In Shutter Priority mode (Tv) it changes the shutter speed. In Aperture Priority mode (Av) it changes the aperture. In Manual mode (M) it changes the shutter speed. In the menu system it scrolls between the coloured tab categories across the top of the screen. You will use this dial constantly throughout your shooting, so it is worth getting comfortable rotating it in both directions smoothly.

Movie Record Button

Just to the left of the shutter button, slightly recessed into the top panel, is the Movie Record Button. It is a small round button surrounded by a red ring — the red ring makes it easy to find by feel. Press it once to begin recording video, and press it again to stop. The camera does not need to be in a dedicated video mode to use this button — in most shooting modes, pressing the Movie Record Button will immediately begin recording. A red dot appears on the screen while recording is in progress.

Mode Dial

On the top-left of the camera is a large, ridged rotating dial. This is the Mode Dial and it is one of the most important controls on the camera. Rotating it selects your entire shooting mode — whether the camera is fully automatic, semi-automatic, or fully manual. Each position on the dial has a label printed beside it. You will need to physically rotate the dial with your thumb and index finger to move between modes. The dial clicks firmly into each position so you always know exactly which mode is selected.

The positions on the dial are: A+ (Scene Intelligent Auto), P (Program AE), Tv (Shutter Priority), Av (Aperture Priority), M (Manual), Fv (Flexible Priority), SCN (Scene modes), a Creative Filters icon, and a video camera icon. Each of these modes is explained in full in Part 5 of this guide.

M-Fn Button (Multi-Function Button)

Just in front of the Mode Dial — on the very top edge of the camera, closer to you as you hold it — is a small, low-profile button. This is the M-Fn Button, which stands for Multi-Function. Pressing and holding this button while rotating the Main Dial lets you quickly cycle through and change a set of common settings without opening any menu. By default, those settings are ISO sensitivity, White Balance, Drive Mode, AF Operation, and Flash Exposure Compensation. Think of it as a shortcut that keeps your hands on the camera and your eye at the viewfinder. The exact functions it controls can also be customised in the Custom Controls menu, which is covered in Part 16.

Hot Shoe

Between the Mode Dial and the top of the viewfinder housing, you will see a rectangular metal bracket recessed slightly into the top of the camera. This is the Hot Shoe. It provides both a physical mounting point and an electrical connection for external accessories. The most common accessory you would attach here is a Canon Speedlite external flash unit, which slides into the hot shoe from behind and locks in place with a rotating collar. The camera can then communicate with the flash to control power, timing, and exposure automatically. You can also mount other accessories such as microphones, wireless transmitters, or monitors in the hot shoe. When nothing is attached, the hot shoe sits empty and unprotected — some photographers place a small plastic hot shoe cover over it to keep dust out.

Stereo Microphone (Top)

On the top panel you will also find two more small holes, positioned symmetrically near the front edge. These are the top-mounted stereo microphone inlets. They work together with the front microphones to capture directional stereo audio during video recording. As with the front microphones, these pick up camera handling noise, so for clean audio in professional video work an external microphone is always preferable.

Back of the Camera

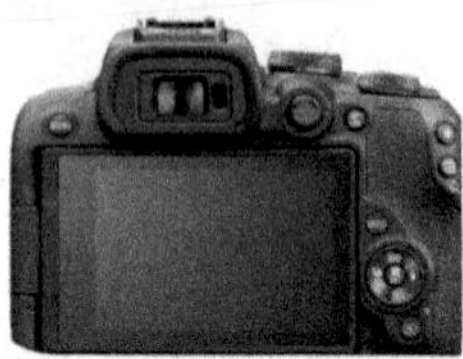

Now turn the camera around so you are looking at the back. This surface has the most controls of any face on the camera, so take your time working through each one.

Electronic Viewfinder (EVF)

In the upper-left area of the back, you will see a raised eyepiece with a rubber eyecup surrounding it. This is the Electronic Viewfinder, usually referred to as the EVF. Put your eye up to it — you will see a small, high-resolution display inside showing exactly what the camera's sensor is seeing in real time. This is your live view through the lens. The EVF shows your subject, the focus point, your exposure settings, and various shooting information all at once. Using the EVF instead of the rear screen is particularly useful outdoors in bright sunlight where the screen can be hard to see, and it also gives you a more stable shooting position because the camera is pressed against your face.

Diopter Adjustment Dial

On the right side of the EVF eyepiece housing — a very small dial recessed just beside the viewfinder — is the Diopter Adjustment Dial. Its purpose is to sharpen the image you see inside the EVF to match your particular eyesight. If the text and image inside the viewfinder appears blurry to you even when the subject is in focus, this is what needs adjusting. Rotate the dial slowly in small increments, looking through the EVF at a stationary subject with text or clear edges, until the display appears crisp and sharp. This is a personal setting — each person who uses the camera may need to adjust it for their own eyes. You only need to do this once, and the setting is retained indefinitely.

Eye Sensor

Below the EVF eyepiece there is a tiny sensor — a small dark window set into the camera body just below the rubber eyecup. This is the Eye Sensor. When it detects that something (your eye, your face, your hand) is close to the viewfinder, it automatically switches the display from the rear LCD screen to the EVF. When you move away, it switches back to the LCD screen. This switching happens automatically and nearly instantaneously. You can adjust how sensitive this sensor is, or disable it entirely and switch between EVF and LCD manually, by going to the Setup Menu and selecting Screen/Viewfinder display.

LCD Touch Screen

The large, dominant screen on the back of the camera is the LCD Touch Screen. It measures 3 inches diagonally and has a resolution of approximately 1.04 million dots. It shows your live view while shooting and displays images and videos during playback. It is fully touch-sensitive — you can tap the screen to move your focus point, tap a face to tell the camera to focus on it, and tap menu items to navigate. The screen can also be physically moved. It is mounted on a fully articulating hinge on the left side, meaning it can tilt upward for overhead shots, tilt downward for low-angle shots, and flip completely around to face forward for selfies or vlogging. To move the screen, hold the left edge and pull it outward gently, then rotate it to the position you need.

MENU Button

In the upper-left corner of the back panel, clearly labelled MENU, is a small rectangular button. Pressing this button opens the camera's full menu system, which contains hundreds of settings organised across colour-coded tabs. Every major camera setting that is not controlled by a physical dial or button lives inside this menu. The full menu system is covered in complete detail in Part 3 of this guide.

INFO Button

Directly below the MENU button, labelled INFO, is another small rectangular button. Pressing it cycles through different information display screens during both shooting and playback. While shooting, pressing INFO repeatedly cycles through: a clean display with no overlay information, a basic shooting information overlay, a detailed information screen showing all current settings, an electronic level display for checking if the camera is horizontally straight, and a histogram display showing the exposure distribution of the live scene. During playback, pressing INFO adds or removes data about the photo you are viewing, such as the shooting settings used, the histogram, and GPS data if recorded.

Q Button (Quick Control)

On the right side of the back panel, labelled with the letter Q, is the Quick Control button. Pressing it opens the Quick Control Screen, which is a grid of the most commonly adjusted settings displayed directly on the LCD. Instead of navigating deep into the menu, you can change Image Quality, White Balance, ISO, AF Mode, Drive Mode, Metering Mode, and more all from this single screen. Use the joystick or touch the screen to highlight a setting, then rotate the Main Dial or Quick Control Dial to change its value. The Quick Control screen is your fastest route to adjusting settings while shooting.

Playback Button

Below the Q button, marked with a white triangle (play icon), is the Playback Button. Press it at any time to review the photos and videos stored on your memory card. The most recently captured image appears first. Rotate the Main Dial or swipe left and right on the touch screen to move through your images. To exit playback and return to shooting mode, press the Playback button again or half-press the shutter button.

Delete Button

Below the Playback button, marked with a small trash can icon, is the Delete Button. During playback, press it once and a confirmation screen appears asking whether you want to cancel or delete the image. Press it a second time, or select Delete on screen, to permanently remove the image from your memory card. Deleted images cannot be recovered from within the camera, so always confirm before deleting. Protected images (marked with a lock icon) cannot be deleted even with this button — the camera simply ignores the command.

AF-ON Button

Near the upper-right of the back panel you will find a button labelled AF-ON. This button activates autofocus independently of the shutter button. When you press it, the camera begins to focus, just as if you had half-pressed the shutter. Many experienced photographers use this for a technique called back-button focus, where they assign all focusing to this button and use the shutter button only to take the photo. This separation allows you to focus on a subject, hold the focus lock with your thumb, recompose the shot, and then press the shutter — all without losing the focus. Back-button focus takes some practice to get used to but becomes highly effective once learned. It is explained in detail in Part 6.

AE Lock / FE Lock Button (★)

Just to the left of the AF-ON button is a button marked with a star symbol (★). This is the AE Lock and FE Lock button. AE stands for Auto Exposure and FE stands for Flash Exposure.

When you press this button during shooting, the camera locks its current exposure reading — meaning the brightness of the photo will be fixed at that level even if you move the camera to recompose. The asterisk symbol (*) appears on the display to confirm the lock is active. This is useful when your subject is positioned against a very bright or very dark background that would otherwise confuse the camera's metering.

When an external flash is attached, pressing this button fires a small pre-flash to measure the flash exposure, and locks that reading for the next shot.

Magnify Button (+)

Near the upper area of the back panel there is a button marked with a magnifying glass and a plus sign (+). During playback, pressing this button zooms into the currently displayed image. Each press zooms in further, up to a maximum of approximately 10x magnification. Once zoomed in, use the joystick to move around the image and inspect different areas for sharpness. This is the standard way to check whether a photo is acceptably sharp after shooting.

Reduce Button (–)

Paired with the Magnify button is the Reduce button, marked with a minus sign (–). During playback, it zooms back out. Pressing it repeatedly reduces magnification until the image returns to its standard single-image view. Pressing it once more from the standard single view switches to a thumbnail index display showing multiple images at once — useful for quickly scanning through a large number of shots.

SET Button

At the very centre of the large textured ring on the back of the camera is a round button labelled SET. This is the confirm button — the equivalent of pressing Enter on a keyboard. Whenever a menu is open and you have highlighted an option you want to select, press SET to confirm it. When adjusting settings on the Quick Control screen, pressing SET opens a more detailed control panel for the highlighted setting. In shooting mode, pressing SET can be customised to perform a function of your choice via the Custom Controls menu.

Navigation Ring / Quick Control Dial

Surrounding the SET button is a large, textured rotating ring. This is the Quick Control Dial, also called the Navigation Ring. You rotate it with your right thumb. In the menu system, rotating it scrolls up and down through the list of items in the current menu tab. On the Quick Control screen, it changes the value of the highlighted setting. In shooting mode, it typically adjusts exposure compensation — making the photo brighter or darker. In Manual mode, rotating it changes the aperture value. This ring is one of the most-used controls on the camera and it is positioned precisely where your thumb rests naturally.

Multi-Controller (Joystick)

Between the AF-ON button and the SET ring you will find a very small raised nub — a tiny thumb-operated stick that can be pushed in eight directions. This is the Multi-Controller, also called the joystick. During shooting, pushing it in any direction moves the active autofocus point across the frame so you can place it exactly where you want to focus. In the menu system, pushing it up, down, left, and right navigates between items. During zoomed-in playback, it pans around the image. The Multi-Controller is particularly valued by photographers who use single-point AF, since it allows fast, precise repositioning of the focus point without taking your eye away from the viewfinder.

Left Side of the Camera

With the camera facing you, the left side is the panel facing your right. Flip open the rubber protective flap that runs along this side to reveal the connection ports underneath.

USB-C Port (Digital Terminal)

The top port on this side, beneath the protective flap, is a USB-C port. The USB-C plug from the included Interface Cable IFC-600PCU connects here. You use this connection for two purposes: transferring photos and videos directly to a computer, and charging the camera battery while it remains inside the camera using a compatible USB power adapter or power bank. This is the only charging option other than removing the battery and placing it in the dedicated charger. When connected to a computer, the camera appears as a removable storage device and you can drag image files off it, or use Canon's EOS Utility software for more control.

HDMI Mini Port

Below the USB-C port, also beneath the protective flap, is a smaller port. This is the HDMI Mini output port. Using an HDMI mini-to-standard HDMI cable (not included), you can connect the camera to a television, computer monitor, or external video recorder. When connected, the camera's live view and playback display appear on the external screen. This is used most commonly for showing a group of people your photos on a larger screen, for outputting clean video to an external recorder while shooting, or for monitoring the live view on a large display.

External Microphone Terminal (3.5mm)

At the bottom of this same side panel, behind a separate small rubber cap, is a standard 3.5mm stereo mini-jack port. This is where you connect an external microphone for video recording. Plugging a microphone into this port automatically disables the camera's built-in microphones and routes all audio recording through the external mic instead. Any standard 3.5mm microphone is compatible. Shotgun microphones that mount on the hot shoe and connect via a cable to this port are the most popular choice for video, as they are directional and pick up sound from directly in front of the camera while rejecting noise from the sides.

Right Side of the Camera

This is the panel on your left as you hold the camera normally. It has a single door on it.

SD Card Slot Door

The entire right side panel is dominated by a hinged door covering the memory card compartment. To open it, find the small ridged tab at the top-right of the door, grip it, and slide it downward — it springs open. Inside you will see a single SD card slot. The Canon EOS R10 accepts SD, SDHC, and SDXC memory cards in all standard sizes. Push a card in label-side facing toward the back of the camera, with the notched corner of the card going in first, until you feel and hear it click into place. To remove the card, push it inward gently until it pops out partway, then pull it free. Never open this door while the camera is writing to the card — a small light on the back of the camera flickers orange during write operations. Opening the door mid-write can corrupt the card and lose the images being saved.

Bottom of the Camera

Turn the camera upside down to see the base plate.

Battery Compartment Door

The large door on the bottom of the camera covers the battery compartment. To open it, locate the small sliding lock switch on the edge of the door. Slide this switch sideways (toward the edge of the camera) while simultaneously pulling the door downward and outward — it swings open on a hinge. Inside you will see the battery slot. The battery LP-E17 inserts with the gold contact pins going in first and the label facing you, and it clicks into a lock when fully seated. To remove the battery, press the small release lever inside the compartment sideways while pulling the battery out. The door can stay open while the battery is being charged inside the camera via USB, but should be closed whenever the camera is in normal use to protect the contacts.

Tripod Socket

At the base of the camera, slightly offset toward the right (toward the grip side), you will see a metal-threaded hole. This is the Tripod Socket. It uses the universal 1/4-inch 20 UNC thread standard, which is the fitting used by virtually all tripods, monopods, and camera plates sold anywhere in the world. Screw any standard tripod head's mounting bolt into this socket clockwise to secure the camera to the tripod. Do not overtighten — firm hand-tight is sufficient. Many camera bags include a quick-release plate that attaches permanently to this socket, allowing you to snap the camera on and off a tripod head in seconds.

> **Note:** *Now that you have identified every part of the camera body, keep the camera in your hand as you continue to the next section. The more you handle it and locate these controls by feel, the faster and more natural your shooting will become.*

1.3 The Electronic Viewfinder (EVF) and LCD Screen

The Canon EOS R10 gives you two ways to see what the camera is seeing before you take a photo: the Electronic Viewfinder and the rear LCD touch screen. Both show the same live image from the sensor in real time, but they serve different purposes and work best in different situations. Understanding both, and knowing when to switch between them, will immediately make you a more comfortable shooter.

The Electronic Viewfinder (EVF)

The EVF is the small eyepiece at the upper-left of the back panel that you look through by bringing the camera up to your eye. Inside it is a high-resolution miniature display, 2.36 million dots, that shows you a live, real-time preview of exactly what the lens is seeing at that exact moment. Because this preview is electronic rather than optical, it is not merely a window — it is a fully processed image that reflects your current exposure settings, white balance, and picture style as they will actually appear in the final photograph. If you increase the ISO and the image gets brighter on screen, that is exactly how bright the photo will be. This what-you-see-is-what-you-get quality is one of the most powerful advantages of a mirrorless camera like the R10 over older DSLR designs.

Along with the live image, the EVF also displays all of your shooting information in a heads-up style overlay. Depending on which INFO display mode is active, you will see your current shutter speed, aperture, ISO, exposure compensation level, battery level, memory card status, AF point position, focus confirmation indicator, drive mode icon, white balance setting, and more. All of this information is visible while your eye is at the viewfinder, so you never need to pull the camera away from your face to check a setting.

Shooting through the EVF rather than the rear screen offers several practical advantages. In bright outdoor sunlight, the rear LCD screen can be very difficult to see clearly, while the EVF is unaffected by ambient light because your eye is pressed against the eyecup and shielded from the surroundings. Using the EVF also gives the camera a third point of contact with your body — your face — in addition to both hands, which makes for a much more stable hold and reduces camera shake, particularly at slower shutter speeds. Many photographers find that images taken through the EVF are consistently sharper than those taken at arm's length using the rear screen, for exactly this reason.

The EVF activates automatically when the camera detects your eye approaching it, thanks to the small proximity sensor just below the eyepiece. You do not need to press any button to switch to the EVF. Simply bring the camera to your eye and the EVF turns on within a fraction of a second.

The LCD Touch Screen

The rear LCD screen is a 3.0-inch fully articulating touch panel with a resolution of 1.04 million dots. It is mounted on the left side of the camera body on a multi-axis hinge that allows it to move in three distinct ways.

To open the screen from its flat closed position, hold the left edge and pull it straight outward away from the camera body. Once it is extended on its hinge, you can tilt it upward — rotating the screen face up so it points toward the sky — for shooting from low angles without lying on the ground. You can tilt it downward — rotating it so the screen faces down at roughly 45 degrees — for overhead shots where you hold the camera above your head. You can also rotate it fully around, flipping the screen to face forward in the same direction as the lens, which is how it is used for self-portraits and vlogging. In this forward-facing position the screen shows you a mirror image of the live view so you can frame yourself naturally.

The touch screen works in the same way as a smartphone screen. You can tap any face or subject on the screen and the camera will immediately move its focus point to that location and begin tracking it. You can tap menu items to select them rather than using the navigation buttons. You can swipe left or right during playback to move between images, pinch inward with two fingers to zoom out, and spread two fingers apart to zoom in. Double-tapping a photo during playback zooms it to 100 percent for a quick sharpness check.

While the touch screen is the most natural and intuitive way to interact with the camera for many people, it does have one practical limitation: operating it at arm's length while trying to simultaneously frame a moving subject is inherently less stable than using the EVF. For static subjects, landscapes, or any situation where you have time to compose carefully, the rear screen is excellent. For fast-moving subjects, sports, wildlife, or any situation requiring maximum stability, the EVF is the better choice.

Cycling Through Display Modes with the INFO Button

Both the EVF and the LCD screen support multiple display modes, and you switch between them by pressing the INFO button on the back of the camera. Each press of INFO cycles forward to the next display mode. The available modes during shooting are as follows.

The first mode is the shooting information display. This is the standard view most photographers use day-to-day. It shows the live image filling most of the screen with a modest row of key shooting data along the bottom edge — shutter speed, aperture, ISO, exposure level, and a few status icons. It gives you the live image with just enough information visible to keep you informed without cluttering the frame.

The second mode is the detailed information display. This expands the shooting data overlay to show every active setting simultaneously — AF mode, white balance, drive mode, battery level, image quality setting, histogram, remaining shot count, and more. This view is useful when you want a full status check of the camera before beginning a shoot, but it can feel overwhelming during active shooting because so much text occupies the screen.

The third mode, available when you enable it in the menu, is the electronic level display. A graphical spirit level appears at the centre of the screen showing whether the camera is tilted left, right, or pitched forward and backward. This is particularly useful for architecture, landscape, and product photography where a straight horizon is essential. The indicator turns green when the camera is level in both axes.

The fourth mode is the no-information display. The live image fills the entire screen with no overlaid text, icons, or data at all. This is the cleanest view and is preferred by photographers who find on-screen information distracting during composition, or who want to evaluate the image as purely as possible before pressing the shutter.

During playback, pressing INFO repeatedly cycles through: a basic image view with just the file number and protection status shown, a shooting data overlay listing the settings used to take the photograph (shutter speed, aperture, ISO, lens focal length, date, and time), a histogram overlay showing the distribution of tones in the image so you can evaluate the exposure after the fact, and a no-information view of just the image.

> **Note:** *The INFO button cycles through display modes in one direction only — each press moves forward to the next mode. There is no way to go back to the previous mode without pressing INFO repeatedly until you cycle all the way around.*

How the EVF and LCD Screen Work Together

By default, the camera uses the eye sensor beside the EVF to automatically decide which display to use. When no eye is detected near the viewfinder, the rear LCD screen is active and showing the live view. The moment the sensor detects your eye approaching, it turns off the LCD screen and switches the display to the EVF. When you move your eye away, it switches back to the LCD. This transition happens in under half a second and is completely silent.

This automatic switching is the default behaviour and suits most users perfectly well. However, if you find the sensor triggering unexpectedly — for example, if something brushes past the viewfinder while the camera is hanging around your neck, accidentally activating the EVF — you can change this behaviour. To do so, press the MENU button, navigate to the yellow Setup tab, scroll to Screen/viewfinder display, and press SET. From here you can choose to keep the LCD screen always on regardless of the eye sensor, keep the EVF always on, or restore the automatic switching behaviour. You can also adjust the sensitivity of the eye sensor on the same screen.

> **Note:** *When the LCD screen is closed flat against the camera body with the screen face inward — a position sometimes used to protect the screen during transport — the eye sensor still controls the EVF normally. The EVF will activate when your eye approaches even with the LCD folded away. This is intentional and is not a fault.*

1.4 Understanding the Camera's Mode Ecosystem

Before you begin shooting, it helps enormously to understand what the different modes on your Canon EOS R10 are actually for and how they relate to each other. Many beginners feel overwhelmed looking at the Mode Dial and seeing a dozen unfamiliar labels. In reality, every mode on that dial fits into one of five clear categories, and once you understand what each category is trying to do, the individual modes begin to make immediate sense.

Think of the Mode Dial as a spectrum of control. At one end, the camera makes every decision for you. At the other end, you make every decision yourself. Everything in between is a negotiation — you control some things and the camera handles the rest. The category a mode falls into tells you exactly where on that spectrum it sits.

Fully Automatic Modes — The Camera Decides Everything

At the fully automatic end of the spectrum sits Scene Intelligent Auto, which is the mode marked A+ in green on the Mode Dial. When you rotate the dial to this position, the camera takes complete control of every exposure setting — shutter speed, aperture, ISO sensitivity, white balance, autofocus behaviour, and drive mode. It analyses the scene in front of it many times per second, determines what type of scene it is looking at (a portrait, a landscape, a moving subject, a low-light environment), and applies the settings it calculates will produce the best result.

In this mode, your only job is to point the camera at your subject and press the shutter button. You cannot override the camera's choices — there are no dials to turn or settings to adjust. This is the right mode for absolute beginners, for occasions when you simply need a photo quickly without thinking, or for handing the camera to someone else who has never used it.

The trade-off is creative control. Because the camera decides everything, you cannot force a blurry background, freeze a fast-moving subject, or create any particular visual effect deliberately. The camera will produce technically correct photos reliably, but they may not always match your creative intention.

Semi-Automatic Modes — A Partnership Between You and the Camera

The middle of the dial is occupied by three semi-automatic modes: P, Tv, and Av. These modes divide responsibility between you and the camera. You control one specific aspect of the exposure and the camera handles everything else. This gives you creative influence over the image while still providing a safety net.

Program AE, labelled P on the dial, lets the camera set both the shutter speed and the aperture, but you can then rotate the Main Dial to shift to a different combination of the two that produces the same overall exposure. You also retain full control over ISO, white balance, and other settings. P mode is the most flexible semi-automatic mode and is a good starting point for photographers who are just beginning to move away from fully automatic shooting.

Shutter Priority, labelled Tv on the dial (Tv stands for Time Value), puts you in charge of the shutter speed and leaves the aperture to the camera. This is the mode to use when controlling motion is your priority. Set a fast shutter speed — 1/500 second or faster — to freeze a subject in motion such as a child running, a bird in flight, or a ball being thrown. Set a slow shutter speed — 1/30 second or slower — to capture the blur of motion deliberately, such as a silky waterfall, light trails from cars at night, or the sense of speed in a panning shot. The camera will select whichever aperture produces a correct exposure at the shutter speed you have chosen.

Aperture Priority, labelled Av on the dial (Av stands for Aperture Value), puts you in charge of the aperture — the size of the opening inside the lens — and leaves the shutter speed to the camera. This is the mode most photographers use most of the time, because aperture directly controls depth of field, which is one of the most fundamental creative decisions in photography. A wide aperture (a small f-number such as f/1.8 or f/2.8) creates a sharp subject against a beautifully blurred background — the look most associated with professional portrait photography. A narrow aperture (a large f-number such as f/11 or f/16) brings everything from near to far into sharp focus simultaneously — the look of classic landscape photography. The camera will select a shutter speed to match the aperture you have chosen.

Manual Mode — You Control Everything

At the opposite end of the spectrum from Scene Intelligent Auto sits Manual mode, labelled M on the dial. In Manual mode, you set both the shutter speed and the aperture yourself. The camera meters the scene and shows you an exposure indicator on screen telling you whether your chosen settings will produce an image that is too bright, too dark, or correctly exposed, but it does not intervene — it takes the photo exactly as you have set it up, even if those settings would produce a very dark or very bright result.

Manual mode requires you to understand the relationship between shutter speed, aperture, and ISO well enough to balance them yourself. It is the most demanding mode to use but also the most powerful, because it gives you complete, repeatable control over every aspect of the exposure. It is the preferred mode for studio photography with flash, for night and astrophotography, for any situation where the lighting is consistent and you want every frame to be identically exposed, and for video recording where automatic exposure changes during a shot would be distracting.

A variant of Manual mode also exists on the R10 called Flexible Priority AE, labelled Fv on the dial. This mode allows you to set any combination of shutter speed, aperture, and ISO manually while leaving the settings you have not touched on automatic. You could, for example, set only the aperture and leave shutter speed and ISO on Auto, or set all three yourself for full manual control, or leave all three on Auto for the same result as Program mode. Fv mode is essentially one mode that can behave like all the others, which makes it useful for photographers who frequently switch between approaches.

Video Mode — A Separate World for Moving Images

The video camera icon on the Mode Dial switches the R10 into its dedicated video recording mode. While many of the same concepts — exposure, focus, white balance — apply equally to video as to photography, video has its own distinct set of settings, constraints, and considerations that are different enough to warrant an entirely separate mode.

In video mode, the camera records to your memory card in the MP4 format. You can choose between 4K resolution (3840 by 2160 pixels) and Full HD resolution (1920 by 1080 pixels), and you can select different frame rates within each resolution to achieve different looks and slow-motion effects. The menu system shows a separate set of video-specific settings when the camera is in this mode, and many of the photo-specific settings become unavailable.

Even if you have no immediate interest in recording video, it is worth knowing that the Movie Record Button on the top of the camera can begin recording from almost any shooting mode — not only when the Mode Dial is set to the video icon. However, the dedicated video mode gives you the most control over video-specific settings and is the right choice any time video is your primary goal.

Scene Modes and Creative Filters — Presets for Specific Situations

At the SCN position on the Mode Dial, the camera offers a collection of Scene modes — pre-programmed combinations of settings that are optimised for specific, common shooting situations. Selecting Portrait mode, for example, tells the camera to prioritise a wide aperture for background blur, smooth skin tones in the Picture Style, and continuous face-tracking autofocus. Selecting Sports mode tells the camera to use a fast shutter speed, high-speed continuous drive, and predictive subject-tracking autofocus. Each scene mode removes the need to think about individual settings for its intended situation.

Scene modes are not inferior to the semi-automatic and manual modes — they are simply a different approach. A photographer who understands Aperture Priority mode and a photographer who uses Portrait scene mode may produce nearly identical results in a standard portrait situation. Scene modes are particularly useful when you find yourself in an unfamiliar situation and want a sensible set of defaults applied quickly without having to think through each setting individually.

The Creative Filters mode, represented by a separate icon on the dial, offers a different type of preset. Rather than optimising the technical settings for a situation, Creative Filters apply artistic visual transformations to your images in camera: converting to black and white with added grain, applying a miniature tilt-shift effect that blurs the top and bottom of the frame to make scenes look like small models, simulating a fish-eye lens, creating a soft dreamy glow, and so on. Each filter produces an effect that would otherwise require software editing after the fact. Creative Filters are a way to experiment with different visual styles without any post-processing knowledge.

> **Note:** *As you work through the rest of this guide, you will encounter each of these modes in full detail. For now, the important thing to understand is the overall logic: more dial positions to the left of M mean more camera control, and the M position and Fv position mean more of your own control. No mode is the wrong choice — the right mode is always the one that helps you get the shot you are trying to get.*

PART 2 — First-Time Setup

This part walks you through everything you need to do before the Canon EOS R10 is ready to take its first photograph. Work through each section in order. By the end of section 2.7 your battery will be charged, your memory card will be formatted, your lens will be attached, and the camera will be configured with your language, date, time, and viewfinder set precisely to your eye.

2.1 Charging the Battery

The LP-E17 battery that came in the box is not charged. Before you do anything else, charge it fully. The Canon EOS R10 uses the dedicated LC-E17 charger included in the box. Do not put the battery into the camera yet.

What you need

The LP-E17 battery, the LC-E17 (or LC-E17E) charger that came in the box, and access to a wall power outlet.

Steps

1. Take the LP-E17 battery out of its packaging. On one end you will see a strip of orange plastic covering the gold contact pins — slide this orange cover off and set it aside. You will need it if you ever store the battery separately from the camera.
2. Hold the LC-E17 charger in front of you. On its face you will see a slot with two small metal contact pins at the back. This is where the battery slides in.
3. Orient the battery so the orange-marked end — the end where you just removed the cover — is facing toward the charger's contact pins. The LP-E17 label on the battery should be facing up.
4. Slide the battery into the charger slot, pushing the orange-marked end in first. Press it firmly until it locks into the slot with a click or snaps flush against the charger body.
5. If you received the LC-E17E model (the version with a detachable power cord rather than fold-out prongs), connect the power cord to the back of the charger now.

6. Plug the charger into a wall power outlet. The charge indicator lamp on the charger face lights up orange immediately. Orange means the battery is actively charging.
7. Leave the charger plugged in. A full charge from empty takes approximately two hours. When the lamp changes from orange to solid green, the battery is fully charged.
8. Unplug the charger from the wall. Press the battery release on the charger and slide the LP-E17 out. Replace the orange contact cover if you are not inserting the battery into the camera immediately.

Important: *Never charge the LP-E17 using any charger other than the LC-E17 or LC-E17E that Canon supplied with this camera. Third-party chargers do not regulate voltage correctly for this battery and can cause overheating, reduced battery life, or permanent damage to the battery or camera.*

Note: *While the battery is charging, continue to section 2.3 to prepare your SD card. You do not need to wait for the battery to finish charging before reading ahead.*

2.2 Inserting the Battery

Once the LP-E17 is fully charged, insert it into the Canon EOS R10 before powering the camera on for the first time.

Steps

9. Make sure the ON/OFF switch on the top of the camera is in the OFF position. The switch surrounds the shutter button — rotate it counter-clockwise to OFF if it is not already there. Never insert or remove the battery while the camera is switched on.
10. Turn the camera upside down so the base plate is facing up toward you.
11. Locate the battery compartment door. It is the large door that covers most of the base plate. On the edge of this door you will see a small sliding lock switch with a ridged surface.
12. Slide the lock switch sideways — push it toward the edge of the camera. While holding it there, pull the door outward and downward. It swings open on a hinge.
13. Hold the LP-E17 battery with the LP-E17 label facing toward you and the gold contact pins pointing into the compartment.

14. Insert the battery into the compartment contacts-first, following the direction indicated by the small diagram moulded into the inside of the compartment door. Push the battery straight in until you feel it click and the orange battery lock lever snaps over it.
15. Close the battery compartment door firmly and slide the lock switch back to its original position to secure it. Give the door a gentle tug to confirm it is locked shut.

Note: *The battery level indicator appears on the LCD screen and in the EVF whenever the camera is on. A full battery is shown as a solid white rectangle. As charge decreases, the icon empties and eventually blinks to warn you that the battery needs replacing soon.*

2.3 Inserting and Formatting the SD Card

The Canon EOS R10 stores all photos and videos on an SD memory card. The card is not included in the box and must be purchased separately. The camera accepts SD, SDHC, and SDXC cards. For general photography a UHS Speed Class 1 card (marked U1) is adequate. For 4K video recording and high-speed burst shooting, use a UHS Speed Class 3 card (marked U3) or a Video Speed Class 30 card (marked V30) or faster. A capacity of 64 GB or 128 GB suits most users.

Inserting the Card

16. Look at the right side of the Canon EOS R10. You will see a hinged door covering the memory card compartment. At the top edge of this door there is a small ridged tab.
17. Grip the tab and slide the door downward — it springs open on a hinge toward you.
18. Hold your SD card with the label facing toward the back of the camera (toward the LCD screen side) and the notched corner of the card oriented so it goes into the slot first.
19. Slide the card into the single slot inside the compartment. Push it straight in until you feel and hear it click into place. The card sits flush when correctly seated — it should not protrude.
20. Close the door by pushing it back toward the camera body until it clicks shut.

Formatting the Card

Before using any SD card in the Canon EOS R10 — whether it is brand new or previously used in another device — you must format it inside the camera. Formatting erases all data on the card and prepares the file structure specifically for Canon's image recording system. Skipping this step can cause save errors, corrupted files, or unexpected behaviour during shooting.

21. Make sure the battery is inserted and the camera is powered on. The ON/OFF switch on top of the camera should be in the ON position.
22. Press the MENU button on the upper-left of the camera back. The menu system opens on the LCD screen.
23. Look at the row of coloured tabs running across the top of the screen. Use the Main Dial — the textured wheel behind the shutter button — to scroll right along the tabs until you reach the yellow Setup tab. It is marked with a wrench icon.
24. Once you are on the yellow Setup tab, look through the list of items. Use the Quick Control Dial — the textured ring around the SET button on the back — to scroll down through the list until Format card is highlighted.
25. Press SET to open the Format card screen. You will see information about the card currently inserted, including its total capacity and the amount of space used.
26. The screen shows two options: Cancel and OK. Use the Quick Control Dial or the joystick to highlight OK.
27. Press SET to begin formatting. The camera formats the card in a few seconds. Do not turn the camera off or remove the card while formatting is in progress.
28. When formatting is complete, the camera returns to the menu automatically. Press the MENU button once to close the menu, or half-press the shutter button to return directly to the shooting screen.

Important: *Formatting permanently deletes everything on the card, including any photos or videos stored on it. If the card contains images you want to keep, transfer them to your computer before formatting.*

Note: *Format your SD card inside the Canon EOS R10 each time you begin a new shoot or insert a card that was previously used in a different device. This simple habit prevents the vast majority of card-related errors.*

2.4 Attaching a Lens

The Canon EOS R10 uses the Canon RF lens mount. It is compatible with all RF mount lenses natively. If you own Canon EF or EF-S lenses from an older DSLR system, you can use them on the R10 with the Canon Mount Adapter EF-EOS R, sold separately. This section covers attaching an RF mount lens directly to the camera body.

Removing the Body Cap

29. Hold the Canon EOS R10 with the front of the camera facing you.
30. Locate the Lens Release Button. It is the small oval silver button on the front of the camera body, positioned to the left of the lens mount as you face the camera.
31. Press and hold the Lens Release Button with your right index finger.
32. While holding the button, grip the white plastic body cap with your left hand and rotate it counter-clockwise — turning it to the left — until it comes free from the mount.
33. Release the Lens Release Button. Set the body cap aside in a safe place — you will need it to protect the mount whenever no lens is attached.

Preparing the Lens

34. Remove the rear lens cap from the back of the lens. This is the cap that covers the rear glass element and the lens mount contacts. Rotate it counter-clockwise and lift it free.
35. Keep the front lens cap on the lens for now to protect the front glass element while you handle the lens.

Attaching the Lens to the Camera

36. Hold the camera in your right hand with the lens mount facing away from you.
37. Hold the lens in your left hand with the rear of the lens facing the camera mount.

38. Look at the rear edge of the lens. You will see a small red dot on the edge of the lens barrel. Now look at the camera's lens mount ring — there is also a small red dot on its outer edge, positioned at approximately the 12 o'clock position (pointing straight up when the camera is held upright).
39. Align the red dot on the lens directly with the red dot on the camera mount. This alignment is essential — the lens will not seat correctly if the dots are not matched.
40. With the dots aligned, bring the rear of the lens against the camera mount and press the two surfaces firmly together.
41. While keeping the lens pressed against the mount, rotate the lens clockwise — turning it to the right — until you feel and hear a firm click. The click means the lens lock has engaged and the lens is fully secured.
42. Give the lens a gentle counter-clockwise tug to confirm it is locked. It should not move. If it rotates freely, the lens has not seated correctly — rotate it counter-clockwise to remove it and repeat from step 3.
43. Remove the front lens cap by pinching the two tabs on its sides and pulling it straight off. The camera is now ready to shoot.

Removing a Lens

44. Make sure the camera is switched OFF before removing the lens, particularly in dusty environments. This prevents the sensor's static charge from attracting airborne dust particles as the lens is lifted away.
45. Press and hold the Lens Release Button on the front of the camera with your right index finger.
46. While holding the button, grip the lens barrel with your left hand and rotate it counter-clockwise — to the left — until it stops.
47. Lift the lens straight away from the camera mount.
48. Immediately replace the body cap on the camera and the rear lens cap on the lens to protect both from dust.

Important: *Never force a lens onto the mount or attempt to rotate it without first aligning the red dots. Forcing the lens can damage the mount contacts on both the camera and the lens. Never remove a lens while the camera is powered on unless it is absolutely unavoidable.*

2.5 First Power-On and Initial Settings

The first time you power on the Canon EOS R10, it will walk you through a short setup sequence to configure the language, time zone, and clock. You need to complete this before the camera will let you take photos, as the date and time are embedded into the file data of every image you record.

Steps

49. Make sure the battery is inserted, the SD card is inserted, and a lens is attached.
50. Locate the ON/OFF switch on the top of the camera. It is the rotating collar that surrounds the shutter button. Rotate it clockwise to the ON position. The rear LCD screen lights up and the Canon EOS R10 logo appears briefly, followed by the language selection screen.
51. The language selection screen shows a list of available languages. Use the Quick Control Dial — the textured ring around the SET button on the back of the camera — to scroll up and down through the list until your preferred language is highlighted. Alternatively, tap your language directly on the LCD touch screen.
52. Press SET to confirm the language. The screen moves to the time zone and region selection.
53. Scroll through the list of regions and cities to find your time zone. Highlight it using the Quick Control Dial or by tapping the screen, then press SET to confirm.
54. The next screen asks you to choose your date display format — the order in which the day, month, and year are shown. The three options are year/month/day, month/day/year, and day/month/year. Scroll to your preferred format and press SET.
55. The date and time entry screen appears. It shows six fields: year, month, day, hour, minute, and second. The first field is already highlighted.
56. Use the Main Dial — the textured wheel just behind the shutter button — to change the value in the highlighted field. Rotate right to increase the number and left to decrease it.
57. Press SET to move to the next field. Repeat — adjust with the Main Dial, confirm with SET — until all six fields show the correct current date and time.

58. After confirming the final field, the screen displays a summary showing your selected time zone and the current date and time. If everything is correct, press SET one final time to save the settings. The camera exits the setup sequence and goes directly to the shooting screen.

Note: *If you need to correct the date or time after this initial setup, you can do so at any time by pressing MENU, navigating to the yellow Setup tab, scrolling to Date/Time/Zone, and pressing SET.*

2.6 Enabling the Touch Screen

The LCD touch screen on the Canon EOS R10 is enabled by default from the factory, so in most cases you will not need to change anything here. However, if touch input is not responding, or if a previous user disabled it, follow these steps to turn it on and set its sensitivity.

Steps

59. Press the MENU button on the upper-left of the camera back to open the menu system.
60. Use the Main Dial to scroll right along the coloured tabs at the top of the screen until you reach the yellow Setup tab. It is marked with the wrench icon.
61. Use the Quick Control Dial to scroll down through the items on the Setup tab until Touch control is highlighted.
62. Press SET to open the Touch control options. Three choices appear on screen: Disable, Enable, and Sensitive.
63. Highlight your preferred option using the Quick Control Dial. Select Enable for standard touch response. Select Sensitive if you want the screen to react faster to light or brief touches — this setting is useful if you find the standard sensitivity requires you to press too firmly. Select Disable only if you want to turn off touch input entirely, which some photographers prefer to avoid accidentally moving the focus point when the screen is pressed against clothing while the camera hangs from a strap.
64. Press SET to confirm your choice.

65. Press the MENU button once to close the menu, or half-press the shutter button to return to the shooting screen.

Note: *Enabling the Sensitive setting uses marginally more battery power than the standard Enable setting. The difference is small enough that most users will not notice it in practice.*

2.7 Setting the Viewfinder Diopter

The Electronic Viewfinder on the Canon EOS R10 has a built-in diopter correction adjustment. This is a lens system inside the eyepiece that can be shifted to compensate for your individual eyesight. If the image and text you see inside the viewfinder look blurry even when your subject is correctly in focus, the diopter needs adjusting. This is not a fault with the camera — it is a personal calibration that every user should set once for their own eyes.

Steps

66. Attach a lens to the camera if you have not already done so, and power the camera on.
67. Bring the camera up to your eye and look through the EVF eyepiece. The eye sensor will detect your eye and activate the viewfinder display.
68. Point the camera at something in front of you that has clear edges and distinct contrast — a wall with text on it, a window frame, a printed page, or any stationary subject with visible detail. This gives you a reference to judge the sharpness of the EVF image.
69. Locate the diopter adjustment dial. It is a very small ridged dial positioned on the right side of the EVF housing — between the eyepiece and the right edge of the camera back. Keep your eye at the viewfinder while you find it with your right thumb.
70. While continuing to look through the EVF, slowly rotate the diopter dial. Turn it one way and then the other in small increments. As you rotate it, watch the sharpness of the information text and the image inside the viewfinder.
71. Stop rotating when the viewfinder display — both the shooting data text and the live image — appears as sharp and clear as possible to

your eye. The exact dial position varies from person to person depending on their eyesight.

72. No confirmation press is required. The diopter setting is mechanical, not a menu option — the position of the dial itself holds the adjustment.

Note: *If you wear glasses and normally shoot with them on, set the diopter while wearing your glasses. If you shoot without glasses, set it without them. The diopter has a limited correction range of approximately minus 3 to plus 1 dioptre, which covers most common vision prescriptions. If you require a stronger correction than the built-in range provides, Canon offers optional correction lenses that attach to the eyepiece.*

Note: *The diopter dial on the R10 is small and positioned close to the eyepiece rubber. It is easy to accidentally nudge it while handling the camera. If the EVF ever looks softer than usual, check the diopter position and readjust it before assuming there is a focus problem with the lens.*

PART 3 — The Menu System (Full Walkthrough)

The menu system is where the majority of the Canon EOS R10's settings live. Everything that cannot be changed with a physical dial or button on the camera body is found inside this menu. It can feel overwhelming the first time you open it — there are hundreds of settings spread across more than a dozen tabs. But the menu is logically organised by colour and category, and once you understand the structure, you will be able to find any setting quickly without guessing.

This part of the guide walks through every menu tab and every item inside it. Read through it once to get your bearings, then use it as a reference whenever you need to find or understand a specific setting.

3.1 How to Open and Navigate the Menu

The menu system on the Canon EOS R10 is accessible at any time the camera is powered on, regardless of which shooting mode is active.

Opening the Menu

1. Press the MENU button. It is located on the upper-left area of the camera back, clearly labelled MENU in white text. The menu opens immediately on the LCD screen. If your eye is at the EVF when you press MENU, the menu opens inside the viewfinder instead.

Understanding the Tab Structure

Across the top of the menu screen you will see a row of small coloured icons — these are the menu tabs. Each tab is a category that groups related settings together. The tabs are colour-coded to make them easier to identify at a glance. There are more tabs than can fit on screen at once, so you need to scroll through them.

To move between tabs, rotate the Main Dial — the textured wheel just behind the shutter button on the top of the camera. Rotating it to the right moves you forward through the tabs; rotating left moves you back. You can also tap directly on any visible tab icon along the top of the touch screen to jump to it immediately.

Inside each tab, the settings are listed vertically. To scroll up and down through them, rotate the Quick Control Dial — the textured ring around the SET button on the back of the camera. You can also swipe up or down on the touch screen.

Opening a Setting

When the setting you want is highlighted — shown with a blue or orange selection bar — press SET to open it. A sub-screen appears showing the available options for that setting. Use the Quick Control Dial to highlight your preferred option, then press SET again to confirm. Some settings open a further sub-menu with additional choices. The process is always the same: highlight, press SET, choose, press SET.

You can also tap any listed item directly on the touch screen to open it without using the dials at all.

Going Back and Closing the Menu

To go back one level — from a sub-menu to the main menu tab — press the MENU button once. To close the menu entirely and return to the shooting screen, press the MENU button a second time, or half-press the shutter button at any point.

> Note: *Any setting you change inside the menu takes effect immediately when you press SET to confirm it. You do not need to save or apply changes separately — they are stored as soon as you confirm them and are retained even after you power the camera off.*

3.2 Menu Tab Overview

The Canon EOS R10 menu is divided into five colour-coded groups of tabs. Here is what each group contains before you dive into the individual items.

Red Tabs — Shooting Menu (Tabs 1 through 9)

The red tabs control everything related to capturing still photographs. This is the largest group in the menu and covers image quality, file format, autofocus behaviour, exposure settings, white balance, picture styles, drive modes, flash control, and more. There are nine red tabs in total, numbered 1 through 9 along the top. Each tab is represented by a small camera icon with the tab number beside it.

Pink Tab — Movie Menu

The pink tab contains all settings specific to video recording — resolution, frame rate, audio levels, video stabilisation, and time-lapse setup. Many of these settings are only accessible when the camera is set to video mode, though some can be reached from this tab in any mode.

Blue Tab — Playback Menu

The blue tab controls how you review, manage, and process images after they have been captured. Settings here cover image protection, deletion, in-camera RAW conversion, creative filter application to existing images, slideshow playback, and how information is displayed during review.

Yellow Tabs — Setup Menu

The yellow tabs contain the camera's system-level settings — everything that affects how the camera itself operates rather than how it captures images. This includes the date and time, display brightness, power saving timers, Wi-Fi and Bluetooth connectivity, file numbering, SD card formatting, firmware updates, and custom function settings.

Green Tab — My Menu

The green tab is a blank menu that you populate yourself. You can add up to six items from anywhere in the menu system to My Menu, creating a personal shortcut page for the settings you access most frequently. You can also configure the camera to open My Menu first every time you press the MENU button, which makes it a very efficient way to reach your most-used settings without navigating through multiple tabs.

3.3 Shooting Menu (Red Tabs 1–9) — Every Item Explained

To reach the Shooting Menu, press MENU and look for the red camera icons along the top of the screen. There are nine of them, labelled with a small number beside the camera icon. Use the Main Dial to scroll between them or tap the tab number you want.

Shooting Menu 1

- **Image quality** — This is where you choose the file format and compression level for every photo the Canon EOS R10 captures. Press SET to open it. You will see two rows of options. The top row sets the RAW file format — RAW (full uncompressed), C-RAW (compressed RAW, smaller file with comparable quality), or a dash meaning no RAW file is saved. The bottom row sets the JPEG or HEIF format — L (large), M (medium), S1, or S2 for JPEG; or HEIF for the high-efficiency format. You can choose a RAW option and a JPEG option simultaneously to save both file types with each shot, which doubles the storage used but gives you both a processed-ready JPEG and a fully editable RAW file from every shutter press. For maximum editing flexibility, select RAW alone. For quick sharing without editing, select Large Fine JPEG. For the best balance of quality and file size, select C-RAW.
- **Still img aspect ratio** — This sets the shape of the image frame. The Canon EOS R10 sensor is natively a 3:2 rectangle — the same proportions used by 35mm film and the most common format for printing standard photo sizes. The other options are 4:3 (closer to a square, matching tablet screens), 16:9 (widescreen, matching TV and monitor screens), and 1:1 (a perfect square, popular for certain social media formats). When you select a non-native ratio, the camera applies a crop — the EVF and LCD show lines or a dimmed area indicating what will be cut from the final image. The sensor still records a 3:2 image in RAW format regardless of which ratio you choose, so if you shoot RAW, the crop is only applied to the embedded preview; you can restore the full frame when editing. JPEG files are cropped permanently.
- **Image review** — After you press the shutter and take a photo, the Canon EOS R10 displays the captured image on the LCD screen for a brief moment so you can check it. This setting controls how long that review lasts. The options are 2 sec, 4 sec, 8 sec, Hold, and Off. At 2 sec the image flashes briefly and then the live view resumes. At Hold the image stays on screen indefinitely until you half-press the shutter or press another button. Off disables the review entirely so the camera goes straight back to live view without showing the captured image. Setting it to 2 sec is recommended for most shooting — it gives you enough time to check the result without interrupting your shooting rhythm. Setting it to Off saves a small amount of battery power and is preferred by photographers shooting fast-moving subjects who cannot afford any delay between shots.

- **Lens aberration correction** — All lenses introduce small optical imperfections into an image — slight darkening at the corners, subtle distortion of straight lines, colour fringing along high-contrast edges, and softening at small apertures. The Canon EOS R10 can correct these automatically for RF and EF lenses it recognises by reading the lens data stored in the camera. Press SET to open this setting and you will find five individual correction switches, each of which can be turned on or off independently.
  - **Peripheral illumination correction** — Brightens the corners of the image to compensate for vignetting — the natural darkening that most lenses produce at the edges of the frame, particularly at wide apertures. Recommended setting: Enable.
  - **Distortion correction** — Straightens barrel distortion (where straight lines bow outward near the edges) and pincushion distortion (where they bow inward). Most noticeable with wide-angle lenses and in architectural photography. Enabling this may crop the edges of the frame very slightly to allow room for the correction. Recommended setting: Enable.
  - **Digital lens optimizer** — The most comprehensive correction. It uses Canon's precise optical formula data for your specific lens to correct diffraction softening, remaining chromatic aberration, and spherical aberration simultaneously. It requires a compatible Canon lens to function and takes slightly longer to apply during processing. When enabled, it supersedes several of the other corrections. Recommended setting: Standard or High for maximum image quality.
  - **Chromatic aberration correction** — Removes colour fringing — the red, green, or purple outlines that appear along high-contrast edges, particularly in bright backlighting conditions. Recommended setting: Enable.
  - **Diffraction correction** — At very small apertures (f/11 and smaller), light waves bend as they pass through the narrow aperture opening, softening the entire image. The R10 applies sharpening to compensate for this. Most useful for landscape and architectural photography where small apertures are common. Recommended setting: Enable.

Note: *Lens aberration corrections apply only to JPEG and HEIF output. If you shoot RAW, the corrections are noted in the file's metadata but are applied* *only when you process the RAW file in Canon's Digital Photo Professional software or another compatible editor — the original RAW data itself is not altered.*

Shooting Menu 2

- **Expo. comp./AEB** — This item controls two related but distinct functions. Press SET to open it. A scale appears across the screen ranging from minus 3 to plus 3 stops, with zero at the centre. The first function is Exposure Compensation. Rotating the Main Dial moves a single marker left or right along this scale. Moving it toward the plus side makes the camera expose the photo brighter than its automatic reading; moving it toward the minus side makes it darker. Use this whenever the camera's automatic exposure is producing results that are consistently too bright or too dark. The second function is Auto Exposure Bracketing (AEB). Rotate the Quick Control Dial to spread a bracket of three markers across the scale. When AEB is active and you press the shutter, the Canon EOS R10 takes three consecutive shots — one at the negative exposure, one at the base exposure, and one at the positive exposure — giving you three versions of the scene at different brightnesses. AEB is used for HDR merging in post-processing and as a safety net in tricky lighting.

- **ISO speed settings** — Press SET to open the ISO speed settings sub-menu. Inside you will find three options. ISO speed lets you set the current ISO value directly — from 100 to 32000, with expansion to 51200 available. ISO speed range sets the upper and lower limits that the camera can use when Auto ISO is active, so you can prevent it from going above a level where noise becomes unacceptable for your purposes. Auto ISO range is where you set the minimum shutter speed below which the camera will raise the ISO rather than allow the shutter to drop further — this is important for preventing motion blur in low light while using Auto ISO.

- **Auto Lighting Optimizer** — When the Canon EOS R10's automatic metering exposes a scene correctly overall but certain areas of the image — particularly shadows — come out darker than they look to your eye, the Auto Lighting Optimizer can automatically brighten those darker regions to create a more balanced result. It analyses the image after capture and applies a selective brightness boost. The strength is adjustable: Disable turns it off entirely, Low applies a gentle correction, Standard is the default and suits most situations, and High applies the strongest correction. Leave it at Standard for general shooting. Disable it when you are deliberately shooting high-contrast images or when you want full predictability over your exposure, such as in studio work.

- **HDR mode** — When this mode is active, pressing the shutter causes the Canon EOS R10 to take three rapid exposures at different brightness levels and merge them into a single file that retains detail in both the bright highlights and the dark shadows simultaneously — a result that a single exposure cannot achieve in high-contrast scenes. Press SET to open it. The Adjusting range options (Auto, plus or minus 1 EV, plus or minus 2 EV, plus or minus 3 EV) determine how far apart the three exposures are. Auto allows the camera to judge the range needed based on the scene contrast. Wider ranges recover more extreme highlights and shadows but require the three shots to align well — use a tripod or very steady hands when shooting at wider HDR ranges. The merged result is saved as a JPEG. Note that in HDR mode the camera cannot shoot RAW files.

- **HDR PQ settings** — This setting configures output for HDR PQ (Perceptual Quantizer) — a colour and brightness format used by HDR-compatible televisions and monitors. When enabled, the Canon EOS R10 records images or video in a format that preserves an extended range of brightness and colour for playback on HDR displays. On a standard non-HDR screen, HDR PQ images may appear washed out or dim, because the format is not designed for standard display output. Enable this only if you are specifically capturing content for playback on an HDR-compatible screen.

Shooting Menu 3

- **White balance** — White balance tells the Canon EOS R10 what colour temperature the light in your scene is, so that it can make white objects appear genuinely white in your photos rather than orange, blue, or green. Press SET to open it. The options are AWB (Auto White Balance, with sub-options for Ambience priority or White priority), Daylight, Shade, Cloudy, Tungsten light, White fluorescent light, Flash, Colour temperature (where you enter a specific Kelvin value from 2500K to 10000K), and Custom. A full explanation of each option and when to use it is in Part 9 of this guide. For most everyday shooting, AWB Ambience priority produces natural, accurate results.

- **Custom White Balance** — This option lets you set a precise white balance by photographing a neutral white or grey reference card under your specific lighting conditions and telling the camera to use that image as its reference. Press SET to open it. The screen shows your most recent images. Use the Main Dial to scroll to the photo of your white or grey card, press SET, and confirm. The camera extracts the colour information from that image and stores it as the custom white balance. You then need to go back to the White balance setting and select the Custom option (shown as two triangular arrows) to actually apply it. Custom white balance is most useful in mixed artificial lighting environments where no preset matches accurately — indoors under theatre lighting, in a studio with unusual coloured LED panels, or under sodium vapour street lights.

- **White balance correction** — This setting allows you to add a persistent shift toward a specific colour across all your shots, without changing your base white balance preset. Think of it as a fine-tuning layer on top of whatever white balance you have selected. Press SET and a colour grid appears — a blue-amber axis and a magenta-green axis. Use the joystick to move the correction point away from centre. Moving it toward amber (A) adds warmth; toward blue (B) adds coolness; toward magenta (M) adds pink; toward green (G) adds green. This is useful when you find that your chosen white balance is consistently slightly off in a particular direction and you want to correct it without switching to a different preset.

- **Color space** — This setting determines the range of colours that the Canon EOS R10 can record in a JPEG or HEIF file. Press SET to choose between sRGB and Adobe RGB. sRGB is the standard colour space used by virtually all web browsers, social media platforms, and consumer photo printers. It covers the range of colours that most screens and printers can reproduce, and images in sRGB look correct on almost any device without any conversion. Adobe RGB covers a wider range of colours, particularly in the green and cyan regions, and is used in professional print workflows where wide-gamut printing equipment can reproduce those additional colours. Choose sRGB for all photos intended for online sharing, screen display, or standard consumer printing. Choose Adobe RGB only if your entire workflow — from editing software to printer — supports and uses the Adobe RGB colour space. Note that Adobe RGB images shown on a non-colour-managed screen or application will appear dull and desaturated, because the wider gamut is being squeezed into a smaller display range.

- **Picture Style** — Picture Style controls how the Canon EOS R10 processes and presents colour, contrast, sharpness, and tone in JPEG and HEIF images. It is the equivalent of choosing between different film stocks. Press SET and a list of styles appears. Highlight any style and press the INFO button to see a breakdown of its sharpness, contrast, saturation, and colour tone values. You can also press SET on a style to customise those individual values if none of the presets suit you exactly. The available styles are: Auto (the camera analyses the scene and chooses the most appropriate processing), Standard (vivid colour and strong sharpness, the default for most everyday shooting), Portrait (slightly softer sharpness and accurate skin tone rendering, best for people), Landscape (punchy blues and greens with high sharpness, best for outdoor scenes), Fine Detail (the highest sharpness setting, best for subjects with intricate texture such as fabric, architecture, or foliage), Neutral (minimal processing with low contrast, designed as a starting point for extensive post-processing in editing software), Faithful (attempts to reproduce colours as they appear under standard 5200K daylight, prioritising accuracy over vibrancy), Monochrome (records in black and white — you can further adjust filter effects to change how colours translate to grey tones, and add toning effects such as sepia), and User Def. 1 through 3 (three empty slots where you can save your own custom combinations of any style's parameters).

Note: *Picture Style affects JPEG and HEIF files only. If you shoot in RAW format, the selected Picture Style is recorded in the file's metadata but does not alter the actual image data. You can apply or change the Picture Style to a RAW file when processing it in Canon Digital Photo Professional.*

Shooting Menu 4

- **Clarity** — Clarity adds or removes mid-frequency contrast — the contrast between medium-sized details in the image rather than overall brightness or fine edge sharpness. Increasing clarity (toward plus 4) makes textures such as skin pores, fabric weave, stone, or bark look more pronounced and three-dimensional. Decreasing clarity (toward minus 4) softens these mid-tones and creates a slightly hazy, ethereal quality sometimes used in portrait work to smooth skin. Press SET and use the Main Dial to move the slider. The effect is visible in real time on the screen as you adjust it. Clarity applies to JPEG output. Zero is the neutral starting point and produces unaltered rendering.

- **Long exp. noise reduction** — At exposures of one second or longer, a type of noise called fixed-pattern noise appears in images — a scattering of coloured or bright dots that are fixed in the same positions regardless of the scene content. This noise comes from heat generated by the sensor during a long exposure. When Long exp. noise reduction is enabled, the Canon EOS R10 automatically takes a second exposure of equal length immediately after your photo, but this time with the shutter closed — a dark frame. It then subtracts the noise pattern found in the dark frame from your actual image, significantly reducing the fixed-pattern noise in the final result. Press SET to choose Auto (the correction applies only when the camera detects a level of noise worth correcting) or Enable (the correction always applies to exposures of one second or longer). The trade-off is that with Enable selected, the camera is unavailable for the full length of your exposure after the shot while it processes the dark frame — a 30-second exposure requires a further 30 seconds of processing before the camera is ready again.

- **High ISO speed NR** — When you shoot at high ISO values, the Canon EOS R10's sensor amplifies its signal to compensate for low light, but this amplification also magnifies electronic noise — the grain-like texture that appears in smooth areas of the image. High ISO speed noise reduction applies luminance smoothing to reduce this grain. Press SET to choose from four levels: Multi Shot Noise Reduction (takes four frames in rapid succession and merges them for the most effective noise reduction without softening fine detail — only available in JPEG), High (aggressive smoothing, most effective at reducing noise but may slightly soften fine detail), Standard (balanced default, recommended for most shooting), Low (gentle smoothing, preserves more fine detail at the cost of slightly more visible noise), and Disable (no noise reduction applied). Standard is the right choice for general use. Switch to Multi Shot NR when you are shooting stationary subjects at very high ISO and want the cleanest possible JPEG output.

- **Dust Delete Data** — Over time, dust particles can settle on the image sensor and appear as small dark spots in your photos — most visible in out-of-focus areas and at small apertures. The Canon EOS R10's self-cleaning system removes most dust automatically at startup and shutdown, but some particles may remain. Dust Delete Data is a reference capture that records the exact position of any remaining dust spots on the sensor. When you later open your RAW files in Canon's Digital Photo Professional software, it uses this reference data to automatically erase the corresponding spots from your images. To use it, press SET and follow the on-screen instructions — you will need to photograph a plain white surface (a blank white wall or white paper) at a specific distance. Update the Dust Delete Data any time you notice new spots appearing in your images or after cleaning the sensor.

Shooting Menu 5

- **Optical VF simulation** — The Canon EOS R10's electronic viewfinder can display the live image in two different ways. In its default mode, the EVF shows a fully processed preview that reflects your current exposure settings — brightening when ISO is high, darkening when the aperture is small, and showing the image with the selected white balance and Picture Style applied. This is the what-you-see-is-what-you-get behaviour that makes mirrorless cameras distinctive. Optical VF simulation changes the EVF so that it maintains a consistent, natural-looking brightness regardless of your exposure settings — similar to looking through the optical viewfinder of a DSLR, where the scene always appears at its natural brightness even if your settings would produce an over or under-exposed photo. Enable this if you find the exposure-reactive EVF disorienting, or if you prefer to judge exposure purely from the settings rather than from the live preview.
- **Shooting info disp.** — This setting controls what information is visible on the LCD screen and EVF during shooting. Press SET to open the configuration screen. You can customise two separate layouts: one for the EVF and one for the LCD screen. Within each layout you can toggle individual information elements on or off — items such as the electronic level, a grid overlay, the histogram, the shooting mode icon, the remaining shot count, and various status indicators. The camera shows a live preview of how your changes affect the display as you make them. Press the INFO button within this setting to switch between configuring the EVF layout and the LCD layout.
- **VF display format** — This setting offers two layout options for the shooting information displayed inside the EVF: Display 1 and Display 2. Display 1 presents shooting data across the bottom of the EVF image, keeping the upper portion of the frame unobstructed. Display 2 places data in a separate panel below the live image rather than overlaying it on the image itself. Press SET, use the Quick Control Dial to highlight your preferred layout, and press SET to confirm. The difference is a matter of personal preference — try both and use whichever keeps the viewfinder display feeling uncluttered for you.

- **Display performance** — This controls the frame rate at which the live view image updates on the LCD screen and in the EVF. Press SET and choose between Smooth and Resource saving. Smooth sets the live view to 60 frames per second, producing a fluid, lag-free preview that makes it easier to track moving subjects and assess focus. Resource saving drops the frame rate and reduces processing demand, which extends battery life at the cost of a slightly choppier live view — the image updates less frequently. Use Smooth as your default. Switch to Resource saving only in situations where battery conservation is a priority and you are not tracking fast movement.

Shooting Menu 6

- **AF operation** — This setting determines the fundamental behaviour of the autofocus system on the Canon EOS R10. Press SET and choose from three options. One-Shot AF locks focus at a single point when you half-press the shutter or press AF-ON. Once focus is locked, a green frame confirms it and a beep sounds if the beep is enabled. The focus does not change even if the subject moves after the lock — you must release and re-press to refocus. This is the correct mode for stationary subjects. Servo AF keeps the autofocus active and continuously adjusting as long as you hold the shutter half-pressed or keep the AF-ON button held. The camera predicts subject movement and shifts the focus point to stay on the subject, even as it moves toward or away from the camera. No confirmation beep sounds in Servo AF. This is the correct mode for any moving subject — wildlife, sports, children, vehicles. AI Focus attempts to give you the best of both: it starts in One-Shot AF and automatically switches to Servo AF if it detects that your subject has begun to move. It is a useful compromise when you are unsure whether your subject will stay still. A full explanation of how to choose between these modes in practice is in Part 6.

- **AF area** — This setting determines where on the frame the Canon EOS R10 looks for its focus target. Press SET and a graphical representation of the frame appears with the available area modes listed. Spot AF focuses on an extremely small, precise point — a smaller area than 1-Point AF — useful for locking onto a specific tiny detail within a larger subject. 1-Point AF focuses on a single, user-positioned square point and ignores everything outside it; use the joystick to position it wherever you need. Expand AF area uses your selected point plus a small ring of surrounding points to help maintain focus if the subject drifts slightly off the primary point. Zone AF divides the frame into nine zones and focuses on the nearest or most prominent subject within whichever zone you select. Whole Area AF hands over full control to the camera, which searches the entire frame and applies its subject detection logic to find and track a face, eye, body, animal, or vehicle automatically. A full explanation of each area mode and when to use each one is in Part 6.

- **Subject to detect** — When Whole Area AF or any of the expanded area modes are active, the Canon EOS R10 can apply intelligent detection to recognise specific types of subjects and prioritise them for focus tracking. Press SET to choose your subject type. People causes the camera to look for human faces, eyes, heads, and bodies — it will lock onto and track the nearest or most prominent person in the frame and specifically seek out their eye for the sharpest possible focus. Animals causes the camera to detect and track dogs, cats, and birds, focusing preferentially on their face or eye when one is visible. Vehicles causes the camera to detect and track cars and motorcycles, prioritising the driver's helmet or face and the vehicle's front end. Selecting None disables subject detection and the camera focuses using contrast and phase detection only, without attempting to identify what it is looking at.

- **Eye detection** — When subject detection is set to People, the Canon EOS R10 can lock onto and track a specific eye within a detected face. Press SET to choose from three options. Left eye priority instructs the camera to always seek out and prioritise the subject's left eye when both eyes are visible. Right eye priority prioritises the right eye. Auto allows the camera to decide which eye to focus on — it generally chooses the eye nearest to the camera. A small eye-detection frame appears over the tracked eye in the viewfinder. You can switch between left and right eye priority quickly while shooting by pressing the M-Fn button and rotating the Quick Control Dial, without needing to return to the menu.

- **Continuous AF** — When Continuous AF is enabled and the camera is in live view on the shooting screen — before you have half-pressed the shutter or pressed AF-ON — the autofocus system runs continuously in the background, constantly searching for and adjusting to changes in the scene. This means that when you do press the shutter, the camera is already close to or on focus and can confirm and lock it faster. The trade-off is that continuous AF uses the sensor and processor actively, which draws more battery power than having the AF system idle. Enable it if you frequently shoot fast-moving subjects and want the shortest possible lag between pressing the shutter and achieving focus. Disable it if battery life is a concern or if you are shooting stationary subjects where the extra responsiveness is not needed.

- **Touch & drag AF settings** — This setting allows you to use the LCD touch screen to reposition the active autofocus point while your eye is at the EVF — without moving the camera away from your face. Press SET to open the configuration screen. Touch & drag AF must first be set to Enable. Once enabled, you can touch anywhere on the LCD screen with your thumb while looking through the EVF and the AF point will move to correspond with where you touched. The Active touch area setting lets you limit which portion of the screen responds to touch — choosing the right half of the screen prevents accidental touches from your nose moving the AF point. The Positioning method can be set to Absolute (the AF point jumps to exactly where you touch on the screen) or Relative (the AF point moves in the direction you drag, from wherever it currently sits, like a trackpad). Relative is generally more intuitive and precise for repositioning the AF point while shooting.

Shooting Menu 7

- **Metering mode** — Metering determines how the Canon EOS R10 measures the light in the scene to calculate the correct exposure. Press SET to choose from four metering patterns. Evaluative metering divides the entire frame into a grid of zones, measures each one, analyses the overall pattern of brightness, and calculates an exposure that balances the whole scene. It gives extra weight to the area around the active AF point. This is the default mode and works well in the vast majority of situations. Partial metering measures from approximately 5.5 percent of the frame area at the centre, ignoring the surrounding brightness — useful when your subject is surrounded by areas that are significantly brighter or darker and you want to expose purely for the subject. Spot metering is a further refinement of partial metering, measuring from only about 2.5 percent of the frame at the centre — a very precise tool for reading the light from a specific small area of the scene, such as a face in a backlit scene. Centre-weighted average metering measures brightness across the entire frame but gives approximately 75 percent of the total weight to the central portion of the image, blending centre and edge measurements into a single reading. A full explanation of when to use each mode is in Part 7.

- **Exposure smoothing** — This setting is relevant primarily to video recording and live view shooting. When the camera is using Auto exposure and the light level in the scene changes — a cloud passing in front of the sun, for example, or moving from shade into direct light — the exposure normally adjusts immediately, which can cause a sudden jump in brightness visible in live view and recorded video. Exposure smoothing causes the Canon EOS R10 to transition between exposure values gradually rather than snapping to the new level instantly, producing a smoother and more natural-looking change. Enable this setting if you are recording video or shooting in conditions where the light level fluctuates. For still photography with manual exposure, it has no practical effect.

- **Drive mode —** Drive mode determines what happens when you press the shutter button — specifically, how many shots the camera takes and how quickly. Press SET and choose from: Single shooting (one photo per press of the shutter, the camera waits for the next press before firing again), High speed continuous plus (the fastest available rate — up to 15 frames per second using the electronic shutter), High speed continuous (up to 15 fps but using the mechanical or electronic first-curtain shutter, which is slightly more compatible with artificial lighting than the fully electronic shutter), Low speed continuous (approximately 4 frames per second, useful for sequences where the highest burst rate is not necessary), Self-timer 10 sec (a 10-second countdown before the shutter fires — use this for group photos where you need time to walk into frame), Self-timer 2 sec (a 2-second countdown — use this for tripod shots to eliminate camera shake caused by pressing the shutter), and Self-timer continuous (counts down then fires a sequence of 2 to 10 shots — useful for capturing a series of expressions or poses in a self-portrait session). Drive mode can also be changed quickly via the Q menu or by pressing the M-Fn button and rotating the Main Dial, without opening the full menu.

- **Anti-flicker shooting —** Fluorescent and certain LED artificial light sources do not produce constant light — they cycle between bright and dim many times per second, driven by the alternating current frequency of the electrical supply. At fast shutter speeds, the Canon EOS R10's shutter can open during a dim phase of this cycle, causing some frames in a burst to come out darker or with a banded gradient across the image even though all other settings are identical. Anti-flicker shooting detects the cycling frequency of the light source and times each shutter release to coincide with the peak brightness phase of the cycle, ensuring consistent exposure across all frames. Press SET to enable it. When enabled, a brief delay may occur between pressing the shutter and the camera firing, as it waits for the correct phase. Anti-flicker is most useful for sports and event photography under artificial lights.

- **Shutter mode —** The Canon EOS R10 offers three different shutter mechanisms, and this setting lets you choose between them. Press SET to select. Mechanical shutter uses the camera's physical curtain mechanism — a set of metal blades that physically open and close over the sensor. It produces a quiet click sound with each shot and is compatible with all lighting conditions including fluorescent and LED lights. Electronic first-curtain shutter uses the mechanical curtain only for the closing stroke — the opening of the shutter is simulated electronically by resetting the sensor's charge all at once, which reduces the vibration that a fully mechanical first curtain would create. This is slightly quieter than full mechanical and reduces a form of blur called shutter shock in long telephoto shooting. Electronic shutter is entirely silent — no physical curtains move at all. Both the opening and closing of the exposure are handled electronically within the sensor. This is the mode that enables the 15 fps maximum burst rate and is completely silent, making it useful in quiet environments such as concerts, ceremonies, or wildlife watching. The trade-off is that electronic shutter can produce a rolling shutter distortion — a skewed or wavy appearance — when photographing fast horizontal motion, and may cause banding under artificial light sources that cycle rapidly. Use Mechanical for reliability in all conditions. Use Electronic first-curtain for telephoto shooting on a tripod. Use Electronic only in situations where silence is essential or the maximum burst rate is needed, and where the lighting is consistent natural or flash light.

Shooting Menu 8

Shooting Menu 8 contains all flash-related settings. These settings are only relevant when an external Speedlite flash unit is attached to the hot shoe on top of the Canon EOS R10. The R10 does not have a built-in flash. If no flash is attached, these settings are greyed out and cannot be adjusted.

To reach Flash control: press MENU, scroll with the Main Dial to the eighth red Shooting tab, scroll down to Flash control, and press SET.

- **Flash firing —** The master switch for the attached flash. Set to Enable to allow the flash to fire. Set to Disable to prevent the flash from firing even though it is physically attached and switched on — useful when you want the flash mounted for quick access but do not want it to fire for certain shots.

- **E-TTL II metering —** E-TTL II (Evaluative Through-The-Lens) is the system the Canon EOS R10 uses to automatically calculate how much flash power is needed for a correct exposure. The camera fires a brief pre-flash before the main exposure, measures the light that returns through the lens, and sets the flash output accordingly. This setting lets you choose how that measurement is made. Evaluative divides the scene into zones and gives extra weight to the area around the active focus point, making it more responsive to the actual subject's reflectivity. Average measures the entire scene evenly without weighting for the focus point — useful in controlled studio situations where you want a consistent flash output regardless of subject position.
- **Flash sync speed in Av mode —** In Aperture Priority mode, the camera normally selects the shutter speed automatically. This setting limits the range of shutter speeds available for flash synchronisation. The options are Auto (the camera freely selects any speed from 1/250 sec down to 30 seconds as needed), or fixed speeds from 1/250 down to 1/60 sec. Choosing a fixed speed prevents the camera from selecting shutter speeds slower than that value in Av mode with flash, which avoids the risk of blurred ambient light in the background of flash-lit shots.
- **Flash exposure compensation —** Adjusts the output of the attached flash brighter or darker relative to the E-TTL II calculated level, without changing the overall camera exposure. The range is minus 3 to plus 3 stops in third-stop increments. Turn it down (toward minus) if flash-lit portraits appear washed out or unnaturally bright — a setting of minus 1 or minus 1.3 stops often produces more natural-looking flash portraits. Turn it up (toward plus) if the flash is not illuminating the subject sufficiently at the current distance. This adjustment can also be made from the Q menu without opening the full menu.
- **Flash exposure bracketing —** Similar to exposure bracketing for ambient light, Flash exposure bracketing causes the Canon EOS R10 to take three consecutive flash shots with the flash output varied across the three frames — one darker, one at the metered level, and one brighter. This is useful in critical flash photography situations where getting the flash output exactly right matters and you want insurance across multiple frames.

- **Wireless flash settings** — When using compatible Canon Speedlite units that support wireless operation, this setting configures the Canon EOS R10 to act as a controller for a multi-flash wireless setup. You can set flash groups, assign individual flash units to each group, and set the power ratios between groups. This enables off-camera flash arrangements — for example, one flash as a key light, a second as a fill light, and a third as a background light — all controlled from the camera without physical connections between the flash units.

Shooting Menu 9

- **Bulb timer** — In Manual exposure mode, setting the shutter speed beyond 30 seconds brings you to BULB mode — the shutter stays open for as long as you hold the shutter button down, and closes when you release it. For exposures of many minutes (star trails, light painting, very long night exposures) holding the shutter button continuously is impractical and introduces camera shake. The Bulb timer solves this by letting you specify an exact exposure duration in advance. Press SET, then use the Main Dial to set the hours, minutes, and seconds. When you press the shutter button in BULB mode with the timer active, the shutter opens and the timer counts down automatically — the shutter closes at the end of the set duration without you needing to hold the button or time it manually.

- **Remote control** — Enables wireless remote shooting using the Canon BR-E1 Bluetooth Remote Controller, sold separately. Press SET and choose Enable to activate remote control reception. Once enabled and paired via the Bluetooth settings in the Setup menu, pressing the button on the BR-E1 triggers the Canon EOS R10's shutter without any physical contact with the camera — useful for self-portraits, long exposures on a tripod, wildlife photography from a distance, or any situation where touching the camera would introduce vibration or disturb a scene.

- **Image stabilizer** — This setting controls the Image Stabilisation behaviour of any IS-equipped Canon lens attached to the R10. Press SET to open the IS settings. IS mode lets you switch between the stabilisation modes available on your lens — Mode 1 stabilises in all directions for general handheld shooting, Mode 2 stabilises only vertically and is designed for horizontal panning shots, and Mode 3 activates stabilisation only at the moment of exposure for erratic movement. You can also set IS to Off from here if you are shooting on a tripod and want to prevent the IS system from introducing subtle movement. Note that the Canon EOS R10 itself does not have in-body image stabilisation — this setting only applies to IS-equipped lenses.

- **Shooting info display** — A secondary access point to the same shooting information display customisation available in Shooting Menu 5. From here you can toggle which data elements appear on the shooting screen and configure separate layouts for the LCD screen and the EVF. The function is identical to the Shooting info disp. item in Shooting Menu 5 — it is duplicated here for convenience.

Note: *Shooting Menu 9 is the last of the nine red shooting tabs. The next tab in the menu system — reached by continuing to rotate the Main Dial to the right — is the pink Movie menu tab, covered in Part 12 of this guide.*

3.4 Movie Menu — Every Item Explained

The Movie menu is accessed via the pink tab in the menu system. To reach it, press MENU and rotate the Main Dial to the right past the nine red Shooting tabs until you reach the single pink tab marked with a video camera icon. This tab contains all settings specific to video recording on the Canon EOS R10. Some of these settings are only adjustable when the Mode Dial is set to the video camera icon — if a setting appears greyed out, rotate the Mode Dial to video mode and return to the menu.

- **Movie rec quality** — This is where you set the resolution and frame rate for every video the Canon EOS R10 records. Press SET to open it. The options are presented in a list showing resolution, frame rate, and the resulting file format and compression type together. The available resolutions are 4K (3840 by 2160 pixels) and Full HD (1920 by 1080 pixels). Within each resolution, different frame rates are available depending on whether your Video system is set to NTSC or PAL in the Setup menu. Under NTSC the frame rates available are 23.98 fps (cinematic, standard for film-style video), 29.97 fps (standard broadcast frame rate for NTSC regions), and 59.94 fps (smooth motion, suitable for slow-motion playback at half speed). Under PAL the available rates are 25 fps (standard broadcast for PAL regions) and 50 fps (smooth motion and slow-motion capability at half speed). 4K at 23.98 or 25 fps is the highest quality option for documentary-style footage. Full HD at 50 or 59.94 fps is the most practical choice for capturing action or any subject you want to slow down in editing. Note that 4K recording on the R10 uses a crop of the sensor at certain frame rates — the full-width 4K option is available at 23.98 and 25 fps, while higher frame rates apply an additional crop.

- **Movie rec format** — This sets the compression format used to encode the video file. Press SET to choose between MP4 with IPB compression, MP4 with ALL-I compression, or Canon Log options if applicable. IPB (Interframe compression) creates smaller files by recording only the differences between successive frames — it is the most storage-efficient option and plays back on virtually any device without needing specialised software. ALL-I (All-Intra compression) records every frame as a complete, independent image, producing significantly larger files but greater editing flexibility and more data per frame for colour grading. Use IPB for everyday video and casual sharing. Use ALL-I when you plan to do serious colour correction in post-production and need more data per frame to work with.
- **High Frame Rate** — When High Frame Rate is enabled, the Canon EOS R10 records Full HD video at 119.88 fps (under NTSC) or 100 fps (under PAL) — four times the standard frame rate. Video recorded at this speed is intended to be played back at a standard rate such as 29.97 or 25 fps, which slows the motion down to one quarter of real-time speed, producing smooth slow-motion footage. Press SET to enable or disable it. When High Frame Rate is active, the selected Movie rec quality setting is overridden and the camera records in Full HD at the high frame rate regardless. Audio is not recorded during High Frame Rate shooting — the file is video-only. The file size per minute of recording is substantially larger than standard frame rate footage.
- **HDR movie recording** — When enabled, the Canon EOS R10 records video in the HDR PQ (Perceptual Quantizer) format, which is designed for playback on HDR-compatible televisions and monitors. HDR PQ preserves a wider range of brightness than standard video encoding, keeping detail in very bright highlights and very dark shadows that standard video would clip to pure white or pure black. Press SET and select Enable to activate it. When HDR movie recording is on, Canon Log and some other settings become unavailable simultaneously. Video recorded in HDR PQ will appear washed out or flat on a standard non-HDR display, because the extended brightness range is not supported by that display. Only enable this setting if the final destination for your video is an HDR-compatible screen.
- **Canon Log** — Canon Log is a gamma curve — a flat, low-contrast, desaturated colour profile applied to video during recording that

preserves the maximum amount of tonal information from highlights to shadows. Video recorded in Canon Log looks grey and lifeless when viewed directly, but it contains far more data for a colourist to work with in post-production. By applying a LUT (Look-Up Table) in editing software, the flat Canon Log image is transformed into a vivid, graded final result with precisely controlled colour and contrast. Press SET to enable Canon Log. Canon Log 3 is available on the R10. This setting is intended for video professionals who have a colour grading workflow. If you are not grading your footage in editing software, leave Canon Log disabled and use the standard picture profile instead, which produces a ready-to-use image directly from the camera.

- **Movie Servo AF** — When Movie Servo AF is enabled, the Canon EOS R10's autofocus system runs continuously throughout a video recording, constantly adjusting focus to keep the subject sharp even as it moves toward or away from the camera. Press SET and choose Enable to keep it active, or Disable to lock focus at the point it was when you started recording. With Movie Servo AF enabled, the camera applies smooth, gradual focus transitions to avoid abrupt focus-pulling that would be distracting in the final video. Disable it when filming a stationary subject and you want to prevent any focus hunting, or when you are pulling focus manually and do not want the camera to override your adjustments.

- **Movie Servo AF speed** — When Movie Servo AF is active, this setting controls how quickly the Canon EOS R10 moves from the current focus point to the new focus position when the subject moves. Press SET to open a slider from minus 7 (slowest transition) to plus 7 (fastest transition). A slower speed produces gradual, cinematic focus pulls that look intentional and smooth. A faster speed keeps up with quick subject movement but may look mechanical or jerky. The right setting depends on the speed of your subject and the look you want. For interviews and documentary footage, minus 2 to minus 4 produces natural-looking focus shifts. For action where the subject is moving quickly toward or away from the camera, a faster setting around plus 3 to plus 5 may be needed to maintain sharp focus.

- **Movie Servo AF tracking** — This setting adjusts how quickly the Canon EOS R10 responds to changes in subject position during video recording — specifically, how easily the camera switches its focus target to a newly prominent subject when something comes between the camera and the original subject. Press SET to open a slider from minus 2 (most persistent, sticks to the originally tracked subject even when something passes in front) to plus 2 (most responsive, switches focus quickly to whatever is currently closest or most prominent). A more persistent setting is better for subjects that occasionally step behind other objects but remain your intended focus target. A more responsive setting suits rapidly changing scenes where the nearest subject is always the correct focus target.

- **Audio** — This item opens a sub-menu containing all microphone and audio recording settings for the Canon EOS R10. Press SET to enter it. The following items are available inside the Audio sub-menu.
  - **Recording** — The master switch for audio. Set to Enable to record sound alongside your video. Set to Disable for silent video files. When disabled, no audio track is recorded and the setting cannot be overridden. Leave this at Enable for all standard video recording.
  - **Recording level** — Sets the input sensitivity of the microphone — how loudly the audio is captured. The range is 1 to 64, displayed as a number alongside a live audio level meter visible on the recording screen. Watch the meter while your subject speaks or the ambient sound is at its typical level. The bar should peak roughly in the upper third of the scale during the loudest expected sounds — reaching the red zone at the far right means the audio will distort and clip. Reduce the level if the meter consistently hits the red. Increase it if the meter barely moves and the audio sounds quiet. For most outdoor and indoor interview situations, a level between 30 and 45 is a reasonable starting point.
  - **Wind filter** — Activates a low-frequency cut filter on the built-in stereo microphone to reduce the rumbling sound produced by wind blowing directly across the microphone inlets. Press SET and choose Enable to activate it. The filter effectively removes bass-heavy wind noise while preserving most speech and ambient sound above the affected frequency range. Enable it whenever you are shooting outdoors in any wind conditions. Disable it in windless indoor environments to preserve the full frequency range of the audio.
  - **Attenuator** — When sudden, unexpectedly loud sounds — a shout, a clap, a vehicle horn — would normally push the audio level into distortion, the Attenuator automatically reduces the microphone input level by 12 dB at the moment of the loud sound to prevent

clipping. Press SET and choose Enable to activate it. This is a useful safety net for unpredictable recording environments such as live events, street shooting, or any situation where you cannot monitor and manually adjust the recording level in real time. For controlled recording environments where you have set the level carefully, the Attenuator is not necessary.

- **Movie digital IS —** The Canon EOS R10 does not have in-body image stabilisation. Movie digital IS compensates for this during video recording by applying electronic stabilisation — the camera crops slightly into the sensor and uses the cropped area as a buffer, shifting the captured region of the frame electronically to counteract camera shake. Press SET and choose from three options. Off applies no electronic stabilisation — only the optical IS of the attached lens is active. Enable applies a moderate level of electronic stabilisation with a small crop to the frame. Enhanced applies stronger stabilisation with a more noticeable crop, designed for walking handheld shots where camera movement is greater. The Enhanced setting significantly reduces the field of view compared to Off, so be aware of the tighter framing. Use Enable for general handheld video. Use Enhanced for walking or moving shots. Use Off on a tripod or gimbal where the stabilisation is unnecessary and the crop is undesirable.

- **Time-lapse movie —** Time-lapse movie automates the process of taking a sequence of still photos at set intervals and assembles them directly into a finished video file inside the Canon EOS R10, without any external software needed. Press SET to open the time-lapse configuration screen. Scene sets the shooting interval and total number of shots automatically based on a simplified scene selection — choose from options such as buildings and scenery, streets, flowers and plants, or sky and weather. For manual control, select Custom and set the Interval (the time gap between each shot, in seconds), the Number of shots (how many frames the sequence will contain), and the Movie rec quality for the output video. The camera calculates and displays the estimated total shooting time and the length of the finished video based on your settings. A tripod is essential — any camera movement between frames creates jarring jumps in the final video. Fully charge the battery or power the camera via USB before starting, as long time-lapse sequences can run for hours. Do not open the SD card door or power off the camera while the time-lapse is in progress.

- **Video snap —** Video snap is a mode that records a fixed-length video clip each time you press the Movie Record button, rather than starting an open-ended recording that you stop manually. Press SET to configure it. Choose a clip length of 2 seconds, 4 seconds, or 8 seconds. Once set, each press of the Movie Record button records exactly that duration and then stops automatically. The R10 can string consecutive video snaps together into a single compilation file, building a highlight reel of short clips in-camera as you shoot. This is a useful tool for travel documentation, events, or any shooting where you want to capture brief moments without managing separate start and stop presses for each clip.

Note: *The Movie menu tab is separate from the Shooting menu tabs. Settings you configure in the Movie menu apply only to video recording and do not affect still image capture. Conversely, changes to still image settings in the red Shooting tabs do not affect video output.*

3.5 Playback Menu — Every Item Explained

The Playback menu is accessed via the blue tab. Press MENU and rotate the Main Dial to the right past the nine red Shooting tabs and the pink Movie tab to reach it. The blue tab is marked with a right-pointing triangle — the standard play icon. All settings in this tab relate to reviewing, managing, and processing images and videos after they have been captured.

- **Protect images** — Applies a protection lock to selected images, preventing them from being accidentally erased by the Delete button or by the Erase images function. Press SET and choose from Select images (you review images one by one and press SET on each one you want to protect — a key icon appears on protected images), All images in folder (protects every image in the currently active folder), Unprotect all in folder (removes protection from all images at once), All images on card, or Unprotect all on card. Protecting an image does not prevent it from being erased when the SD card is formatted — format always erases all data regardless of protection status.
- **Rotate** — Manually rotates the currently displayed image 90 degrees clockwise with each press of SET. This is a display-only rotation — it does not alter the image file itself, only how it is presented on screen and in compatible viewing software. Use this if an image was captured in a way that the camera's auto-rotate did not correctly identify, or if

you want to view a landscape image rotated to portrait orientation for inspection.

- **Erase images** — Permanently deletes images from the SD card. Press SET and choose from Select and erase images (you scroll through images and mark each one for deletion, then confirm all at once — use this for selective deletion of multiple images), All images in folder (deletes every unprotected image in the current folder), or All images on card (deletes every unprotected image on the entire card). Protected images are skipped. Deleted images cannot be recovered from within the camera. If you need to recover accidentally deleted images, stop using the card immediately and use data recovery software on a computer before any new images overwrite the deleted data.

- **Print order** — Marks specific images for printing using the DPOF (Digital Print Order Format) standard, which is recognised by compatible photo printers and print services. Press SET to choose images, set the number of copies for each, and whether to print the date on the image. Take the SD card to a DPOF-compatible printer or photo kiosk and it will automatically print the marked images in the specified quantities without you needing to select them manually on the printer.

- **Photobook Set-up** — Similar to Print order but specifically for creating photobooks. Press SET to mark up to 998 images from the SD card for photobook production. The marked images can then be ordered through Canon's online photobook service or processed in Canon's printing software. This is a convenience function for photographers who regularly create printed photobooks from their work.

- **Creative filters** — Applies artistic filter effects to existing JPEG images stored on the card, producing a new filtered copy without altering the original. Press SET, scroll to the image you want to apply a filter to, and press SET again to open the filter selection. The available filters mirror those in the Creative Filters shooting mode: Grainy B/W, Soft focus, Fish-eye effect, Water painting effect, Toy camera effect, Miniature effect, and the HDR art variations. Use the Main Dial to scroll between filters and see a live preview of each effect on your image. Press SET to confirm and the camera saves a new JPEG copy with the filter applied. The original image is not modified. This is useful when you shot in the standard mode but later decide a creative effect would suit a particular image.

- **Resize** — Creates a smaller JPEG copy of a selected image at a reduced resolution. Press SET, select the image, and choose the target size from the available options — the specific sizes available depend on the resolution of the original image. The reduced copy is saved as a separate file alongside the original. Use this to produce a smaller version of an image for email or messaging without needing a computer, when the full-resolution file is too large to send directly.
- **Cropping** — Crops a JPEG image in-camera and saves the cropped area as a new file. Press SET and select the image you want to crop. A crop frame appears on screen. Use the Magnify and Reduce buttons to change the size of the crop frame, and use the joystick to move it to the area you want to keep. Rotate the Quick Control Dial to rotate the crop frame if needed. Press SET when the crop is positioned correctly and the camera saves the cropped image as a new file. The aspect ratio of the cropped area is shown on screen and the saved file's resolution depends on how large the crop area is. The original image is unchanged.
- **RAW processing** — Converts a RAW image file into a JPEG directly inside the Canon EOS R10, giving you control over the processing parameters without needing a computer. Press SET and scroll to the RAW image you want to process — only RAW files are listed, not JPEGs. Press SET to open the processing options screen. You can adjust: Brightness (exposure compensation for the conversion), White balance (choose any of the standard presets or the custom value), Picture Style, Auto Lighting Optimizer, High ISO speed NR, Lens aberration correction, Clarity, and Cropping. Each adjustment shows a live preview update on the image thumbnail. When you are satisfied, select Save to create the JPEG. The original RAW file is not altered. This is a powerful feature for photographers who shoot RAW but occasionally need a processed JPEG from a specific image while away from their computer.
- **HEIF to JPEG conversion** — Converts images saved in the HEIF format into JPEG files, creating a new JPEG copy while leaving the original HEIF file intact. Press SET, select the HEIF image, and confirm. The JPEG is saved to the card immediately. Use this when you need to share or use a HEIF image with a device or application that does not support the HEIF format — converting to JPEG ensures compatibility with all standard viewing and editing software.

- **Slide show —** Plays all images in the current folder as an automatic slideshow on the LCD screen. Press SET to open the slideshow settings. Set the display duration for each image (1, 2, 3, 5, 10, or 20 seconds), choose whether to repeat the slideshow continuously, and select whether to include videos in the playback sequence. Select Start to begin. The slideshow runs automatically — press SET to pause, and press MENU to stop it. This is useful for reviewing a shoot's output without pressing a button for each image, or for showing a client or group a selection of images on the camera screen.

- **Set image search conditions —** Filters which images are displayed during playback according to criteria you specify. Press SET and choose filter parameters: Rating (show only images with a specific star rating), Date (show only images taken on a specific date), Folder (show only images in a specific folder), Protected (show only protected images), Card (show images from the current card), or File type (show only stills or only movies). Once a filter is active, playback navigates only through images that match the criteria, ignoring all others. This is particularly useful on a full card when you want to review only today's shots, only your five-star selects, or only video files. To clear all filters and return to viewing all images, return to this setting and select All images.

- **Image jump with dial —** Sets how far the Main Dial jumps through images during playback each time it is rotated. Press SET and choose from: 1 image (moves one image at a time — the default), 10 images (jumps ten images per click), 100 images (jumps one hundred images per click), Date (jumps to the first image of the next or previous shooting date), Folder (jumps to the first image in the next or previous folder), Movies (jumps between video files only, skipping stills), Stills (jumps between still images only, skipping videos), or Rating (jumps between images that have been given a star rating). When jump by Date, Folder, or Rating is active, rotating the Quick Control Dial during playback still moves one image at a time, while the Main Dial performs the jump function.

- **Playback information display —** Configures what information overlays appear on screen when you press the INFO button during image playback. Press SET to open the configuration screen. You can toggle each of the following overlays independently: the basic shooting information panel (shutter speed, aperture, ISO, lens, focal length, date, time), the histogram, the highlight and shadow alert, the AF point overlay, the white balance data, the GPS information panel if GPS data was recorded, and the ratings display. Enable only the overlays you regularly use — having all of them active means pressing INFO many times to cycle back to a clean image view.

- **Highlight alert —** When enabled, any areas of a playback image that are overexposed — recording as pure white with no recoverable detail — blink rapidly between black and white on the LCD screen. This makes it immediately obvious which parts of your image have lost highlight detail, allowing you to judge whether to reshoot with less exposure. Press SET and choose Enable to activate it. The blinking areas appear only during playback and do not affect the image file. This is sometimes called the blinkies by photographers and is one of the most useful review tools the camera offers. Leave it enabled as a default.

- **AF point display —** When enabled, the autofocus point or points that were active at the moment the photo was taken are shown as a red or white frame overlay on the image during playback. This lets you see exactly where the camera focused, which is useful for diagnosing focus errors — if the image is sharp in the wrong place, the AF point display shows you which point was active and why. Press SET and choose Enable to activate it.

- **Playback grid —** Overlays a grid of lines on your image during playback to assist with composition evaluation. Press SET and choose from Off, 3x3 Grid (nine equal sections — useful for checking rule-of-thirds composition), 6x4 Grid (a finer grid for more precise alignment checks), or 3x3+Diagonal Grid (the standard grid with diagonal lines added for checking diagonal balance and leading lines). The grid is a display overlay only and does not appear in the image file.

- **Magnification —** Sets the default zoom level that appears the first time you press the Magnify button during playback. Press SET and choose from 1x (no magnification, full image view), 2x, 4x, 8x, or 10x. If you typically press the magnify button to check critical focus on faces or fine detail, setting the default to 10x saves you multiple button presses to reach full magnification. Choose the level that matches your most common playback review use.

- **HDMI HDR output —** When the Canon EOS R10 is connected to a television or monitor via the HDMI mini port, this setting configures whether the output signal is sent in standard dynamic range or HDR

PQ format. Press SET and choose On to send HDR PQ output if your connected display supports it, or Off to send a standard signal. This affects both live view output and image playback over HDMI. Set it to On only if your connected monitor or television is HDR-compatible — on a standard display, the HDR output will appear flat and washed out.

3.6 Setup Menu — Every Item Explained

The Setup menu is accessed via the yellow tabs. Press MENU and rotate the Main Dial to the right past the red, pink, and blue tabs to reach the yellow wrench icon tabs. There are multiple yellow tabs — rotate the Main Dial to move between them. The Setup menu contains the camera's system-level settings that govern how the Canon EOS R10 operates as a device, independent of how it captures images.

- **Record func+card/folder sel.** — Controls how the Canon EOS R10 organises the files it saves to the SD card. Press SET to open it. The Rec. func. option does not apply to the R10 in the same way as dual-card cameras — the R10 has a single card slot, so this setting primarily governs file type separation. The Card sel. option lets you check the card currently in the slot. The Folder options allow you to create a new folder manually, select an existing folder to save into, or rename folders. The Auto-create folder setting determines whether the camera creates a new folder automatically when the current folder reaches 9999 images. Leaving this at its default setting is suitable for most users — the camera manages folders automatically without any intervention needed.
- **File numbering** — Controls how the Canon EOS R10 numbers each image file it saves. Press SET and choose from three options. Continuous numbering causes files to be numbered in sequence across all cards and sessions — the counter continues from where it left off after every power cycle and card change, running from 0001 up to 9999 before resetting. This ensures no two files from the same camera ever share the same number, which is useful when managing large libraries. Auto reset resets the file number to 0001 every time the camera is powered on or a new card is inserted. Manual reset immediately resets the counter to 0001 on the next shot. Use Continuous for standard shooting to avoid duplicate file names. Use

Manual reset if you want to start a clean numbered sequence for a specific project or shoot day.

- **Format card** — Erases all data on the SD card and prepares it with a fresh Canon file structure. Press SET, then select OK on the confirmation screen to begin. Formatting takes only a few seconds. All images, videos, and any other files on the card are permanently erased, including protected images. This is the same operation covered in Section 2.3. Format the card at the start of each new shoot once you have confirmed all previous images have been backed up.
- **Auto rotate** — When you hold the Canon EOS R10 vertically to take a portrait-orientation photo, the camera records which direction it was rotated. Auto rotate uses this information to display the image the correct way up in playback. Press SET and choose On (camera and computer rotation) — the image is rotated for display both on the camera's LCD screen during playback and in compatible software on a computer. On (computer only) — the rotation tag is embedded in the file for software to use, but the camera itself displays the image in the orientation it was physically captured. Off — no rotation information is recorded. Leave this set to On (camera and computer) for the most convenient experience.
- **Date/Time/Zone** — Sets the internal clock and time zone for the Canon EOS R10. Press SET to open the configuration screen. The date and time are embedded in every image file the camera produces as part of the EXIF metadata — this data is how photo management software sorts your images by date and time. Set this accurately whenever you travel to a different time zone to keep your image timestamps correct. The process for setting the date and time is the same as described in Section 2.5.
- **Language** — Sets the language used for all menu text, button labels, error messages, and on-screen prompts. Press SET and scroll through the list of available languages to find your preferred one. Press SET to confirm. The change takes effect immediately. All subsequent menus and displays will appear in the selected language.
- **Video system** — Sets the electrical video output standard the Canon EOS R10 uses. Press SET and choose NTSC or PAL. NTSC is the standard used in North America, Japan, South Korea, and parts of South America. PAL is the standard used in Europe, Australia, China, India, and most of Africa and Asia. This setting affects the available frame rates in video

recording — NTSC enables 29.97 and 59.94 fps, while PAL enables 25 and 50 fps. It also affects the HDMI video output signal. Set this to match the standard used in your country or region. If you change this setting, restart the camera to ensure all frame rate options update correctly.

- **Beep** — Controls the audible confirmation sounds the Canon EOS R10 makes during operation. Press SET and choose from Enable (the camera beeps to confirm focus lock in One-Shot AF, to indicate the end of a self-timer countdown, and during certain other operations), Touch (the camera beeps only for touch screen operations such as tapping a focus point), or Disable (all beeps are silenced). Disable the beep in quiet environments such as concerts, ceremonies, wildlife photography, or any situation where an audible beep would be disruptive or unwanted.

- **Headphone volume** — Controls the audio output level when headphones are connected to the Canon EOS R10 via the 3.5mm headphone jack — available through a USB-C to 3.5mm adapter, as the R10 does not have a dedicated headphone port. This setting adjusts the playback volume for reviewing audio during recorded video playback. Press SET and use the Main Dial to increase or decrease the volume level. This setting has no effect on the microphone recording level.

- **Power saving** — Controls how quickly the Canon EOS R10 reduces power consumption when left idle. Press SET to open three individual timers. Auto power off sets how long the camera waits before shutting itself down completely when not in use — options range from 15 seconds to 30 minutes, or Disable to prevent automatic power off entirely. The Viewfinder off timer sets how quickly the EVF display turns off when no eye is detected at the viewfinder. The Display off timer sets how quickly the LCD screen dims and then turns off when no controls are operated. Set Auto power off to 1 or 2 minutes for normal shooting to preserve battery life, or to a longer time if you frequently leave the camera idle for extended periods between shots and find it inconvenient to wait for it to wake up.

- **Eco mode** — A power conservation mode that dims the LCD screen more aggressively when the camera is idle and shortens the auto power off timer automatically, regardless of what the Power saving timers are set to. Press SET and choose On to enable it. In Eco mode, the screen dims noticeably after just a few seconds of inactivity, waking again when you half-press the shutter. Battery life is meaningfully extended in Eco mode, particularly during long sessions where the camera is frequently left idle between shots. The trade-off is that the dimming can be jarring if you are accustomed to the screen staying consistently bright.

- **Screen/viewfinder display** — Controls which display is active and how the eye sensor manages switching between the EVF and the LCD screen. Press SET to open it. The Display option lets you choose between Auto (the eye sensor switches between EVF and LCD automatically), EVF (the EVF is always active, the LCD is always off), and LCD (the LCD is always active, the EVF only activates when you physically look through it). The Brightness and Colour tone sub-options adjust the visual quality of the selected display. Use Auto for normal handheld shooting. Use EVF when mounting the camera on a tripod and shooting exclusively through the viewfinder. Use LCD for video recording with the screen flipped out.

- **Touch control** — Enables, disables, or adjusts the sensitivity of the LCD touch screen. Press SET and choose Enable for standard response, Sensitive for faster and lighter touch response, or Disable to turn off all touch input. This is the same setting described in Section 2.6.

- **LCD brightness** — Adjusts the brightness of the rear LCD screen independently. Press SET and a brightness scale appears with a grey test patch. Adjust the scale with the Main Dial and evaluate the test patch to find the brightness level that looks accurate and comfortable in your current environment. In bright sunlight you will need a higher brightness setting to see the screen clearly. In a dark studio, a lower setting prevents the screen from appearing glaring or affecting your eyes.

- **LCD color tone** — Adjusts the colour tone of the rear LCD screen, shifting it warmer (more amber) or cooler (more blue). Press SET and use the Main Dial to move the slider. This is a calibration setting for the display itself, not a change to your image files — it only affects how images look on the LCD screen. Adjust it if the LCD's colour cast makes it difficult to judge white balance or colour accuracy on screen.

- **Viewfinder brightness** — Adjusts the brightness of the electronic viewfinder display. Press SET and choose Auto — the camera adjusts the EVF brightness based on ambient light conditions automatically using a sensor — or Manual, which lets you set a fixed brightness level using the Main Dial. Auto is appropriate for most shooting. Manual gives you a consistent, unchanging EVF brightness for situations where you need reliable visual consistency between shots.

- **Viewfinder color tone** — Adjusts the colour tone of the EVF display in the same way that LCD color tone adjusts the rear screen. Press SET and use the Main Dial to shift the EVF colour toward warmer or cooler tones. Adjust this if the EVF's colour rendering appears noticeably different from the LCD and you want them to match more closely for consistent evaluation of images.

- **HDMI display** — Configures what is shown on an external monitor or television connected to the Canon EOS R10 via the HDMI mini port. Press SET and choose from Display On (both the camera's LCD screen and the external monitor are active simultaneously — the camera continues to show its normal display while the HDMI output mirrors it) or Display Off (when an HDMI device is detected, the camera's LCD screen turns off and the image is sent only to the external display). Display Off is the standard choice when using a field monitor or external recorder during video production, as it reduces the camera's power consumption and removes any distraction from the external display.

- **GPS device settings** — Configures the Canon EOS R10 to record GPS location data in the EXIF metadata of each image when a compatible Canon GPS receiver is connected via the USB-C port or through a dedicated GPS accessory. Press SET to access the GPS sub-settings: GPS auto time setting (synchronises the camera's clock to GPS satellite time, keeping the timestamp accurate without manual adjustment), GPS information display (shows the current GPS coordinates, altitude, and satellite fix status on screen). Without a connected GPS receiver, these settings have no effect.

- **Wi-Fi settings** — Manages all Wi-Fi connections for the Canon EOS R10. Press SET to open the Wi-Fi configuration screen. Wi-Fi/Bluetooth connection is the primary option — it opens the wireless connection wizard where you can initiate connections to smartphones via the Canon Camera Connect app, to computers, to printers, to Canon's image.canon cloud service, or to other cameras for image transfer. The Nickname setting lets you set a custom name for this camera that appears when other devices search for it — useful if you use multiple Canon cameras. The Clear settings option resets all paired devices and saved connection configurations. A full walkthrough of connecting to a smartphone is in Part 15.

- **Bluetooth settings** — Manages the Bluetooth connection used for pairing the Canon EOS R10 with a smartphone or with the Canon BR-E1 wireless remote. Press SET and choose Bluetooth function to enable or disable Bluetooth entirely. The paired device is listed here — select it to disconnect or remove the pairing. Bluetooth is used for the persistent background connection between the R10 and the Canon Camera Connect app on your phone, which enables automatic image transfer and location logging even when Wi-Fi is not active. Bluetooth uses significantly less power than Wi-Fi and can remain on throughout a shooting session without noticeably affecting battery life.
- **Wireless communication settings** — Contains additional network configuration options. Press SET to access the camera's MAC address, the option to change the camera's wireless nickname, and advanced network settings including manual IP address configuration for connection to specific networks or FTP servers. Most users will not need to adjust anything in this sub-menu — it is primarily relevant for photographers who transfer images directly to a network server on set.
- **Copyright information** — Embeds your name and a copyright notice directly into the EXIF metadata of every image the Canon EOS R10 captures from the moment this information is entered. Press SET and select Enter author's name or Enter copyright details. Use the on-screen keyboard that appears to type your name and copyright text. Once saved, every subsequent image file will contain this information in its metadata, making it visible in editing software such as Adobe Lightroom, Bridge, or Canon Digital Photo Professional. This does not visibly watermark the image — it embeds the text as invisible metadata. Set this once and it is retained permanently until you change or clear it.
- **Certification logo display** — Displays the regulatory and certification logos applicable to the Canon EOS R10 in your region — such as CE marking, FCC compliance, and other standards compliance marks. This is an informational screen only. Press SET to view the logos. There are no adjustable settings here.
- **Custom Functions (C.Fn)** — Opens the Custom Functions sub-menu where you can modify advanced camera behaviours that are not exposed in the main menu. Custom Functions are covered in full in Part 16 of this guide. From here you can access the full C.Fn list and adjust individual parameters.

- **Camera user settings** — Allows you to save the current complete configuration of the Canon EOS R10 — every menu setting, every custom control assignment, every shooting parameter — to a saved user profile stored on the SD card or within the camera. Press SET to access Save settings (saves the current configuration) and Load settings (restores a previously saved configuration). This is useful for photographers who use the camera in different contexts — for example, saving one profile configured for portrait shooting and another for wildlife shooting, and switching between them instantly without manually reconfiguring dozens of individual settings.
- **Clear all camera settings** — Resets every setting in the Canon EOS R10 to its factory default values. Press SET and confirm by selecting OK. This is a complete reset — all menu configurations, custom controls, Wi-Fi pairings, and shooting settings return to the state the camera was in when it left the factory. The date, time, language, and copyright information are also cleared. Use this if the camera is behaving unexpectedly and you cannot identify the cause, or before handing the camera to someone else and want to ensure they start from a clean default state. It cannot be undone.
- **Firmware** — Displays the current firmware version installed on the Canon EOS R10 and allows you to update it. Press SET to see the version number. Canon periodically releases firmware updates that add features, improve autofocus performance, fix bugs, and extend compatibility with new lenses and accessories. To update: download the latest firmware file from Canon's official website to your computer, copy it to the root level of a formatted SD card, insert that card into the camera, return to this menu item, press SET, and select OK to begin the update. The process takes several minutes. The camera must not be powered off during the update — connect via USB power or use a fully charged battery. A full update walkthrough is in Part 17.

3.7 My Menu — Building Your Personal Shortcut Menu

My Menu is a blank menu tab that you fill yourself with the settings you use most often. Instead of navigating to different tabs every time you need a specific setting, you can add up to six items from anywhere in the menu system to My Menu and reach all of them from a single location. You can also configure the camera to open My Menu automatically every time you press the MENU button, bypassing the other tabs entirely and taking you straight to your most-used settings.

How to Open My Menu

Press the MENU button on the upper-left of the camera back. Rotate the Main Dial all the way to the right past all the coloured tabs until you reach the green tab at the far end — it is marked with a star icon. This is My Menu. When you first access it, it is empty except for the configuration options at the bottom.

Adding Items to My Menu

1. With the green My Menu tab open, scroll down using the Quick Control Dial to highlight Add to My Menu and press SET.
2. The screen switches to show the full menu system. The red Shooting tabs appear first. Use the Main Dial to move between tabs and the Quick Control Dial to scroll through items within each tab.
3. Navigate to any setting you want to add — for example, scroll to the red Shooting Menu 2 tab, then scroll down to ISO speed settings.
4. With the item highlighted, press SET. A confirmation message appears. Press SET again to confirm the addition.
5. The camera returns to the Add to My Menu screen. Repeat steps 2 to 4 to add more items. You can add up to six items in total.
6. When you are done adding items, press the MENU button to return to My Menu. Your added items now appear in the list, ready to access directly.

Reordering Items in My Menu

7. On the green My Menu tab, scroll down to Sort and press SET.
8. The list of your added items appears. Highlight the item you want to move and press SET.
9. The item is selected and highlighted differently. Use the Quick Control Dial to move it up or down in the list.
10. Press SET to confirm the new position. Repeat for other items if needed, then press MENU to exit.

Removing Items from My Menu

11. On the green My Menu tab, scroll to Delete from My Menu and press SET.
12. The list of your added items appears with tick boxes. Highlight the item you want to remove and press SET to mark it.
13. Press the Q button to proceed. A confirmation screen appears. Select OK and press SET to remove the marked items.

Making My Menu Open First

14. On the green My Menu tab, scroll down to Display from My Menu and press SET.
15. Select Enable and press SET to confirm.
16. From now on, every time you press the MENU button, the camera opens directly to your My Menu tab instead of the last-used tab. To navigate to the other tabs from here, rotate the Main Dial left toward the red tabs.

Note: *My Menu items are saved permanently and are not cleared when you use Clear all camera settings — this is one of the few settings that survives a full camera reset. However, if you copy settings to an SD card and load them on a different R10 body, My Menu items are included in the transfer.*

3.8 Quick Control Screen (Q Button)

The Quick Control screen is the fastest way to change the most commonly used shooting settings on the Canon EOS R10 without opening the full menu. Think of it as an express panel — it brings together the settings you adjust most often into a single grid that appears directly on the LCD screen. Experienced photographers use the Q screen constantly to switch between settings while keeping the camera ready to shoot.

Opening the Quick Control Screen

Press the Q button on the back of the camera. It is located on the right side of the camera back, clearly labelled Q. The shooting screen is replaced by a grid of settings panels. Each panel shows one setting and its current value.

Navigating and Changing Settings

17. Press the Q button to open the Quick Control screen.

18. To highlight a setting, use the joystick to move the selection across the grid, or tap the setting directly on the touch screen.
19. Once a setting is highlighted, rotate the Main Dial or the Quick Control Dial to change its value. The value updates immediately on screen as you rotate — you can see the change taking effect in real time.
20. To open the full detail screen for the highlighted setting — which shows all available options in a list rather than just cycling through them with a dial — press SET. Make your selection and press SET again to confirm.
21. When you are finished, half-press the shutter button or press the Q button again to close the Quick Control screen and return to the shooting view.

Settings Available on the Quick Control Screen

The following settings appear on the Q screen during still photography. Each can be changed directly from this screen without opening the full menu.

- **Image quality** — Cycles through the available file format and size combinations — RAW, C-RAW, JPEG sizes, HEIF, and dual RAW+JPEG combinations. Rotate the Main Dial to change the setting.
- **Picture Style** — Switches between the available Picture Styles — Auto, Standard, Portrait, Landscape, Fine Detail, Neutral, Faithful, Monochrome, and User Defined styles. Rotate the Quick Control Dial to cycle through them.
- **AF operation** — Switches between One-Shot AF, Servo AF, and AI Focus. Rotate a dial to cycle through the three options.
- **AF area** — Changes the autofocus area mode — Spot, 1-Point, Expand, Zone, Whole Area, and Tracking. Rotate a dial to move between them.
- **Drive mode** — Switches between Single shooting, High-speed continuous plus, High-speed continuous, Low-speed continuous, Self-timer 10 sec, Self-timer 2 sec, and Self-timer Continuous.
- **Metering mode** — Switches between Evaluative, Partial, Spot, and Centre-weighted average metering.
- **White balance** — Cycles through all white balance presets and the Custom white balance option.

- **ISO** — Adjusts ISO sensitivity directly. Rotating the Main Dial changes the ISO value. Pressing SET opens the full ISO speed settings screen where you can also configure Auto ISO range.
- **Exposure compensation** — Moves the exposure compensation slider from minus 3 to plus 3 stops. Rotating the Quick Control Dial adjusts the level. The current value is shown as a position on the scale.
- **Flash exposure compensation** — Appears on the Q screen only when an external Speedlite flash unit is attached to the hot shoe. Adjusts the flash output brighter or darker relative to the E-TTL II metered level.

Note: *The Q screen in video mode shows a different set of settings relevant to video recording — including resolution, frame rate, and audio level — replacing the still-photography items. The operation is identical: highlight a setting and rotate a dial to change it.*

PART 4 — Physical Controls and What They Do

Every button, dial, ring, and switch on the Canon EOS R10 has a specific purpose and, in many cases, behaves differently depending on which shooting mode is active. Part 1.2 of this guide introduced you to where each control is located on the camera body. This part goes further — it explains exactly what each control does, how to operate it correctly, what it controls in each context, and why it works the way it does. Work through this section with the camera in your hands.

4.1 Shutter Button

The shutter button is the large, round, slightly concave button on the top-right of the Canon EOS R10, sitting inside the collar of the ON/OFF switch. It is the control you will use more than any other on this camera, and it has two distinct stages of pressure that serve entirely different functions. Understanding both stages is the single most important habit you can develop as a photographer.

Half-Press — Focus and Metering

Press the shutter button down gently until you feel a soft resistance — approximately halfway. Do not press it all the way down. This is the half-press. When you half-press the shutter button, two things happen simultaneously: the Canon EOS R10 activates its autofocus system and locks focus on the subject, and it takes an exposure reading from the scene to calculate the correct shutter speed, aperture, and ISO combination.

When focus is successfully achieved, a confirmation signal appears. In One-Shot AF mode, a green dot lights up in the lower-left area of the viewfinder or LCD display and a short beep sounds if the beep is enabled. The AF point or points that achieved focus turn green on screen. If the camera cannot achieve focus, the dot blinks orange and no beep sounds — this is the camera telling you that the focus has not locked and the photo should not yet be taken.

You can hold the shutter half-pressed to maintain the focus lock while you make final adjustments to your composition. As long as you keep gentle pressure on the button, the focus stays locked on the point it found. Release the pressure fully and the lock is cancelled.

Full Press — Taking the Photo

Once you have confirmed focus with a half-press, continue pressing the shutter button all the way down in one smooth, controlled motion. The shutter fires and the image is captured and saved to the SD card. The entire process — half-press, confirm focus, full press — should be a fluid, two-stage movement rather than a single hard jab at the button.

Pressing the shutter button all the way down in a single motion without the half-press stage is one of the most common causes of blurry and out-of-focus photos, particularly for new users. The camera needs the half-press moment to lock focus before the shutter fires. Skipping it means the camera takes the photo before it has had time to find and confirm focus, and the result is an image that may be acceptably sharp or may be completely soft depending on whether the AF system happened to be focused in the right area at the moment of the full press.

Practical Technique

Develop the habit of treating every shot as a two-step process: half-press and wait for the green dot, then full press. In the beginning this will feel slow. With practice it becomes a single, almost instantaneous motion. The half-press pause is where the camera does its work — your only job is to give it that moment before firing.

> **Important:** *Never jab the shutter button in one quick full press. Always half-press first, wait for the focus confirmation signal, then follow through to the full press. This single habit is responsible for a larger improvement in image sharpness than any other technique.*

4.2 Mode Dial

The Mode Dial is the large, ridged rotating dial on the top-left of the Canon EOS R10. Grip it between your thumb and forefinger and rotate it to select your shooting mode. Each position clicks firmly into place so you always know exactly which mode is active. The selected mode is indicated by the marking aligned with the white index line at the back of the dial. The currently active mode name or icon also appears on the LCD screen and in the EVF at all times.

Each position on the Mode Dial fundamentally changes how the camera behaves — which settings it controls automatically, which settings you control manually, and what options are available to you. Choosing the right mode for your subject and situation is one of the most important decisions in photography. Here is what each position does on the R10.

A+ — Scene Intelligent Auto

Rotate the Mode Dial to the green A+ marking. In this position, the Canon EOS R10 takes complete control of every setting — shutter speed, aperture, ISO, white balance, autofocus behaviour, drive mode, and flash activation. The camera analyses the scene many times per second, identifies the type of subject and lighting, and applies what it calculates to be the optimal settings automatically. You have no dials to turn and no settings to adjust. Point the camera at your subject, half-press the shutter to lock focus, and press fully to take the photo.

Scene Intelligent Auto is the right choice when you need to take a photo quickly without thinking through settings, when you hand the camera to someone unfamiliar with it, or when you are in a situation where getting the shot matters more than having creative control over how it looks. The trade-off is that you cannot force a particular depth of field, motion blur effect, or any other deliberate creative outcome — the camera makes those decisions.

P — Program AE

Rotate the Mode Dial to P. In Program AE, the Canon EOS R10 automatically selects both the shutter speed and the aperture to produce a correctly exposed photo. Unlike Scene Intelligent Auto, however, you retain control over every other setting — ISO, white balance, drive mode, autofocus mode, and more. You can also perform a technique called Program Shift: rotate the Main Dial while the shutter is half-pressed and the camera will shift to a different combination of shutter speed and aperture that produces the same overall exposure. For example, if the camera initially selects 1/125 sec at f/5.6, you can shift to 1/250 sec at f/4 for a faster shutter or 1/60 sec at f/8 for more depth of field, while keeping the brightness of the photo identical. Program Shift resets after each shot.

Tv — Shutter Priority

Rotate the Mode Dial to Tv. Tv stands for Time Value — Canon's naming for shutter speed. In this mode, you set the shutter speed using the Main Dial and the Canon EOS R10 automatically selects the appropriate aperture to produce a correct exposure at the shutter speed you have chosen.

Set a fast shutter speed — 1/500 sec, 1/1000 sec, or faster — to freeze a subject in motion: a bird in flight, a football being kicked, a child running. The subject appears completely sharp with no motion blur. Set a slow shutter speed — 1/30 sec, 1/15 sec, or slower — to capture the blur of motion deliberately: a silky-smooth waterfall, light trails from passing cars at night, the flowing movement of a dancer. The background may appear slightly blurred at these slower speeds if you are handholding the camera, so use a tripod for any shutter speed slower than about 1/60 sec.

If the aperture value in the viewfinder or on the LCD screen blinks, it means the scene is too bright or too dark for the camera to find a correct aperture at the shutter speed you have set — the exposure is beyond the lens's available range. Adjust your shutter speed or raise or lower the ISO until the blinking stops.

Av — Aperture Priority

Rotate the Mode Dial to Av. Av stands for Aperture Value. In this mode, you set the aperture using the Main Dial and the Canon EOS R10 automatically selects the shutter speed needed for correct exposure.

Aperture controls depth of field — the range of distance in front of and behind your subject that appears acceptably sharp in the photo. A wide aperture (a small f-number such as f/1.8 or f/2.8) produces a shallow depth of field: the subject is sharp and the background is blurred into a smooth, out-of-focus wash. This is the look most associated with professional portrait photography. A narrow aperture (a large f-number such as f/11 or f/16) produces a deep depth of field: everything from the nearby foreground to the distant background appears sharp simultaneously. This is the look of classic landscape photography.

Av mode is the most widely used semi-automatic mode because depth of field is one of the most fundamental creative decisions in photography, and once you have set the aperture you want, the camera handles all the exposure arithmetic automatically. If the shutter speed displayed blinks in the viewfinder, the lighting conditions exceed what the camera can compensate for at that aperture — adjust the aperture or ISO until it stops blinking.

M — Manual

Rotate the Mode Dial to M. In Manual mode, you set both the shutter speed and the aperture yourself. Rotate the Main Dial to change the shutter speed and rotate the Quick Control Dial to change the aperture. The Canon EOS R10 still meters the scene and shows you an exposure indicator scale at the bottom of the viewfinder and LCD — a bar that moves left toward minus when your settings will underexpose the photo, and right toward plus when they will overexpose it. The centre position indicates a metered correct exposure. The camera shows you this information but does not override your settings — it takes the photo exactly as you have configured it, even if that results in a very dark or very bright image.

Manual mode gives you complete, repeatable control. Every shot is exposed exactly as you intend, regardless of changes in the scene brightness. It is the preferred mode for studio flash photography, for astrophotography and long-exposure night work, for video where automatic exposure shifts during recording would be distracting, and for any situation where consistency across multiple frames is essential.

Fv — Flexible Priority AE

Rotate the Mode Dial to Fv. Flexible Priority AE is a single mode that can behave like any of the semi-automatic or manual modes depending on how many values you set yourself. By default, shutter speed, aperture, and ISO are all set to Auto — the camera controls all three, similar to Program AE. Rotate the Main Dial to set a specific shutter speed, and it locks at that value while the others remain automatic, like Shutter Priority. Rotate the Quick Control Dial to set a specific aperture, and it locks while the others remain automatic, like Aperture Priority. Set all three manually and the mode behaves like full Manual. Press the assigned function button (the SET button by default in Fv mode) to return any individual value back to Auto. Fv mode suits photographers who frequently move between different levels of control within a single session without wanting to rotate the Mode Dial between P, Tv, Av, and M.

SCN — Scene Mode

Rotate the Mode Dial to SCN. In Scene mode, you select from a list of preset situations and the Canon EOS R10 applies a complete package of settings optimised for that specific type of subject. To select a scene type, press the INFO button after rotating to SCN, or tap the scene icon on the LCD touch screen. Use the Quick Control Dial to scroll through the available scenes and press SET to confirm your selection. Each scene mode is explained in full in Part 5 of this guide.

Creative Filters Icon

Rotate the Mode Dial to the position marked with the Creative Filters icon — it appears as a small overlapping circle design. This mode applies an artistic visual transformation to your images in-camera at the moment of capture. Select the filter type by pressing the INFO button or using the Q screen. The available filters and what each one does are explained in Part 5 of this guide.

Video Camera Icon — Movie Mode

Rotate the Mode Dial to the video camera icon to switch the Canon EOS R10 into its dedicated movie recording mode. In this position, the camera reconfigures itself for video capture: the drive mode changes to continuous recording, the menu system displays the Movie menu settings, and all shooting parameters are adjusted for video output. Press the Movie Record button — the small button with the red ring on the top of the camera — to begin recording. Press it again to stop. The full video recording system is covered in Part 12 of this guide.

4.3 Main Dial and Quick Control Dial

The Canon EOS R10 has two rotating controls used for adjusting settings: the Main Dial and the Quick Control Dial. They work together as a pair, and understanding what each one controls in each situation is fundamental to operating the camera quickly and confidently.

Main Dial

The Main Dial is a small, textured rotating wheel positioned just behind the shutter button on the top of the camera. It is designed to be rotated with the pad of your right index finger without moving your hand away from the shooting grip. Rotate it clockwise to increase a value and counter-clockwise to decrease it —

though this direction can be reversed in the Custom Functions menu if you prefer the opposite convention.

What the Main Dial adjusts changes depending on the active shooting mode and context.

- **In Tv (Shutter Priority) mode:** rotates the shutter speed through the available values from 1/4000 sec at the fast end down to 30 sec at the slow end, and then to BULB for manual long exposures.
- **In Av (Aperture Priority) mode:** rotates the aperture through the f-stop values available on the attached lens — from the widest available aperture (lowest f-number) to the narrowest (highest f-number).
- **In M (Manual) mode:** rotates the shutter speed, while the Quick Control Dial handles the aperture.
- **In P (Program AE) mode:** performs Program Shift — changing the combination of shutter speed and aperture while maintaining the same overall exposure level.
- **In Fv (Flexible Priority) mode:** sets and adjusts the shutter speed value.
- **In the menu system:** scrolls left and right between the coloured tab categories across the top of the menu screen.
- **During image playback:** moves forward and backward through the images stored on the SD card — one image per click in the default setting, or by a larger jump amount if Image jump with dial is configured in the Playback menu.
- **On the Quick Control screen:** changes the value of the currently highlighted setting.
- **With the M-Fn button held:** cycles through the settings assigned to the M-Fn function — by default ISO, White Balance, Drive mode, AF operation, and Flash exposure compensation.

Quick Control Dial

The Quick Control Dial is the large, textured rotating ring that surrounds the SET button on the back of the camera. It is designed to be rotated with the pad of your right thumb while your eye is at the viewfinder, keeping the camera stable against your face. Rotate it clockwise to increase a value and counter-clockwise to decrease it.

- **In M (Manual) mode:** sets the aperture value while the Main Dial handles shutter speed. This division — shutter speed on the Main Dial, aperture on the Quick Control Dial — is the standard arrangement for Manual mode.
- **In Av, Tv, P, and Fv modes:** adjusts exposure compensation — moving the exposure level brighter (toward plus) or darker (toward minus) from the camera's metered reading. The change is visible on the exposure indicator scale on screen.
- **In Fv mode:** also sets the aperture when you rotate it after selecting that value to control.
- **In the menu system:** scrolls up and down through the items within the currently active tab.
- **On the Quick Control screen:** changes the value of the highlighted setting, identical in function to the Main Dial on that screen.
- **During image playback:** moves one image at a time when Image jump with dial is set to a jump function — the Quick Control Dial always moves one image at a time regardless of the jump setting applied to the Main Dial.

Note: *If you rotate either dial while the camera is in an auto mode and nothing on screen appears to change, check whether the selected mode allows that particular adjustment. In Scene Intelligent Auto (A+) for example, both dials are inactive because the camera controls all settings.*

4.4 AF-ON Button

The AF-ON button is located on the upper-right area of the camera back, positioned where your right thumb rests naturally when holding the camera in a shooting grip. It is labelled AF-ON in white text. Pressing this button activates the autofocus system on the Canon EOS R10 in exactly the same way that a half-press of the shutter button does — the camera begins focusing on the subject in the active AF area.

What It Does

By default on the Canon EOS R10, both the half-press of the shutter button and the AF-ON button activate autofocus. Pressing either one starts the focus process. The AF-ON button gives you a dedicated thumb-operated control for focus that is physically separate from the shutter button.

Back-Button Focus Technique

Many experienced photographers configure the Canon EOS R10 so that only the AF-ON button activates autofocus, removing the focus function from the shutter button entirely. This technique is called back-button focus and it fundamentally changes the way you operate the camera — giving you independent control over when the camera focuses and when it takes a photo.

With back-button focus set up, the workflow becomes: press and hold the AF-ON button with your right thumb to focus and track your subject, then press the shutter button with your right index finger to take the photo. Because focusing and shooting are completely separated, you can do the following things that are difficult with the default shutter-button focus arrangement.

You can focus on a subject, release the AF-ON button to lock that focus, then recompose the shot by moving the camera to place the subject off-centre — and the focus stays exactly where you set it, because the shutter button does not re-activate AF. With default shutter-button focus, half-pressing the shutter to recompose risks re-triggering AF and losing your focus lock.

You can switch between One-Shot AF and Servo AF behaviour within a single mode simply by how you press the AF-ON button. Hold it continuously to track a moving subject (behaves like Servo AF). Press it once and release to lock focus on a stationary subject (behaves like One-Shot AF). You do not need to change the AF operation setting in the menu.

You can take multiple photos of a stationary subject after locking focus with one AF-ON press, without the camera re-evaluating focus between shots, because the shutter button is only triggering the shutter — not AF.

How to Set Up Back-Button Focus on the R10

1. Press MENU and rotate the Main Dial to the yellow Setup tab.
2. Scroll down to Custom controls (shooting) and press SET.
3. A diagram of the camera back appears showing each assignable button. Highlight the shutter button half-press function and press SET.

4. From the list of available functions, select Metering start — this removes AF activation from the shutter half-press, leaving only metering.
5. Return to the button diagram and highlight the AF-ON button, then press SET.
6. Confirm it is set to Metering and AF start (or AF start only if you prefer). Press SET to confirm.
7. Press MENU to close the menu. From this point, the shutter button half-press only meters the scene and the AF-ON button is the sole control for autofocus.

Note: *Back-button focus takes several days of practice to feel natural if you are accustomed to the default shutter-button focus. Many photographers find it significantly improves their keeper rate once the new muscle memory is established, particularly for sports, wildlife, and any subject that alternates between moving and stationary.*

4.5 AE Lock / FE Lock Button (★)

The AE Lock button is positioned on the upper-right of the camera back, just to the left of the AF-ON button. It is marked with a star symbol (★). AE stands for Auto Exposure. FE stands for Flash Exposure. This button performs different functions depending on whether a flash is attached to the camera.

AE Lock — Locking the Exposure Without Flash

The Canon EOS R10 continuously re-evaluates the exposure as you move the camera and as the light in the scene changes. In most shooting situations this is what you want — the camera adjusts the exposure as you point it at different parts of the scene. However, there are situations where you want to measure the exposure from one specific area and then recompose the shot to place your subject somewhere else in the frame, without the exposure changing when you move the camera.

AE Lock freezes the current exposure reading so you can recompose freely. Here is how to use it.

8. Point the camera at the area of the scene you want to expose for — typically your subject's face, or a mid-tone area of the scene.
9. Half-press the shutter button to activate metering. The camera takes an exposure reading from the scene.
10. While keeping the shutter half-pressed, press the ★ button once with your right thumb. The asterisk symbol (*) appears on the LCD screen and in the EVF, confirming the exposure is now locked.
11. Without releasing the shutter half-press or the ★ lock, move the camera to recompose your shot — place your subject wherever you want in the frame.
12. Press the shutter button fully to take the photo. The exposure remains at the locked value regardless of where the camera is now pointing.
13. The exposure lock is released automatically after you take the shot, or when you release the shutter button completely and the ★ lock times out.

AE Lock is most useful when shooting subjects in front of very bright or very dark backgrounds. A person standing in front of a bright window, a subject lit by a spotlight against a dark stage, a snow-covered landscape — these are all situations where the camera's automatic metering will be skewed by the dominant background brightness. By pointing at the subject first to lock the exposure, then recomposing, you get the exposure right for what matters most.

FE Lock — Locking Flash Exposure

When an external Speedlite is attached and active, pressing the ★ button performs Flash Exposure Lock instead of AE Lock. The camera fires a brief pre-flash at low power to measure how much light reflects back from the scene, calculates the correct flash output needed for a properly exposed photo, and locks that calculation until you take the shot.

Use FE Lock when your subject is positioned off-centre and you are concerned that the flash metering system will bias its reading toward the centre of the frame where the subject is not located. Point the camera at the subject so it is in the centre, press ★ to pre-flash and lock the flash exposure, then recompose and shoot. The locked flash output ensures your off-centre subject is correctly illuminated.

Note: *The ★ button also serves as the index button during magnified playback — pressing it while zoomed into a photo during playback returns immediately to the full single-image view from any zoom level.*

4.6 Multi-Function Button (M-Fn)

The M-Fn button — Multi-Function button — is a small, low-profile button on the top of the Canon EOS R10, positioned just in front of the Mode Dial on the top-left edge of the camera. It is close enough to be reached with your left index finger while your right hand maintains the grip, or it can be pressed with your right thumb when the camera is held at waist level.

How It Works

The M-Fn button does not do anything on its own when pressed. It works in combination with the Main Dial. Press and hold the M-Fn button, then rotate the Main Dial — each click of the dial cycles through a set of settings. Release the M-Fn button when the setting you want is active, then rotate the Main Dial again (now without the M-Fn button held) to change the value of that setting.

Think of it as a mode selector for the Main Dial. Instead of opening the menu or the Q screen to access a specific setting, you hold M-Fn and flick the dial to the setting you want, then adjust it. Once you are familiar with the sequence, a complete setting change takes under two seconds without moving the camera from your eye.

Default Settings Accessible via M-Fn

By default, the Canon EOS R10 cycles through the following settings each time you click the Main Dial while the M-Fn button is held.

- **ISO sensitivity:** The current ISO value is shown on screen. Release M-Fn and rotate the Main Dial to change the ISO from 100 up to 32000 (or 51200 in expanded mode).
- **White Balance:** The current white balance setting is shown. Release M-Fn and rotate the Main Dial to cycle through all white balance presets.

- **Drive mode:** The current drive mode icon is shown. Release M-Fn and rotate the Main Dial to switch between Single, High-speed continuous, Low-speed continuous, and Self-timer options.
- **AF operation:** The current AF mode is shown. Release M-Fn and rotate the Main Dial to switch between One-Shot AF, Servo AF, and AI Focus.
- **Flash exposure compensation:** Only appears in the M-Fn cycle when an external Speedlite is attached. Shows the current flash compensation level. Release M-Fn and rotate the Main Dial to adjust the flash output.

Customising the M-Fn Button

The M-Fn button's function can be changed so that it performs a completely different action — or so that it controls a different set of settings when held with the Main Dial. To customise it: press MENU, navigate to the yellow Setup tab, scroll to Custom controls (shooting), and press SET. Highlight the M-Fn button in the camera diagram and press SET to see the available alternative functions. Custom Controls are covered in full in Part 16 of this guide.

4.7 INFO Button

The INFO button is on the upper-left area of the camera back, directly below the MENU button, clearly labelled INFO. Each press of this button cycles through a different information display mode. It functions during shooting, during menu navigation, and during playback — and what it cycles through is different in each context.

During Shooting

Each press of INFO cycles the shooting screen through the following display modes in sequence. After the last mode, the next press returns to the first.

- **Shooting information display:** The live view fills most of the screen. A row of key shooting data appears along the bottom edge — shutter speed, aperture, ISO, exposure compensation level, remaining shot count, battery level, and a row of mode icons. This is the standard display for everyday shooting.

- **Detailed shooting information:** A more comprehensive data overlay shows every active camera setting simultaneously — AF mode, white balance, drive mode, image quality, metering mode, and more. Useful for a full status check before beginning a session but can feel cluttered during active shooting.
- **No information display:** The live view fills the entire screen with no text, icons, or data overlaid. The scene appears completely unobstructed. Use this when you want to evaluate composition without any distractions, or when you find the on-screen data visually overwhelming.
- **Electronic level display:** A horizontal and vertical spirit level graphic appears at the centre of the screen. The indicator turns green when the camera is level in both the left-right (roll) and front-back (pitch) axes. Use this for landscape photography to ensure a straight horizon, for architecture, for any shot where a tilted frame would be visible and unwanted.
- **Histogram display:** A live histogram appears in the corner of the screen showing the distribution of tones in the current scene. The left side of the graph represents shadows and the right side represents highlights. This is the most accurate tool for evaluating exposure while shooting — more reliable than judging brightness by eye on the LCD screen, which changes in appearance depending on ambient light conditions.

During Playback

While an image is displayed in playback, pressing INFO cycles through the information overlays configured in the Playback information display setting in the Playback menu. By default this includes: basic image view with file number and protection status, shooting data panel showing the settings used to capture the photo, histogram overlay for evaluating the recorded exposure, and a no-information full-image view.

Inside a Menu Setting

When you have opened a specific menu setting and are on its detail screen, pressing INFO provides additional context or help text about that setting in some cases. For example, inside the Shooting info disp. setting, pressing INFO switches the configuration preview between the LCD screen layout and the EVF layout.

4.8 Magnify and Reduce Buttons

The Magnify button and the Reduce button are positioned on the upper area of the camera back. The Magnify button is marked with a magnifying glass and a plus sign (+). The Reduce button is marked with a magnifying glass and a minus sign (–). Their primary use is during image playback, though they also function during certain menu screens and during manual focus live view.

During Playback — Zooming In to Check Sharpness

Checking whether a photo is sharp at the point of focus — particularly on a face or eye in a portrait, on a small detail in a macro shot, or on a distant subject in a wildlife photo — is one of the most important habits in photography. The Canon EOS R10's LCD screen is not large enough to judge fine sharpness at the standard single-image playback view. You must zoom in to the critical area to confirm focus.

14. Press the Playback button to enter playback mode. The most recently captured image appears on screen.
15. Press the Magnify button (+) once. The image zooms in to a preset magnification level — by default, approximately 1.5x to 2x. A small navigation thumbnail appears in the corner of the screen showing your current position within the full image.
16. Continue pressing the Magnify button to increase magnification further. Each press zooms in by one step. The maximum magnification is 10x — at this level you can assess individual pixels and verify that the precise detail you cared about (an eye, a blade of grass, text on a sign) is acceptably sharp.
17. Use the joystick — the small raised thumb-control on the camera back — to pan around the zoomed image. Push it in the direction you want to move and the view shifts accordingly.
18. Press the Reduce button (–) to zoom back out one step at a time. Pressing it repeatedly returns to the standard single-image view.
19. From the standard single-image view, pressing the Reduce button one more time switches to a thumbnail index showing multiple images at once — four, nine, or 36 images depending on how many more times

you press Reduce. This index view is useful for quickly scanning a large number of shots to identify the best ones.

During Manual Focus Live View

When the lens is set to manual focus (MF), pressing the Magnify button while on the shooting screen zooms the centre of the live view image to help you achieve precise manual focus. Rotate the lens focus ring while zoomed in until the subject appears sharp, then press the Reduce button or press SET to return to the full-frame live view and take the shot.

Note: *The default zoom level that appears on the first press of the Magnify button during playback can be changed in the Playback menu under Magnification. Setting it to 10x means the first press immediately goes to maximum zoom, which saves multiple button presses if your standard review workflow always involves checking focus at full magnification.*

4.9 Multi-Controller (Joystick)

The Multi-Controller — commonly called the joystick — is a small, raised rubber-tipped nub on the back of the Canon EOS R10, positioned between the AF-ON button and the Quick Control Dial ring. It can be pushed in eight directions: up, down, left, right, and the four diagonal directions between them. It does not rotate and it does not click as a button in the standard configuration, though it can be assigned a press-function via Custom Controls.

During Shooting — Moving the AF Point

The joystick's primary use during shooting is to move the active autofocus point across the frame. When a single-point AF area mode is active (Spot AF or 1-Point AF), push the joystick in any direction and the AF point — shown as a small square on the LCD or in the EVF — moves in that direction. Push it up to move the point toward the top of the frame, left to move it toward the left edge, diagonally to position it in a corner, and so on. The point stops at the edges of the available AF area.

This is how you place the active focus point directly over your subject when it is positioned away from the centre of the frame — for example, placing the AF point over a person's eye in a portrait where the subject is composed to one side, or targeting a specific bird in a group where multiple subjects are visible.

Push the joystick toward the centre of the frame to return the AF point to the centre position quickly. Alternatively, pressing SET while on the shooting screen recentres the AF point in many AF area configurations.

During Menu Navigation

Inside the Canon EOS R10's menu system, the joystick moves the selection highlight. Push it up or down to move through a vertical list of items within a tab. Push it left or right to jump between the option columns in a grid-style menu screen, such as the white balance correction grid or the Custom Controls camera diagram. The joystick is faster than the Quick Control Dial for navigating grid-based menu screens because it moves diagonally.

During Zoomed Playback

When you have pressed the Magnify button during playback and the image is zoomed in beyond the single-image view, the joystick pans the view around the image. Push it in any direction and the displayed portion of the image shifts accordingly. This lets you inspect any area of the frame — move to the face to check sharpness, move to the background to check for distractions, move to the edges to check for vignetting or unwanted cropping.

> **Note:** *If pressing the joystick during shooting moves the AF point unexpectedly or feels too sensitive, you can adjust or disable the joystick's AF point movement function via the Custom Controls menu. Some photographers prefer to move the AF point using only the touch screen, leaving the joystick inactive.*

4.10 Touch Screen Gestures

The Canon EOS R10's rear LCD screen is fully touch-sensitive and supports a range of tap and swipe gestures that can replace or supplement the physical buttons and dials. Touch operation is particularly intuitive for moving the AF point, browsing images during playback, and selecting menu items. All touch gestures work with a single fingertip.

Tap

A single short tap on any location of the LCD screen during shooting moves the active autofocus point immediately to where you tapped. If subject detection is active, tapping a face or animal locks onto that specific subject. During menu navigation, tapping an item on screen selects it — equivalent to pressing SET. On the Quick Control screen, tapping a setting panel highlights it for adjustment.

Double-Tap

During image playback, double-tapping (two quick taps in the same location) zooms the image to 100 percent magnification centred on the location you tapped. This is the fastest way to jump directly to full magnification at a specific area — for example, double-tapping on a subject's eye to immediately check whether it is sharp at pixel level. Double-tapping again returns to the standard single-image view.

Swipe Left and Right

During image playback, swiping your finger horizontally across the screen — moving it quickly from right to left or left to right — moves between images. Swipe left to advance to the next image. Swipe right to go back to the previous image. This is the most natural and fluid way to browse through a large number of shots quickly.

Swipe Up and Down

During menu navigation, swiping vertically scrolls through the list of items in the current menu tab — equivalent to rotating the Quick Control Dial. Swipe upward to move down the list and swipe downward to move up. This gesture is most useful when navigating long menu tabs where you need to scroll past many items quickly.

Pinch In (Zoom Out)

During image playback, placing two fingers on the screen and bringing them toward each other — a pinch gesture — zooms the image out. If the image is currently magnified, pinching in reduces the magnification step by step. From the standard single-image view, pinching in further switches to the thumbnail index displaying multiple images.

Spread Apart (Zoom In)

During image playback, placing two fingers on the screen and spreading them apart — the reverse of pinching — zooms the image in. The zoom centres on the area between your two fingers, so spreading apart on the face area of a portrait zooms directly into that region. Continue spreading to increase magnification up to the maximum available level.

Touch and Drag AF — Moving AF Point While Using the EVF

When Touch and drag AF is enabled in the menu (covered in Section 3.3, Shooting Menu 6), you can drag your thumb across the LCD screen to reposition the active AF point while your eye is at the EVF. The screen acts like a trackpad for your AF point. Touch it anywhere and drag in the direction you want to move the focus target — the point moves correspondingly in the viewfinder without you needing to pull the camera away from your face. This is an efficient way to reposition focus quickly during portrait or documentary shooting without interrupting your view through the EVF.

> Note: *If you find the touch screen responding to unintended touches — for example, when your nose contacts the screen while you look through the EVF — go to Setup Menu, select Touch control, and set it to Sensitive with the active touch area restricted to the right half of the screen in the Touch and drag AF settings. This prevents inadvertent nose-touches from moving your AF point.*

4.11 Lens Controls

The Canon EOS R10 is a camera body — the lens is a separate, attachable component that has its own set of physical controls. Different lenses have different rings and switches, but RF mount lenses designed for the Canon EOS R10 share a consistent set of controls described here. Check your specific lens manual for details unique to that lens.

Focus Ring

The Focus Ring is a rotating ring on the lens barrel. On most RF lenses, it is the ring closest to the camera body. Rotating it changes the focus distance of the lens — moving the plane of focus closer or further from the camera.

The Focus Ring is active only when the lens (or the camera) is set to manual focus (MF). In autofocus mode, rotating the Focus Ring has no effect on most RF lenses — the ring is electronically coupled and the camera ignores manual input to the ring while AF is controlling focus. To use the Focus Ring manually, switch the lens to MF using the AF/MF switch on the lens barrel (if present), or set the camera to manual focus via the Quick Control screen or the AF operation setting in the menu.

When manual focus is active, rotate the Focus Ring slowly and observe the subject in the EVF or on the LCD screen. The image sharpens as the focus approaches the correct distance and softens again as it passes through it. Use MF peaking (enabled in the menu as described in Part 6) to see coloured highlights appear on the edges of in-focus objects, making it easier to identify exactly when focus is correct.

Zoom Ring

On zoom lenses, the Zoom Ring is the wider ring on the lens barrel that changes the focal length of the lens — in effect, zooming the lens in or out to make the subject appear closer or further away within the frame. Rotating the Zoom Ring toward the higher focal length end narrows the field of view and magnifies the subject. Rotating it toward the lower end widens the field of view and shows more of the scene.

The Zoom Ring is always active regardless of whether the camera is in autofocus or manual focus mode — zooming and focusing are independent operations. Prime lenses (lenses with a fixed focal length) do not have a Zoom Ring.

When you zoom in to a longer focal length, the minimum aperture available on the lens typically becomes narrower (a higher f-number) — this is normal behaviour for variable-aperture zoom lenses. If your aperture display changes when you zoom, this is expected and not a fault

Control Ring

The Control Ring is a feature specific to Canon RF mount lenses and is the ring at the front of the lens barrel — closest to the end of the lens, furthest from the camera body. It rotates smoothly and clicks into position with each increment, similar to the camera's dials. On most RF lenses the Control Ring is electronically coupled to the camera and its function is fully programmable.

By default on the Canon EOS R10, the Control Ring adjusts exposure compensation when the camera is in an auto or semi-automatic mode, and adjusts ISO when in Manual mode. To change what the Control Ring controls, go to MENU, navigate to the yellow Setup tab, select Custom controls (shooting), and in the camera diagram select the Control ring option to reassign it. Available functions include Exposure compensation, ISO sensitivity, Aperture, Shutter speed, and Disabled (which prevents accidental rotation from changing any setting).

The Control Ring gives photographers who prefer to operate the camera with their left hand on the lens a natural way to adjust a key setting without reaching across to the camera body dials. Rotating the Control Ring while maintaining a stable lens support with the left hand is an efficient and ergonomic technique for adjusting exposure parameters during portrait and documentary shooting.

> **Note:** *Some RF lenses have a physical switch that can lock the Control Ring in place to prevent accidental rotation. If the Control Ring on your lens does not appear to respond when you rotate it, check the lens barrel for a small switch labelled LOCK and slide it to the unlocked position.*

PART 5 — Shooting Modes Explained One by One

The Mode Dial on the top-left of the Canon EOS R10 gives you access to ten distinct shooting modes, each designed for a different balance of camera control and creative decision-making. Part 4.2 introduced what each position on the dial is called. This part goes further — it explains how to activate each mode, what to do once you are in it, what the camera is doing for you versus what you are doing yourself, and which real-world subjects and situations each mode suits best.

Work through this part with the Mode Dial in your hand, rotating to each position as you read about it.

5.1 Scene Intelligent Auto (A+)

How to Activate It

Rotate the Mode Dial to the green A+ marking. The green colour distinguishes this from all other modes — it is the fully automatic position. When the Mode Dial is here, the text or icon shown on the LCD screen and in the EVF confirms that Scene Intelligent Auto is active.

What the Camera Does

In Scene Intelligent Auto, the Canon EOS R10 takes complete control of every exposure and capture setting simultaneously. The camera analyses the live view image many times per second and evaluates multiple factors: whether faces are present in the frame, whether the subject is moving or stationary, how bright or dark the scene is overall, what colour the dominant light source is, whether the camera itself is moving, and what category of scene is being photographed. Based on this analysis it selects the shutter speed, aperture, ISO sensitivity, white balance, autofocus behaviour, and drive mode entirely on its own.

It also applies subject detection automatically — if a face is visible in the frame, the camera locks onto it and tracks it continuously. If it detects motion, it shifts to a faster shutter speed and continuous autofocus. If the scene is dark, it raises the ISO and slows the shutter appropriately. You do not configure any of this — it happens without any input from you.

The flash does not exist on the R10 as a built-in unit, so no flash fires automatically in this mode. If you attach an external Speedlite and switch it on, Scene Intelligent Auto will activate and control it automatically when the camera determines that fill flash would improve the exposure.

What You Do

Your only responsibilities in Scene Intelligent Auto are to point the camera at your subject, half-press the shutter button to give the camera a moment to lock focus and take an exposure reading, and then press the shutter fully to take the photo. There are no dials to turn, no settings to check, and no decisions to make about exposure. The camera handles all of it.

What You Cannot Do

In Scene Intelligent Auto you cannot override any of the camera's decisions. Rotating the Main Dial does nothing. Rotating the Quick Control Dial does nothing. You cannot force a specific shutter speed, aperture, ISO, or white balance. You cannot change the autofocus mode or the drive mode. If the camera makes a choice you disagree with — for example, if it chooses a slightly too-slow shutter speed and the subject blurs — you have no mechanism to correct it from within this mode. To gain any control, you must rotate the Mode Dial to a different position.

When to Use It

Scene Intelligent Auto is the right choice when you need a photo quickly without any preparation — handing the camera to a stranger to photograph your group, capturing a spontaneous moment before you have time to adjust settings, or shooting in a completely unfamiliar environment where you are not yet sure what settings to use. It is also useful when the camera is being used by a child or a family member who is unfamiliar with it. For these situations, Scene Intelligent Auto reliably produces correctly exposed, in-focus photos without requiring any knowledge of how to operate the camera.

> **Note:** *Scene Intelligent Auto does not lock any of the Mode Dial's adjacent positions. It is easy to accidentally rotate away from A+ if the dial is knocked.*

Check the mode indicator on the screen when you pick the camera up to confirm you are in the mode you intend.

5.2 Program AE (P)

How to Activate It

Rotate the Mode Dial to the P position. The letter P appears on the LCD screen and in the EVF alongside the shutter speed and aperture values the camera has currently selected. Both values are shown in white text when the camera is in P mode, indicating that the camera is controlling both.

What the Camera Does

In Program AE, the Canon EOS R10 automatically selects both the shutter speed and the aperture required for a correctly exposed image based on its evaluative metering reading of the scene. As you move the camera or the light changes, the camera continuously adjusts these two values to maintain a correct exposure. The camera applies its own logic to the balance — in bright light it tends to favour faster shutter speeds and narrower apertures, in dim light it uses slower speeds and wider apertures.

What You Control

You retain full control over ISO, white balance, drive mode, autofocus operation, autofocus area, picture style, and every other setting not directly related to the shutter speed and aperture balance. You can access and change all of these through the Q screen, the M-Fn button, or the menu system exactly as you would in any other mode.

You can also perform a technique called Program Shift that temporarily overrides the camera's chosen shutter speed and aperture combination without changing the overall exposure level. Here is how to use it.

1. Half-press the shutter button to activate metering. The camera selects and displays its chosen shutter speed and aperture combination.
2. While keeping the shutter half-pressed, rotate the Main Dial. Each click of the dial shifts to a different combination of shutter speed and aperture that produces the same overall brightness. Rotating right

shifts toward a faster shutter speed and wider aperture. Rotating left shifts toward a slower shutter speed and narrower aperture.

3. When the displayed combination suits your creative intent — for example, you want a slightly faster shutter to reduce the risk of motion blur — take the photo by pressing the shutter fully.
4. Program Shift resets automatically after the shot is taken. The camera returns to its own chosen combination for the next frame.

When to Use It

Program AE is the most convenient mode for general everyday shooting when you want reliable automatic exposure but also want the ability to adjust other settings manually. It gives you more creative access than Scene Intelligent Auto while still removing the need to think about the shutter speed and aperture specifically. Use it for street photography, social events, casual travel, and any situation where you want to be ready to shoot immediately without configuring exposure settings first.

> **Tip:** *If you find that Program AE is consistently choosing a shutter speed that is too slow for sharp handheld photos, set the ISO to Auto and configure the Auto ISO minimum shutter speed (in Shooting Menu 2 under ISO speed settings) to a value such as 1/125 sec. The camera will raise the ISO automatically before allowing the shutter to drop below that threshold.*

5.3 Shutter Priority (Tv)

How to Activate It

Rotate the Mode Dial to Tv. The letters Tv stand for Time Value — Canon's term for shutter speed. In the EVF and on the LCD screen, the shutter speed value appears in white text indicating you control it, and the aperture value appears in white or grey depending on whether the camera has found a valid exposure. The shutter speed is displayed in fractions — 1/500, 1/125, 1/60 — or as whole seconds for slow exposures — 1", 2", 30".

Setting the Shutter Speed

5. Rotate the Mode Dial to Tv.

6. Rotate the Main Dial — the textured wheel just behind the shutter button — to change the shutter speed. Rotate it clockwise for a faster shutter speed and counter-clockwise for a slower one.
7. Watch the aperture value on screen. As long as it appears as a normal number without blinking, the camera has found a valid aperture to match your chosen shutter speed and the exposure will be correct.
8. Half-press the shutter to lock focus, then press fully to take the photo.

Choosing Your Shutter Speed

The shutter speed controls how motion is recorded in the image. Understanding this relationship is the key to using Tv mode effectively.

At 1/500 sec and faster — 1/1000 sec, 1/2000 sec, 1/4000 sec — the shutter opens and closes so quickly that almost any moving subject is frozen completely sharp in the final image. A child running across the garden, a bird in flight, a ball at the moment of impact, a sprinter mid-stride — all of these are recorded with crisp, sharp edges and no motion blur. The subject appears as if frozen in time. Use these fast shutter speeds any time the sharpness of a moving subject is your priority.

At 1/125 sec — a mid-range shutter speed — most everyday subjects appear sharp when handholding the camera, even with moderate movement. Walking subjects, slow-moving vehicles, people talking, and general outdoor scenes at this speed are reliably sharp.

At 1/60 sec and slower — 1/30 sec, 1/15 sec, 1/8 sec, 1 sec, and beyond — the shutter is open long enough to record the movement of anything that is in motion during that time as a blur. This blur can be an unwanted defect (if the subject was supposed to be sharp) or a deliberate creative choice that conveys speed, flow, or passage of time. A 1-second exposure of a waterfall turns the rushing water into a smooth, milky veil. A 20-second exposure of a coastal scene at night records the waves as a misty fog over the rocks. A half-second exposure of a busy intersection at night records passing car headlights as flowing light trails. None of these effects are possible at fast shutter speeds — they require the shutter to stay open long enough to accumulate the motion.

At shutter speeds below 1/60 sec while handholding the camera, camera shake — the natural, unavoidable tremor of your hands — becomes visible in the image as a general softness across the whole frame, not just on moving subjects. To use slow shutter speeds without camera shake, mount the Canon EOS R10 on a tripod and use the 2-second self-timer or a remote control to press the shutter without touching the camera.

When the Aperture Value Blinks

If the aperture value on screen starts blinking — flashing between its number and the word HI or LO, or simply flashing — the camera cannot find a valid aperture within the lens's available range to correctly expose the scene at your chosen shutter speed.

If the aperture is blinking at its smallest value (highest f-number) and shows HI, the scene is too bright at your current shutter speed — even the smallest aperture cannot restrict the light enough. The solution is to use a faster shutter speed, reduce the ISO, or attach an ND (neutral density) filter to the lens to reduce the incoming light.

If the aperture is blinking at its widest value (lowest f-number) and shows LO, the scene is too dark for the current shutter speed — even the widest aperture does not let in enough light. The solution is to use a slower shutter speed or raise the ISO.

> **Tip:** *For wildlife and sports photography, set the ISO to Auto (with a reasonable upper limit such as 3200 or 6400 set in the ISO speed settings) and use Tv mode to lock in a fast shutter speed. The R10 will raise the ISO automatically whenever the light is not bright enough to maintain the aperture within range, keeping the shutter speed constant and the subject sharp.*

5.4 Aperture Priority (Av)

How to Activate It

Rotate the Mode Dial to Av. The letters Av stand for Aperture Value. On the LCD screen and in the EVF, the aperture value — shown as an f-number such as f/2.8, f/5.6, or f/11 — appears in white indicating you control it. The shutter speed appears alongside it and updates continuously as the camera adjusts to maintain correct exposure.

Setting the Aperture

9. Rotate the Mode Dial to Av.
10. Rotate the Main Dial to change the aperture. Rotating clockwise increases the f-number (narrows the aperture). Rotating counter-clockwise decreases the f-number (widens the aperture). The range of available f-numbers depends on the attached lens — a lens with a maximum aperture of f/1.8 lets you go as wide as f/1.8, while a kit zoom lens might only go as wide as f/3.5 at its widest focal length.
11. Watch the shutter speed value on screen. As long as it appears as a normal number without blinking, the camera has found a valid shutter speed to match your chosen aperture.
12. Half-press the shutter to confirm focus, then press fully to shoot.

Understanding Aperture and Depth of Field

Aperture is the size of the opening inside the lens through which light passes to reach the sensor. It is measured in f-stops — and here is the important thing to understand: the f-number and the aperture opening size are inversely related. A small f-number means a large opening. A large f-number means a small opening. f/1.8 is a wide-open aperture that lets in a large amount of light. f/16 is a very narrow aperture that lets in a small amount of light.

Aperture directly controls depth of field — the zone of the scene that appears acceptably sharp in the final image.

When you set a wide aperture — a low f-number such as f/1.8 or f/2.8 — the depth of field is shallow. Your subject at the point of focus appears sharp, and anything in front of or behind that subject falls progressively out of focus. At f/1.8 the out-of-focus areas can be extremely blurred, rendering backgrounds as smooth, diffuse washes of colour and tone with no distracting detail visible. This is the quality sought in portrait photography — it separates the subject cleanly from the background and creates the aesthetic known as bokeh.

When you set a narrow aperture — a high f-number such as f/11 or f/16 — the depth of field becomes deep. A much larger zone of the scene, from relatively close in front of the camera to the far distance, appears sharp simultaneously. This is what you need for landscape photography, architecture, group photos, product shots, and any scene where you want everything from foreground to background in focus.

The relationship between aperture and depth of field is one of the most fundamental creative tools in photography. Aperture Priority mode lets you choose exactly where you want to sit on this spectrum and hands off the shutter speed arithmetic to the camera entirely.

When the Shutter Speed Blinks

If the shutter speed value on screen blinks, the camera cannot find a valid shutter speed to correctly expose the scene at your chosen aperture.

If the shutter speed blinks at 1/4000 sec (or 1/8000 sec if using the electronic shutter), the scene is too bright for the chosen aperture — even the fastest available shutter speed cannot cut the light enough. Narrow the aperture by increasing the f-number, or lower the ISO.

If the shutter speed blinks at 30 sec, the scene is too dark for the chosen aperture — even the longest available auto shutter speed cannot gather enough light. Widen the aperture by lowering the f-number, raise the ISO, or switch to Manual mode and use BULB for exposures beyond 30 seconds.

> **Tip:** *Av mode is also the most intuitive mode to use when learning about exposure compensation. Set an aperture you like, and if the camera's automatic shutter speed produces an image that is slightly too dark or too bright, simply rotate the Quick Control Dial to add exposure compensation — plus to brighten, minus to darken — and the camera adjusts the shutter speed accordingly while keeping your aperture exactly as you set it.*

5.5 Manual (M)

How to Activate It

Rotate the Mode Dial to M. In Manual mode, both the shutter speed and aperture values on the LCD screen and in the EVF appear in white, indicating that you control both. An exposure indicator scale — a horizontal bar with a zero at the centre, plus values to the right, and minus values to the left — appears at the bottom of the screen or viewfinder display. This indicator is the camera communicating whether your chosen combination of settings will produce an image that is correctly exposed, overexposed, or underexposed based on its metering reading. It is advisory only — the camera does not intervene.

Setting Shutter Speed and Aperture

13. Rotate the Mode Dial to M.
14. Rotate the Main Dial to set the shutter speed. Clockwise for faster, counter-clockwise for slower. Watch the exposure indicator as you rotate — the marker moves right (toward overexposure) as the shutter slows and moves left (toward underexposure) as it quickens.
15. Rotate the Quick Control Dial to set the aperture. Clockwise for a narrower aperture (higher f-number), counter-clockwise for a wider aperture (lower f-number). The marker on the exposure indicator shifts accordingly.
16. Aim to position the exposure indicator marker at the centre zero point for a metered-correct exposure. You can deliberately position it to the left for a darker image or to the right for a brighter one — in Manual mode, intentional over or underexposure is a valid creative choice and the camera will not override you.
17. Half-press the shutter to lock focus, then press fully to shoot.

Setting ISO in Manual Mode

In Manual mode, ISO is the third variable you control. If you have fixed the shutter speed and aperture and the exposure indicator is not where you want it, adjust the ISO to compensate.

To change ISO without opening the menu: press and hold the M-Fn button on the top of the camera with your left hand, then rotate the Main Dial with your right index finger. The first click of the Main Dial while M-Fn is held selects the ISO function. Release M-Fn, then rotate the Main Dial to change the ISO value. Alternatively, press the Q button to open the Quick Control screen, highlight the ISO panel, and rotate a dial to adjust it.

You can also set ISO to Auto in Manual mode. When ISO is set to Auto in M mode, the camera selects the ISO needed to make your chosen shutter speed and aperture combination produce a correctly exposed image — effectively making the ISO the one automatic variable while shutter and aperture remain fixed. This is sometimes called ISO Auto Manual mode and is useful for event photography or run-and-gun documentary work where the light changes unpredictably but you want to keep your depth of field and motion rendering consistent.

Using the Exposure Indicator

The exposure indicator scale runs from minus 3 at the far left to plus 3 at the far right, with zero at the centre. Each major division represents one stop of exposure. The marker shows where your current settings fall according to the camera's metering. Centre means the camera's metering system evaluates your settings as producing a correctly exposed image under current lighting. One stop to the left means the image will be one stop darker than the metered correct exposure. One stop to the right means one stop brighter.

Understanding what the indicator is telling you versus what you want is important. The camera's metering system averages the scene and aims for a mid-tone result. If your subject is supposed to be dark — a person in black clothing, a dark background — the camera may indicate that the exposure is wrong when it is actually exactly right for your intent. In Manual mode, you make that judgment yourself and the camera records what you set.

When to Use Manual Mode

Manual mode suits any situation where you need complete, repeatable control over the exposure and cannot afford to have the camera change anything automatically between frames.

In a photography studio shooting with flash at a fixed power level, Manual mode keeps the exposure absolutely consistent from shot to shot — the flash power is fixed, the aperture is fixed, the shutter speed is fixed, so every image receives identical exposure regardless of where in the frame the subject moves.

For astrophotography and night sky shooting, the exposures required — often 15 to 30 seconds at f/2 and ISO 3200 or higher — are beyond what any automatic mode handles reliably. Manual mode gives you full control to dial in the precise combination needed for star trails, the Milky Way, or aurora photography.

For video recording, automatic exposure changes mid-shot are visible and distracting to the viewer. Manual mode keeps the exposure constant throughout the clip, producing a clean, professional result even as subjects move in and out of the frame or the camera pans across a scene.

For high-volume event work — a wedding ceremony, a graduation, a conference — where you shoot the same location repeatedly and want every frame consistently exposed, setting Manual mode at the start of the event and adjusting only when the lighting conditions change is far more efficient than allowing the camera to re-evaluate the exposure for every shot.

5.6 Flexible Priority AE (Fv)

How to Activate It

Rotate the Mode Dial to Fv. The Fv marking appears on the dial between M and the SCN position. On screen, you will see shutter speed, aperture, and ISO all displayed — each showing either a specific value you have set or the word AUTO indicating the camera is controlling that parameter automatically.

How Fv Mode Works

Fv mode begins with all three primary exposure variables — shutter speed, aperture, and ISO — set to Auto. In this state it behaves identically to Program AE (P): the camera controls everything and selects appropriate values for correct exposure. From this starting point, you can lock any one, two, or all three variables to a value of your choice, and any variable you leave on Auto remains camera-controlled.

This creates a mode that encompasses all other exposure modes within itself, selectable by how many values you choose to fix.

If you fix only the shutter speed, Fv behaves like Tv — Shutter Priority.

If you fix only the aperture, Fv behaves like Av — Aperture Priority.

If you fix both shutter speed and aperture, Fv behaves like M — Manual, with ISO on Auto.

If you fix all three, Fv behaves like full Manual mode with a fixed ISO.

Setting Values in Fv Mode

18. Rotate the Mode Dial to Fv. All values show as AUTO.

19. To set the shutter speed: rotate the Main Dial. The first rotation changes the shutter speed from AUTO to a specific value and locks it there. The shutter speed is now fixed — the camera will not change it.
20. To set the aperture: rotate the Quick Control Dial. The first rotation changes the aperture from AUTO to a specific value and locks it.
21. To set the ISO: press and hold the M-Fn button and rotate the Main Dial to reach ISO, then release M-Fn and rotate the Main Dial to set the value.
22. To return any fixed value back to Auto: highlight that value on the Q screen and press the assigned reset button, or press the INFO button while the value is selected on the Fv screen. The value reverts to AUTO and the camera resumes controlling it.

When to Use Fv Mode

Fv mode is most useful for photographers who work across different types of subjects within the same shooting session and want to adjust their level of control fluidly without rotating the Mode Dial between positions. A photographer covering a wedding, for example, might fix only the aperture for a ceremony (to control depth of field) and then fix both the aperture and shutter speed during the first dance (to control both blur and background rendering), and then return everything to Auto during candid reception moments — all without changing the Mode Dial. Everything is achievable within Fv by simply fixing or releasing individual values as needed.

> **Note:** *If you are new to manual exposure, Fv mode is also a good learning tool. Start with all values on Auto, then fix one variable at a time and observe how the camera compensates with the remaining automatic values. This teaches the relationship between shutter speed, aperture, and ISO interactively.*

5.7 Scene Modes (SCN)

How to Activate and Select a Scene

23. Rotate the Mode Dial to SCN.
24. The last-used scene type is shown on the LCD screen. To change it, press the INFO button to open the scene selection screen. A grid of scene icons appears.

25. Use the joystick or tap the touch screen to highlight the scene you want. The right side of the screen shows a brief description of the highlighted scene and a sample image illustrating what it is optimised for.
26. Press SET or double-tap the touch screen to confirm your scene selection. The camera is now configured with all settings optimised for that scene type.
27. Compose your shot and press the shutter as normal. The selected scene mode applies until you change it or rotate the Mode Dial away from SCN.

Available Scene Modes and What Each One Does

- **Portrait** — Selects a wide aperture to blur the background behind your subject. The Picture Style shifts to produce softer, more flattering skin tones. Autofocus targets faces automatically and tracks them as they move. Drive mode defaults to Single shooting. Use this for any photo where a person is the primary subject and a clean, blurred background would improve the result — formal portraits, environmental portraits, candid people shots.
- **Landscape** — Sets a narrow aperture to maximise depth of field, keeping everything from near ground to distant horizon in sharp focus. The Picture Style shifts to emphasise vivid blues and greens. Autofocus uses a broad area mode. Use this for open-air scenes, mountain vistas, city skylines, coastal photography, and any outdoor subject where foreground-to-background sharpness is important.
- **Close-up** — Optimises autofocus behaviour for subjects at close focusing distances — the kind of photography sometimes called macro, where you are photographing flowers, insects, jewellery, food details, or any small object filling a large portion of the frame. The camera sets a moderately narrow aperture to maintain adequate depth of field across the subject, since at close distances even a few millimetres of focus shift can render part of the subject out of focus.
- **Sports** — Switches to Servo AF, which continuously tracks and predicts the position of a moving subject, adjusting focus constantly between frames. The drive mode shifts to high-speed continuous shooting so multiple frames are captured with a single hold of the shutter button. The shutter speed is biased toward the faster end of the range to freeze movement. Use this for athletes, cyclists, runners,

animals in motion, vehicles, or any fast-moving subject where a single shot is unlikely to capture the peak moment.

- **Night Portrait —** Designed for photographing a person in a dimly lit environment when you want both the subject and the background to be properly exposed. The camera combines a slow shutter speed — long enough to gather sufficient ambient light from the background — with an external flash (if attached) to illuminate the person in the foreground. The result, when the camera and subject are both still, is a portrait where the person is clearly lit and the background retains its natural atmosphere rather than disappearing into blackness. A tripod is recommended because the slow shutter speed needed for the background will cause camera shake blur in the overall image if the camera moves.
- **Handheld Night Scene —** Addresses the camera shake problem of shooting in low light without a tripod. Instead of one long exposure, the Canon EOS R10 takes four rapid frames in succession and merges them automatically into a single image. Each frame is taken at a fast enough shutter speed to minimise camera shake individually — but by combining four frames, the camera accumulates enough light to produce a brighter result than any single fast shot could. The merging process also reduces random digital noise. The final result is a single JPEG file. Keep the camera as steady as possible during the four-shot burst — excessive movement between frames will degrade the merge quality.
- **HDR Backlight Control —** Used when your subject is in front of a significantly brighter background — a person standing in front of a bright window, a subject outdoors against a bright sky — that would normally cause either the subject to go dark (if exposed for the background) or the background to blow out (if exposed for the subject). The camera takes three consecutive exposures at different brightnesses and merges them into a single JPEG that retains detail in both the bright background and the darker subject simultaneously. The camera must be held steady during the three-shot sequence.
- **Silent Scene —** Switches to the electronic shutter, eliminating all mechanical shutter sound and vibration. The camera operates in complete silence. Use this in environments where shutter noise would be disruptive — a sleeping baby, a library, a quiet ceremony, a wildlife hide, a museum. Be aware that the electronic shutter can produce

rolling shutter distortion when photographing fast lateral motion, and may cause banding under certain artificial light sources.

- **Food** — Shifts the white balance toward warmer tones and adjusts colour rendering to make food appear more vivid, appetising, and accurately coloured under the mixed artificial lighting typical of restaurants. Saturation is slightly boosted in the warm tones — reds, oranges, and yellows — that appear most prominently in food photography. Use this for restaurant meals, food styling, recipe photography, and any situation where you want food to look as appealing in the photo as it does in real life.

- **Kids** — Applies fast continuous autofocus with face and subject detection to track the unpredictable movements of children, combined with a fast shutter speed to freeze their motion. Drive mode shifts to continuous shooting so you capture sequences rather than single frames, increasing the chance of catching the right expression or peak action. Use this for photographs of children playing, running, laughing, or any situation where the subject is small, fast, and unpredictable.

- **Candlelight** — Optimises the white balance and tone rendering for scenes lit primarily by candles or other warm orange-toned flame sources. Rather than correcting the warm colour cast toward a neutral white — which would remove the atmospheric quality of the scene — this mode preserves and enhances the warmth of the light, producing images with the characteristic amber-orange glow that makes candlelit scenes feel intimate. Use this for birthday cakes, holiday candles, lanterns, fireside scenes, and any subject where the warm light is part of the mood you want to capture.

- **Night Scene** — Optimises for photographing dimly lit environments without flash — city streets at night, illuminated buildings, neon signs, bridges, and urban nightscapes. The camera uses a slower shutter speed and a higher ISO to gather the low ambient light without introducing flash, which would overexpose the foreground and destroy the atmosphere of the scene. Use a tripod for exposures longer than approximately 1/30 sec to avoid camera shake. The camera will select the appropriate combination automatically based on the available light level.

- **Fireworks** — Sets a slow shutter speed to record the complete arc of firework trails from launch to burst, and locks focus at infinity so the camera does not waste time hunting for focus in the dark sky between bursts. The camera waits with the shutter open long enough to capture multiple burst trails in a single frame when the shutter speed allows. Mount the Canon EOS R10 on a tripod, point it at the section of sky where bursts are occurring, and use the 2-second self-timer or a remote to press the shutter without introducing camera shake.

Star Modes — Specialized Night Sky Shooting

The Canon EOS R10 includes four dedicated modes specifically for night sky and astrophotography, each optimised for a different type of celestial subject. All four require a tripod, a clear sky away from significant light pollution, and an appropriate lens — ideally a wide-angle lens with a wide maximum aperture such as f/1.8 or f/2.8.

- **Star Portrait** — Combines a long exposure optimised for recording stars in the sky with flash illumination of a person in the foreground, producing a portrait where both the subject and the star field behind them are properly exposed. The flash illuminates the person and the long exposure records the stars. The subject must remain completely still during the entire exposure — any movement will produce a blurred ghost image of the person against the sharp star background.
- **Star Nightscape** — Optimises the exposure specifically for photographing the Milky Way, star fields, or a starry sky above a dark landscape. The camera selects a shutter speed short enough to render stars as points rather than trails — beyond approximately 15 to 25 seconds (depending on focal length), the Earth's rotation causes stars to draw short trails in the image. The camera applies noise reduction appropriate for the high-ISO, long-exposure conditions of night sky photography.
- **Star Trails** — Intentionally uses a very long exposure to record the movement of stars across the sky as continuous trails, producing the distinctive arcing star trail images in which stars appear as long curved lines rotating around the celestial pole. The camera takes a series of long exposures and merges them automatically. Place the camera on a sturdy tripod pointed toward an interesting foreground element with the sky above, and leave it running while the camera works through the sequence.
- **Star Time-Lapse** — Automates the capture of a sequence of night sky images at set intervals and assembles them into a time-lapse video showing the movement of stars across the sky over hours. The camera

handles the timing, merging, and video assembly automatically. Set it up on a tripod, configure the interval and number of frames via the on-screen prompts, and leave it to run through the night.

Note: *All four Star modes require darkness and significant time to capture properly. Ensure the battery is fully charged or that USB power is available before beginning any of these modes. Star Trails and Star Time-Lapse in particular can run for several hours.*

5.8 Creative Filters

How to Activate and Select a Filter

28. Rotate the Mode Dial to the Creative Filters position — the icon showing overlapping circles, located between the SCN position and the video camera icon on the dial.
29. The screen shows the live view with the last-used Creative Filter applied. A filter name appears at the top or bottom of the screen.
30. To change the filter: tap the filter name on the touch screen, or press the Q button and highlight the Creative Filter setting, then rotate a dial to scroll through the available options. You can also press the INFO button to open a selection screen showing all filters in a list with a live preview of each effect on the current scene.
31. Once the desired filter is shown on screen, half-press the shutter to lock focus and press fully to take the photo. The photo is saved as a JPEG with the filter applied permanently. RAW files are not available in Creative Filters mode.

Available Filters and What Each One Does

- **Grainy B/W** — Converts the image to black and white and adds a visible film grain texture, simulating the look of high-ISO analogue film photography from the pre-digital era. The strength of the grain effect — Low, Standard, or High — can be adjusted before shooting by pressing SET when the filter is selected. The low-contrast, textured monochrome result is well suited to street photography, documentary work, and any subject where atmosphere matters more than technical perfection. The grain adds visual weight and a sense of immediacy to the image.

- **Soft focus —** Applies a gentle, diffusing glow to the entire image — particularly prominent in the highlights, which bloom and spread into the surrounding areas. Sharp edges remain visible but are softened, and the overall image takes on a luminous, dreamlike quality. Three strength levels (Low, Standard, High) are available. This effect was historically produced in the darkroom using soft-focus lenses or by placing glass, gauze, or petroleum jelly over the lens. It suits romantic portraits, flowers, and any subject where a delicate, ethereal mood is appropriate.

- **Fish-eye effect —** Simulates the extreme distortion of a fisheye lens — straight lines near the edges and corners of the frame bow dramatically outward, and the centre of the image appears to bulge forward. The field of view appears greatly exaggerated. The effect is most pronounced on scenes with clearly straight elements such as buildings, corridors, or horizon lines. It suits creative urban photography, skateboarding and action sports documentation, and any context where an exaggerated, unusual perspective is desirable. Two distortion strengths are available.

- **Water painting effect —** Applies a desaturated, soft-edged rendering that gives the image the appearance of a watercolour painting — edges are slightly blurred, detail is reduced, and colours are muted and blended. The overall effect removes the photographic precision of a standard image and replaces it with a hand-made, painterly quality. It works particularly well on landscapes, gardens, and natural subjects where the softening of fine detail is not distracting.

- **Toy camera effect —** Simulates the optical characteristics of cheap plastic toy cameras — significant vignetting (darkening of the corners and edges of the frame), a colour shift (the available options shift the colour toward Standard, Warm, Cool, or Vivid tones), and a slightly uneven, lo-fi quality across the image. The heavy corner darkening draws the eye strongly to the centre of the frame. It suits portrait work, street photography, and retro or nostalgic themes where the imperfect, casual aesthetic is intentional.

- **Miniature effect —** Simulates the tilt-shift lens technique used to make full-sized scenes appear as though they are scale models or dioramas. The camera applies a blur to the top and bottom of the frame while keeping a horizontal band in the centre sharp — mimicking the shallow depth of field of a macro lens focused on a small object from directly above. The scene that was photographed from a high vantage point — a cityscape, a market, a road, a railway yard — appears to shrink and become toy-like when this blur is applied. The position of the in-focus band can be moved before shooting by dragging it on the touch screen. The effect is most convincing on scenes photographed from above at a steep angle, looking down over a wide area.

- **HDR art standard** — Captures a single exposure and processes it through a high-dynamic-range algorithm that boosts local contrast — increasing the contrast of fine details and textures within specific tonal regions while compressing the global contrast between highlights and shadows. The result is a hyper-detailed, high-contrast look where every surface texture appears exaggerated and the overall image has a painterly, processed quality. Shadows reveal detail that would normally be dark and lost. Highlights retain texture rather than clipping to pure white.
- **HDR art vivid** — Applies the same HDR processing as HDR art standard but adds significant colour saturation, producing an intensely colourful, almost psychedelic result. Colours appear far more vivid than they did in the original scene. Blues become electric, greens become emerald, reds become crimson. The processing is extreme and intentionally so — this is a deliberate creative departure from realistic colour rendering.
- **HDR art bold** — Applies HDR processing with further contrast enhancement and a darker, heavier tone that gives the image a graphic, almost illustrated quality. The tonal range is compressed more aggressively than in the standard or vivid variants, and the result has a strong, dramatic presence. It suits industrial subjects, architecture, cityscapes, and any scene with strong geometric structure that benefits from the added visual weight.
- **HDR art embossed** — Applies an extreme local contrast boost that produces an almost relief-like, three-dimensional appearance in the textures of the image. Edges and textures appear to protrude from the surface of the photo as if embossed onto the frame. Colour saturation is reduced significantly, giving the result a desaturated, monumental quality. It is the most extreme of the four HDR art variants and suits abstract or architectural subjects with strong surface texture.

Note: *All Creative Filter images are saved as JPEGs only — RAW recording is not available in this mode. If you prefer to have a RAW original alongside a filtered version, shoot in any standard mode first and then apply Creative* *filters in post via the Playback menu (covered in Section 3.5), which creates a filtered JPEG copy from the original RAW file without altering it.*

PART 6 — Focus System

Getting sharp focus on the right part of the image is one of the most fundamental skills in photography, and the Canon EOS R10 gives you a powerful and flexible set of tools to control exactly where and how the camera focuses. This part explains how the autofocus system works, how to choose the right focus area for your subject, how to set up subject detection, and how to use manual focus when automatic focus is not the right choice.

Read through this part once to understand the full system, then return to individual sections as a reference when working in the field.

6.1 How Autofocus Works on the R10

Dual Pixel CMOS AF II

The Canon EOS R10 uses a system called Dual Pixel CMOS AF II. To understand what this means and why it matters, it helps to know what the underlying technology does.

In a conventional image sensor, each pixel captures light and records it as image data. In the R10's sensor, virtually every pixel is split into two separate photodiodes sitting side by side behind a single microlens. These paired photodiodes receive light from slightly different angles because of the microlens above them. By comparing the signals from the left and right photodiodes across many pixels, the camera's processor can determine which direction the lens needs to move and by exactly how much to bring the subject into focus. This is phase-detection autofocus — the same fundamental principle used by professional sports and wildlife cameras, but implemented directly on the imaging sensor rather than on a dedicated separate autofocus sensor.

Phase-detection is significantly faster than the contrast-detection autofocus used in older mirrorless and compact cameras, which had to move the lens back and forth to find the sharpest point by searching for maximum contrast. Phase-detection calculates the required lens movement in a single measurement and drives the lens directly to focus in one continuous motion. The result is the fast, smooth, confident focusing behaviour you will notice the first time you half-press the shutter on the R10 — particularly with RF mount lenses, which are specifically optimised for this system.

The Dual Pixel CMOS AF II system covers approximately 100 percent of the frame horizontally and approximately 100 percent vertically, meaning there is almost no area of the image where phase-detection is unavailable. You can place your focus point anywhere in the frame and the system will work at full capability in that position.

Subject Detection and Tracking

Layered on top of the phase-detection hardware is the Canon EOS R10's deep learning subject detection. The camera's processor runs a continuously updated analysis of the live view image, looking for patterns that match the shapes it has been trained to recognise: human faces, human eyes, human bodies, animal faces and eyes (dogs, cats, birds), and vehicles (cars, motorcycles, including their cockpits and headlights). When a matching subject is detected, the camera not only focuses on it but actively tracks its position as it moves across the frame, predicting where the subject will be in the next fraction of a second and pre-positioning the focus accordingly.

This tracking happens automatically when appropriate AF area modes are selected. The camera maintains the focus lock on the detected subject even as it partially leaves the frame, is briefly obscured by another object, turns away, or changes its apparent size as it moves toward or away from the camera.

The AF Frame — What You See on Screen

While the camera is focusing, one or more frames or boxes appear overlaid on the live view image on the LCD screen and in the EVF. These frames show you exactly where the camera's focus system is working at any given moment.

A white or blue square or rectangle indicates an active AF point or zone — this is where the camera is currently focusing or tracking. When focus is confirmed and locked in One-Shot AF mode, the frame turns green and a beep sounds (if the beep is enabled). In Servo AF mode the frame remains white or blue during continuous tracking — it never turns green, because focus is continuously re-evaluated rather than locked.

An orange frame indicates that the camera has detected a subject — a face, an eye, an animal, or a vehicle — and is actively tracking it. You will see the orange frame appear over a face or eye and move with the subject as they move. This tracking frame is independent of your selected AF area mode — even if you are using 1-Point AF, the camera will show an orange tracking frame when it detects a face within the active AF area.

If the AF frame blinks orange or disappears, the camera is unable to confirm focus — the subject is too dark, too low in contrast, moving too fast, or outside the AF coverage area. In these situations, try moving the AF point to a higher-contrast area of the subject, switching to a different AF area mode, or switching to manual focus.

6.2 AF Area Modes

The AF area mode determines the zone of the frame the Canon EOS R10 searches for focus, and how much control you have over exactly where within that zone the focus lands. Different subjects and situations call for different area modes — knowing which to use in each context significantly improves your ability to get the shot you intend.

How to Access and Change AF Area Mode

1. Press the Q button on the back of the camera to open the Quick Control screen.
2. Use the joystick or tap the touch screen to highlight the AF area panel. It shows the current area mode name and a small diagram of the frame illustrating the active area.
3. Rotate the Main Dial or Quick Control Dial to cycle through the available area modes. The diagram updates as you rotate to show which area of the frame each mode covers. Alternatively, press SET to open the full AF area selection screen, which shows all modes in a list with a brief description of each.
4. Once the desired mode is displayed, half-press the shutter or press the Q button again to close the Q screen and return to shooting with the new AF area active.

You can also change the AF area mode directly from Shooting Menu 6 via the MENU button if you prefer to navigate through the menu rather than using the Q screen.

Spot AF

Spot AF focuses on an extremely small, precise point — smaller than a single 1-Point AF square. You position this point yourself using the joystick or by tapping the touch screen. The camera focuses on whatever falls within that tiny area and ignores everything outside it completely.

Use Spot AF when you need to focus on a very specific, small detail within a larger subject — the eye of an insect in a macro photograph, a particular instrument in an orchestra, a small bird perched among foliage where a larger AF point would inadvertently focus on a leaf in front of the bird rather than the bird itself. Spot AF demands that your AF point placement be accurate, because the focused area is so small that even a slight misalignment will produce a miss.

To position the Spot AF point: after selecting Spot AF, use the joystick to push the point in any direction across the frame. It moves one step at a time. For faster repositioning, tap directly on the area of the touch screen where you want the point to land — it jumps immediately to that location. To return the point to the centre, push the joystick inward (press it as a button if assigned) or press SET while on the shooting screen in some configurations.

1-Point AF

1-Point AF focuses on a single square point of a fixed size, which you position across the frame using the joystick or touch screen in the same way as Spot AF. The point is larger than Spot AF, making it easier to use without perfectly precise placement, while still ignoring everything outside the selected area.

1-Point AF is the standard choice for the majority of still-photography situations. It gives you direct, unambiguous control over exactly where the camera focuses — you place the point on your subject and the camera focuses there, with no automatic subject detection or switching to nearby subjects. For portraits, place the 1-Point AF square over the near eye. For architecture, place it on a sharp edge or detail at the primary focal distance. For product photography, place it on the nearest feature of the product you want to be sharpest.

When your subject is not in the centre of the frame, use the joystick or touch screen to move the 1-Point AF square off-centre to where your subject is. This is more reliable than using centre AF and recomposing, particularly in Servo AF mode where recomposing after locking focus can cause the camera to re-evaluate.

Expand AF Area

Expand AF area uses your selected single AF point as the primary focus target, but also activates a small ring of surrounding points that assist in maintaining focus if the subject moves slightly away from the primary point. The camera prioritises the point you placed and uses the surrounding points as a fallback if the primary point loses the subject.

Use Expand AF area for subjects that are mostly stationary but liable to drift slightly — a person who may shift their weight or turn their head slightly between frames, a bird perched in a tree that occasionally shifts position, a dancer at a moment of relative stillness. The expanded surrounding area provides a small buffer that reduces the chance of a missed focus when the subject makes a minor movement without your having time to reposition the AF point.

Expand AF Area (Surrounding)

This mode extends the assisted area further than the standard Expand AF area — your selected point is still the priority target, but the assistance ring now covers all immediately surrounding points rather than just a tight cluster. The effective coverage area is noticeably larger than standard Expand AF area while still being smaller than Zone AF.

Use this mode when your subject is moving with moderate unpredictability and you want more safety margin around your selected point than Expand AF area provides, but you still want to maintain a specific area of focus priority rather than handing over complete control to the camera. It suits slower-moving wildlife, athletes at moderate pace, and documentary photography of people in motion who are not moving fast enough to need Zone AF or Whole-Area AF

Zone AF

Zone AF divides the entire frame into nine rectangular zones arranged in a three-by-three grid. You select which zone is active using the joystick — pushing it in any direction moves the active zone to the adjacent position. The camera focuses on the subject it detects within the selected zone, applying subject detection within that zone if subject detection is enabled.

Zone AF is appropriate when your subject is moving within a defined area of the frame — a goalkeeper moving laterally across the bottom of the frame, a bird flying across a section of sky, a cyclist coming through a specific part of the course. By selecting the zone where the action is concentrated, you let the camera make the fine tracking decisions within that area while you maintain overall compositional control through which zone is active. It is faster to operate than positioning a single point because you are moving between nine large zones rather than a precise pixel-level point.

Large Zone AF (Horizontal and Vertical)

Large Zone AF further expands the coverage into two options: a horizontally elongated zone that covers the full width of the frame but only the central horizontal strip, and a vertically elongated zone that covers the full height of the frame but only the central vertical strip. You switch between horizontal and vertical orientation by rotating a dial after selecting Large Zone AF.

The horizontal orientation suits subjects moving laterally across the frame — a runner crossing from left to right, a car passing through the shot. The vertical orientation suits subjects approaching or receding along the optical axis — a bird flying toward the camera, a subject walking directly toward you. Within the large zone, the camera uses subject detection and tracking to focus on the most prominent detected subject.

Large Zone AF is useful when you cannot predict precisely where in the frame the subject will be at the moment you press the shutter, but you can predict the general axis of movement. It reduces the reaction time needed compared to repositioning a small zone or single point.

Whole-Area AF (Auto)

In Whole-Area AF, the Canon EOS R10 searches the entire frame simultaneously and applies its subject detection system — People, Animals, or Vehicles depending on your Subject to detect setting — to find and lock onto the most appropriate subject automatically. You do not position an AF point at all. The camera selects the focus target itself based on its detection algorithms, then tracks it continuously.

When People detection is active, the camera scans the whole frame for faces. When it finds one, a focus frame appears over the face and a smaller sub-frame appears over the near eye specifically. If multiple faces are present, the camera generally prioritises the largest face or the one closest to the centre, but you can switch between detected subjects by tapping a different face on the touch screen.

Whole-Area AF is the mode that delivers the full capability of the R10's intelligent tracking system. It is the right choice for fast-paced shooting where manually repositioning an AF point between shots is impractical — documentary photography, events, street photography, wildlife in open environments, and any situation where the subject is moving unpredictably and you need the camera to handle the tracking burden so you can concentrate on composition and timing.

The trade-off is that you surrender direct control over which subject the camera focuses on. If the camera chooses the wrong subject — for example, focusing on a person in the background when you want the person in the foreground — you can redirect it by tapping the correct subject on the touch screen, or switch to a smaller AF area mode that excludes the unwanted subject.

> **Note:** *The AF area mode you select persists between shots and across power cycles — the camera remembers the last-used mode when you turn it back on. Before shooting in a new situation, check the AF area indicator on the screen to confirm the mode is appropriate for the subject you are about to photograph.*

6.3 Subject Detection

Subject detection is the layer of the Canon EOS R10's autofocus system that recognises specific categories of subject — people, animals, or vehicles — within the live view image, and directs the autofocus system to lock onto and track them preferentially. It works alongside the AF area mode: when Whole-Area AF is active, subject detection operates across the entire frame. When a smaller AF area mode is active, subject detection operates within the selected area only.

How to Set Subject Detection

5. Press the MENU button on the upper-left of the camera back.
6. Rotate the Main Dial to navigate to the sixth red Shooting tab — Shooting Menu 6.
7. Scroll down using the Quick Control Dial until Subject to detect is highlighted, then press SET.
8. The available options appear: People, Animals, Vehicles, and None. Highlight your choice and press SET to confirm.
9. Press MENU or half-press the shutter to close the menu and return to shooting. The subject detection setting is now active.

Subject detection can also be changed via the Q screen — press Q, navigate to the AF area panel, press SET to open the detailed AF area screen, and the subject detection option appears alongside the area mode selection.

People Detection

When Subject to detect is set to People, the Canon EOS R10's processor continuously analyses the live view looking for human faces, heads, eyes, and bodies. When a person is detected, the camera places a focus frame over the face and, when the face is large enough in the frame and clearly visible, a smaller frame specifically over one eye. The camera tracks this detection as the person moves — the frames follow them across the frame, adjusting position as they turn, approach, recede, or are partially obscured.

People detection prioritises whoever is most prominently featured in the frame — generally the person whose face is largest in the image, or the person closest to the centre. When multiple people are present, the camera tracks the priority subject and shows tracking frames on the others. You can switch the camera's focus to a different person by tapping their face on the LCD touch screen — the camera immediately redirects its tracking to the tapped individual.

People detection is effective even when the subject's face is partially turned away, partially obscured, or partially out of frame, as long as enough facial structure is visible to identify. It is also active at long distances where a face occupies only a small portion of the frame, though detection confidence decreases as face size diminishes.

Animals Detection

When Subject to detect is set to Animals, the camera applies detection optimised for dogs, cats, and birds. For dogs and cats, the camera looks for the characteristic facial structure of those animals and attempts to lock onto an eye when one is clearly visible at sufficient size. For birds, it looks for the head and attempts to track the eye when identifiable.

Animals detection is less universal than People detection — it is calibrated specifically for dogs, cats, and birds and may not reliably detect other animals. It is not designed for large wildlife such as elephants, deer, or horses, though it may incidentally detect and track some of these animals depending on their size in the frame and facial similarity to the trained categories.

When shooting birds in flight, Animals detection combined with Servo AF and Whole-Area AF is one of the most effective combinations the R10 offers. The camera can lock onto and continuously track a bird across the entire frame even when the bird is small and moving rapidly, maintaining accurate focus through direction changes and partial obscurement by branches or other elements.

Vehicles Detection

When Subject to detect is set to Vehicles, the camera looks for cars and motorcycles. For cars, it targets the front end of the vehicle — the grille, headlights, and bumper area. For motorcycles, it targets the front wheel, headlight, and cockpit area. When a vehicle is detected, the tracking frame appears over the relevant part of the vehicle and follows it as it moves. For motorsport and automotive photography this detection is particularly useful, as the camera maintains focus on the approaching front of a vehicle even at high speed and in situations where a human driver might struggle to keep a manually positioned AF point on the subject.

None — No Subject Detection

When Subject to detect is set to None, the subject detection system is disabled. The camera focuses purely using phase-detection contrast evaluation without attempting to identify what it is looking at. The AF area modes still function normally, but no intelligent tracking overlay appears. The camera focuses on whatever is highest in contrast or most prominent within the active AF area, without priority given to faces, eyes, or any other specific subject type. Use this setting when you are shooting abstract subjects, architectural details, landscapes without people or animals, product photography, or any situation where the subject detection categories are irrelevant to your subject matter.

> **Note:** *Switching between subject detection categories takes only a few seconds via the MENU or Q screen. It is worth developing the habit of checking this setting when you change from one type of subject to another — switching from animal photography to portrait work, for example, should prompt a switch from Animals to People detection for the most accurate tracking.*

6.4 Eye AF

Eye AF is the Canon EOS R10's ability to detect a human or animal eye specifically — not just the face — and use that eye as the precise focus target. The eye is the most important point of focus in a portrait: when the eye nearest to the camera is sharp, a portrait looks professional and emotionally connected. When the focus lands on the nose, ear, or shoulder instead — which can happen easily when shooting at wide apertures with a shallow depth of field — the portrait loses impact even if the exposure and composition are perfect. Eye AF eliminates this problem by automatically locking onto the eye itself.

How Eye AF Works on the R10

Eye AF is active automatically whenever Subject to detect is set to People or Animals and the AF area mode is set to Whole-Area AF or one of the larger area modes. When the camera detects a face of sufficient size and clarity, it places the focus frame over the face and then draws a smaller, more precise frame specifically over one eye. This eye frame is what the camera uses as its actual focus target. At wide apertures where depth of field is very shallow, the difference between focusing on the eye versus the nose is the difference between a sharp pupil and a sharp tip of the nose — Eye AF ensures the camera locks on the correct target without any additional input from you.

The eye frame follows the eye as the subject moves, turns their head, blinks, and changes position. Even when the subject turns partially away so that only one eye remains visible, the camera maintains the eye frame on the visible eye and continues tracking. If both eyes are lost — for example, the subject turns fully away — the camera reverts to tracking the face as a whole until an eye becomes visible again.

Setting Eye Detection Priority

By default, the Canon EOS R10 selects which eye to focus on automatically. The automatic selection generally chooses the eye nearest to the camera, or the eye that is more completely visible. In most situations, the automatic selection is appropriate. However, there are situations — particularly in formal portraits or when shooting subjects with a consistent preferred shooting side — where you want to specify which eye the camera should prioritise.

10. Press the MENU button on the upper-left of the camera back.
11. Rotate the Main Dial to navigate to Shooting Menu 6.
12. Scroll to Eye detection and press SET.
13. Three options appear: Left eye priority, Right eye priority, and Auto. Highlight your preferred setting and press SET to confirm.
14. Close the menu by pressing MENU or half-pressing the shutter. The selected eye priority is now active.

Left eye priority instructs the camera to seek out and track the subject's left eye when both are visible. Right eye priority prioritises the right eye. Note that these are from the subject's perspective — the subject's left eye is on the right side of the frame when the subject faces the camera directly.

Switching Eye Priority While Shooting Without the Menu

You can switch between Left eye priority and Right eye priority in real time while shooting without opening the menu. Press the M-Fn button and rotate the Quick Control Dial — each click switches the eye priority between Left and Right. The change takes effect immediately and is visible on screen as the eye frame moves from one eye to the other. This is useful when you are shooting a series of portraits of the same subject and want to vary which eye is closest to the camera across different poses without pausing to enter the menu.

Tip: *For environmental portraits where the subject is positioned at an angle to the camera — the classic three-quarter pose — set the eye priority to the eye facing more directly toward the camera. This is usually the far eye from* *the camera's perspective, which is the one that creates a stronger connection with the viewer. In Left or Right eye priority mode, you can quickly evaluate which setting brings the frame to that eye and lock it in for the session.*

6.5 AF Operations — One-Shot, Servo, AI Focus

The AF operation setting controls the fundamental behaviour of the autofocus system — specifically, whether it locks focus at a single moment or continuously adjusts focus as long as you are pressing the shutter or AF-ON button. This is one of the most important settings in the focus system, and choosing the correct AF operation for your subject is as important as choosing the correct AF area mode.

How to Change AF Operation

15. Press the Q button on the back of the camera to open the Quick Control screen.
16. Use the joystick or tap the touch screen to highlight the AF operation panel. It shows the current mode: ONE SHOT, SERVO, or AI FOCUS.
17. Rotate the Main Dial or Quick Control Dial to cycle between the three options. The change takes effect immediately.
18. Half-press the shutter or press the Q button again to close the Q screen.

AF operation can also be changed by pressing the M-Fn button and rotating the Main Dial (using the M-Fn shortcut cycle described in Section 4.6), or through Shooting Menu 6 in the full menu system.

One-Shot AF

In One-Shot AF, the Canon EOS R10 locks focus at the moment you half-press the shutter button (or press the AF-ON button). The camera evaluates the phase-detection signal, drives the lens to the correct focus distance, and stops. A green frame appears over the focused area and a short beep sounds confirming focus lock (if the beep is enabled in the Setup menu). The focus remains locked at that distance as long as you maintain the half-press.

If the subject moves after focus is locked, the focus does not follow — it stays at the distance that was confirmed when you first half-pressed. To refocus on the moved subject, release the shutter button fully, then half-press again to initiate a new focus evaluation.

One-Shot AF is appropriate for any subject that is stationary or moving very slowly — product photography, still life, landscape, architecture, posed portraits, food photography, and any scene where the subject is not going to move significantly between the moment you lock focus and the moment you take the photo. It is also more energy-efficient than Servo AF because the autofocus motor is only active during the brief focusing event rather than continuously.

One-Shot AF pairs with AE Lock in a specific way: when focus is confirmed in One-Shot AF, the exposure is also locked simultaneously. The green focus frame and the locked exposure remain constant as long as you hold the shutter half-pressed. This combined focus-and-exposure lock is one reason why One-Shot AF with recomposing works reliably — both focus and exposure are frozen at the locked values.

Servo AF

In Servo AF, the Canon EOS R10 begins focusing when you half-press the shutter (or press AF-ON) and continues to track and adjust focus continuously for as long as the button is held. There is no confirmation beep and no locked-focus green frame — the focus frame remains white and continues moving with the subject. Each time you fully press the shutter to take a photo, the camera records the image at whatever focus distance the servo system is tracking at that instant.

The Servo AF system does not just react to where the subject is now — it uses predictive tracking. The Canon EOS R10 analyses how fast the subject is moving and in which direction, and pre-positions the focus slightly ahead of where the subject currently is, anticipating where they will be in the fraction of a second between the last sensor measurement and the shutter opening. This predictive component is what makes Servo AF capable of keeping a fast-moving subject sharp in a burst sequence even when the subject is accelerating toward or away from the camera.

Use Servo AF for any subject that is in continuous motion — athletes in competition, birds in flight, animals running, vehicles, children playing, dancers, and any situation where the subject is unlikely to be in the same position when the shutter fires as they were when you initiated focus. Servo AF combined with high-speed continuous drive mode and Whole-Area AF is the R10's most powerful configuration for this type of shooting.

Servo AF does not lock exposure at the moment focus is initiated the way One-Shot AF does. The exposure is evaluated freshly for each frame in a burst sequence, meaning the camera adjusts the exposure independently for each shot based on current metering. This is the correct behaviour for tracking subjects that move across areas of varying brightness.

AI Focus

AI Focus is a hybrid mode designed for subjects whose behaviour is unpredictable — subjects that are stationary most of the time but may begin to move without warning. When you half-press the shutter in AI Focus mode, the camera begins in One-Shot AF, evaluating and locking focus on the still subject with a green frame and a beep. If the subject begins to move while the focus is locked, the camera detects this movement and automatically transitions to Servo AF, releasing the lock and beginning continuous tracking.

The transition from One-Shot to Servo happens without any action on your part — the camera makes the switch internally when it detects subject movement. A series of short beeps may sound to indicate the transition has occurred.

AI Focus suits situations where you cannot predict whether your subject will be stationary or moving at the moment you press the shutter — a child who may be standing still one moment and running the next, a pet that might lunge into motion unpredictably, a street performer who alternates between still poses and movement. Rather than forcing you to switch between One-Shot and Servo manually, AI Focus handles the transition automatically.

The trade-off is that AI Focus is less decisive than either pure mode. In One-Shot AF it may transition to Servo prematurely if the camera mistakes slight camera shake or a minor subject movement for intentional motion. In Servo it may not track quite as aggressively as pure Servo AF. For subjects that are definitively stationary, use One-Shot AF. For subjects that are definitively in continuous motion, use Servo AF. Reserve AI Focus for the genuinely ambiguous cases in between.

> **Note:** *The AF operation mode is one of the settings accessible via the M-Fn button shortcut. If you find yourself regularly switching between One-Shot and Servo during a session — for example, alternating between posed portraits and candid action — configure the M-Fn button cycle to include AF operation so you can switch between them in under two seconds without opening the Q screen or the menu.*

6.6 Manual Focus

Manual focus is the mode in which you — not the camera — control exactly where the lens focuses by rotating the focus ring on the lens barrel. While the Canon EOS R10's autofocus system is highly capable, there are specific situations where autofocus either cannot operate or does not produce the result you want, and manual focus is the correct tool.

These situations include: macro photography where the depth of field is extremely shallow and the AF system may oscillate between slightly different focus distances rather than settling precisely where you need it; astrophotography where there is insufficient contrast in the dark sky for phase-detection to work; shooting through glass or a net where the AF system focuses on the nearest surface rather than the subject beyond it; creative focus effects where you deliberately want a focus point the camera would not choose on its own; and any situation where the camera is hunting (repeatedly adjusting focus without confirming) and you want to stop the hunting and set focus at a specific distance yourself.

Switching to Manual Focus

There are two ways to switch the Canon EOS R10 to manual focus.

The first way is to use the AF/MF switch on the lens barrel, if your lens has one. Most Canon EF and RF lenses include a small switch on the side of the barrel labelled AF and MF. Sliding this switch to the MF position immediately disables autofocus and activates manual focus for that lens. This is the fastest and most direct way to switch modes — you do not need to navigate any menus.

The second way is through the camera's menu. Press MENU, navigate to Shooting Menu 6, scroll to AF operation, press SET, and scroll to the Manual Focus option at the end of the list. Press SET to confirm. This method is useful if your lens does not have a physical AF/MF switch, or if you want to keep the lens switch in the AF position while disabling AF from the camera body.

Focusing Manually

19. Switch to manual focus using either method described above. The AF frame disappears from the screen and no focus confirmation occurs when you half-press the shutter.
20. Look at the subject on the LCD screen or through the EVF.
21. Rotate the focus ring on the lens barrel — the ring closest to the camera body on most RF lenses. Rotating it in one direction moves the focus closer; rotating the other direction moves it further. The direction is specific to the lens.
22. Watch the image on screen as you rotate. The subject will sharpen as the focus approaches the correct distance and soften again as it passes through. Slow your rotation as you approach apparent sharpness to make precise adjustments.
23. When the subject appears as sharp as possible, stop rotating. Press the shutter fully to take the photo.

MF Peaking — Colour Highlights on In-Focus Edges

Manual focus peaking is a visual aid that overlays coloured highlights on the edges of objects that are currently at the plane of focus. As you rotate the focus ring, the coloured highlights shift across the image, appearing on different elements as they come into focus. When the highlights are concentrated on your intended subject, that subject is at the focus distance. This makes manual focus dramatically easier than trying to judge sharpness by looking at the overall image, particularly when shooting at wide apertures where the transition from sharp to soft is very gradual.

24. Press MENU and navigate to Shooting Menu 6.
25. Scroll to MF peaking settings and press SET.
26. Set Peaking to Enable. The peaking highlight overlay will now appear during manual focus.

27. Set Level to Low, Standard, or High. Low produces subtle highlights visible only on precisely in-focus edges. High produces more prominent, broader highlights that are easier to see but may be imprecise at very shallow depths of field. Standard is the recommended starting point.

28. Set Color to Red, Yellow, or Blue. Choose the colour with the highest contrast against your typical subjects. Red peaking highlights are easiest to see against green foliage and blue skies. Yellow is visible against both dark and light subjects. Blue is most visible against warm-toned subjects.

29. Press MENU to close the settings and return to shooting. The peaking colour highlights will appear on the shooting screen whenever the camera is in manual focus mode.

To evaluate peaking accurately, watch the screen as you rotate the focus ring slowly. The coloured highlights sweep across the image, landing on whatever is at the current focus distance. When the highlights are on your intended subject — the face in a portrait, the stamens of a flower, the label on a product — stop rotating and take the shot.

MF Magnification — Zooming In for Precise Focus

Manual focus magnification temporarily enlarges the centre of the live view image — or the area around the active AF point — to a magnified view so you can evaluate focus at a finer level than the full-frame view allows. At full-frame view, even significant defocus can look acceptable on the small LCD screen. At 5x or 10x magnification, very small focus errors become clearly visible, allowing you to place the focus with precision.

To activate MF magnification on the Canon EOS R10: while in manual focus mode, press the Magnify button (+) on the back of the camera. The display zooms in to the centre of the frame. Press it again to zoom in further. Use the joystick to pan the magnified view to the area of the subject you want to evaluate. Rotate the focus ring until the subject appears sharpest at this magnification. Press the Reduce button (–) or press SET to return to the full-frame view, then take the shot.

MF magnification can also be configured to activate automatically when you begin rotating the focus ring, without pressing the Magnify button manually. To enable this: press MENU, navigate to Shooting Menu 6, scroll to MF peaking settings or the Custom Controls menu depending on your firmware version, and look for the focus ring rotation magnification option. When enabled, the display zooms in automatically as soon as you start turning the focus ring and returns to full frame when you stop — this is a highly efficient workflow for manual focus shooting.

Important: *Magnification shows only the centre of the frame — or the area around a selected focus point. Make sure to pan the magnified view to the actual subject before judging sharpness, particularly when the subject is positioned off-centre in the composition.*

Note: *Manual focus and MF peaking are available during video recording as well as still photography. In video, rotating the focus ring with peaking enabled allows you to pull focus smoothly between subjects — a technique used to draw the viewer's attention from one element of the scene to another. For the smoothest focus pulls, use a lens with a smooth, dampened focus ring rather than a fly-by-wire focus ring that changes focus speed based on how fast you rotate it.*

PART 7 — Exposure Controls

Exposure is the single most technical concept in photography, and understanding it is the difference between taking whatever photo the camera decides to give you and taking the photo you actually intended to make. This part explains what exposure is, how the three controls that determine it work on the Canon EOS R10, how to adjust them, and how to evaluate whether your exposure is correct before and after you press the shutter.

7.1 What Exposure Means

Exposure is the total amount of light that reaches the Canon EOS R10's sensor during the moment the shutter is open. The sensor records that light and converts it into the image data that becomes your photograph. If the right amount of light reaches the sensor, the image is correctly exposed — the bright areas of the scene look bright, the dark areas look dark, and the mid-tones in between are rendered accurately. If too much light reaches the sensor, the image is overexposed — highlights become pure white with no recoverable detail, colours look washed out, and the image as a whole appears too bright. If too little light reaches the sensor, the image is underexposed — shadows block up to pure black, detail in the darker areas of the scene is lost, and the image appears too dark overall.

Three physical controls determine how much light reaches the sensor in any given shot. These three controls are ISO sensitivity, shutter speed, and aperture. Together they are referred to as the Exposure Triangle, because changing any one of them affects the exposure and may require a compensating adjustment in one or both of the others to maintain the same overall brightness.

What makes exposure interesting — and challenging — is that each of the three controls affects not only the brightness of the image but also something else entirely. ISO affects image quality. Shutter speed affects how motion is recorded. Aperture affects how much of the scene is in focus. Choosing a specific combination of settings is therefore not simply a matter of getting the right brightness — it is a creative decision that simultaneously determines the look and character of the image in multiple ways.

The sections that follow explain each control individually in the context of the Canon EOS R10's specific settings, ranges, and operating methods.

7.2 ISO

What ISO Controls

ISO is a measure of how sensitive the Canon EOS R10's sensor is set to be when receiving light. Think of it as a gain amplifier applied to the sensor's output signal. At low ISO values, the signal is recorded at its base level with minimal amplification — the result is a clean, smooth image with fine detail rendered accurately and without visible grain. At high ISO values, the sensor's output signal is amplified to compensate for low light levels — the camera can expose correctly in darker conditions, but the amplification also amplifies any random electronic noise present in the signal, producing the grain-like texture visible in images shot at high ISO. This grain is called digital noise.

The practical consequence is a trade-off: low ISO gives you the best possible image quality but requires adequate light or a longer exposure time to achieve correct brightness. High ISO allows you to shoot in darker environments with faster shutter speeds, at the cost of increased noise and reduced fine detail.

ISO Range on the Canon EOS R10

The R10's native ISO range runs from ISO 100 at the lowest sensitivity to ISO 32000 at the highest. Within this native range, the sensor is operating within its designed parameters and the noise at each level is managed by Canon's noise reduction processing. Below ISO 800, images are typically very clean with noise that is barely perceptible even at large print sizes. At ISO 1600 and 3200, a small amount of fine grain becomes visible in smooth areas such as skies and skin, but remains acceptable for most uses. At ISO 6400, noise is clearly visible but the images remain usable for web display and moderate-sized prints. At ISO 12800 and 25600, noise is prominent and fine detail begins to soften as the noise reduction processing smooths over it. ISO 32000 is available for situations where obtaining any image at all is more important than technical image quality.

An expanded ISO range extends the upper limit to ISO 51200. This expansion is achieved through digital processing rather than additional sensor sensitivity, and images at ISO 51200 show significant noise and detail loss. It is a last resort for extremely dark conditions, not a setting for general use.

ISO 100 is the base ISO — the setting that produces the lowest noise and the widest dynamic range, meaning the greatest ability to simultaneously record detail in both very bright and very dark areas of the same scene. When light conditions allow it, ISO 100 always produces the highest quality result.

How to Set ISO on the R10

There are three ways to set ISO on the Canon EOS R10.

The fastest method is the M-Fn button shortcut. Press and hold the M-Fn button on the top of the camera with your left hand, then rotate the Main Dial with your right index finger. Each click of the Main Dial cycles through the M-Fn function options — ISO is the first in the default sequence. Release the M-Fn button when ISO is shown as the active function. Now rotate the Main Dial again (without holding M-Fn) to change the ISO value. The value updates on the LCD screen and in the EVF in real time as you rotate.

The second method is through the Quick Control screen. Press the Q button on the camera back to open the Q screen. Use the joystick or tap the touch screen to highlight the ISO panel — it shows the current ISO value or the word AUTO. Rotate the Main Dial or Quick Control Dial to change the ISO value directly. The change takes effect as you rotate.

The third method is through the menu. Press MENU, navigate to Shooting Menu 2, scroll to ISO speed settings, and press SET. Inside this sub-menu, select ISO speed to set a specific value, or proceed to the Auto range settings described below.

Auto ISO

When ISO is set to AUTO, the Canon EOS R10 selects the ISO value automatically, raising it when the scene is dark and lowering it when there is sufficient light. Auto ISO is compatible with all shooting modes including Manual — in Manual mode with Auto ISO active, the camera fixes the shutter speed and aperture at your chosen values and adjusts only the ISO to achieve correct exposure.

Leaving ISO entirely on Auto without any limits can result in the camera selecting very high ISO values in dim conditions, producing noisier images than necessary. The ISO speed settings menu allows you to configure two important Auto ISO parameters.

1. Press MENU and navigate to Shooting Menu 2.
2. Scroll to ISO speed settings and press SET.
3. Select ISO speed range to set the minimum and maximum ISO values the camera is permitted to use during Auto ISO operation. For example, setting the maximum to 6400 prevents the camera from ever selecting ISO 12800 or above automatically, keeping noise within a level you consider acceptable.
4. Select Auto ISO range and then Min. shutter spd. This setting controls the slowest shutter speed the camera will use before it begins raising the ISO. Set it to Auto and the camera decides based on the focal length of the attached lens. Set it to a specific value — such as 1/125 sec — and the camera will raise the ISO rather than allow the shutter to drop below that threshold. This prevents camera shake blur in low-light handheld shooting while keeping the ISO as low as possible in brighter conditions.

Tip: *A practical Auto ISO configuration for general handheld shooting: set the maximum Auto ISO to 6400, and set the minimum shutter speed to 1/focal length of your lens (for example, 1/50 sec with a 50mm lens, or 1/200 sec with a 200mm telephoto). This gives the camera enough ISO latitude to handle varied lighting while preventing unacceptably slow shutter speeds or excessively high noise.*

7.3 Shutter Speed

What Shutter Speed Controls

Shutter speed is the duration for which the Canon EOS R10's shutter remains open during each exposure — the length of time the sensor is actively receiving light. It is measured in seconds and fractions of seconds. A shutter speed of 1/1000 sec means the shutter opens and closes in one one-thousandth of a second. A shutter speed of 1 sec means the shutter remains open for a full second. A shutter speed of 30 sec means the shutter stays open for thirty seconds.

Shutter speed controls two things simultaneously: how much light reaches the sensor during the exposure, and how motion is rendered in the image. A very fast shutter speed admits light for only a very brief interval — perfect for freezing a subject in motion with zero blur. A very slow shutter speed admits light for a much longer interval — accumulating more light but also recording the entire path of any moving subject during that time as a blur or trail.

Shutter Speed Values and What They Produce

Understanding what specific shutter speed ranges do to your images makes choosing the right setting intuitive rather than guesswork.

At 1/2000 sec, 1/4000 sec, and 1/8000 sec (the maximum available with the electronic shutter on the R10), virtually any movement is frozen completely. A hummingbird's wings, water droplets mid-splash, a Formula 1 car at full speed — all appear sharp and still. These speeds require bright light or a high ISO to achieve correct exposure.

At 1/500 sec and 1/1000 sec, fast human motion is frozen sharply — a sprinting athlete, a footballer mid-kick, a cyclist at speed, a dog catching a frisbee. These are the workhorse speeds for sports and wildlife photography in good light.

At 1/250 sec, moderate motion is frozen — walking people, a slow-moving vehicle, a child playing at moderate speed. This is also the maximum flash synchronisation speed on the R10 with mechanical shutter, meaning you cannot use flash with a shutter speed faster than 1/250 sec unless your Speedlite supports High Speed Sync.

At 1/125 sec, general handheld shooting at moderate focal lengths produces sharp results for still or slowly moving subjects. This is a reliable all-purpose speed for daylight shooting.

At 1/60 sec, the safe limit for handheld shooting at standard focal lengths is reached. Any slower than this risks introducing camera shake — the natural tremor of your hands becoming visible as a general softness across the entire image. At this speed or slower, use a tripod, lean against a stable surface, or enable image stabilisation on the lens.

At 1/30 sec, 1/15 sec, and 1/8 sec, camera shake from handheld shooting is likely to be visible. A tripod is strongly recommended. Any moving subjects will show noticeable motion blur.

At 1 sec, 2 sec, 4 sec, and longer, the exposure is long enough to accumulate the light from very dark scenes and to record the movement of any subject as a complete blur trail. A waterfall photographed at 1 sec becomes a smooth, solid veil of white. City traffic photographed at 4 sec leaves flowing rivers of red and white light. A night sky photographed at 20 sec begins to record faint stars. These speeds require a tripod without exception.

At 30 sec — the maximum automatic shutter speed available in the menu-driven exposure settings — the camera can gather light in very dark scenes. Beyond 30 sec, switch the shutter speed dial to BULB.

BULB Mode

BULB is a special shutter setting available in Manual mode. To access it, rotate the Mode Dial to M, then rotate the Main Dial past the 30 sec setting — the display shows BULB. In BULB mode, the shutter opens when you press the shutter button fully and stays open for as long as you hold it. The shutter closes when you release the button. The duration of the exposure is determined entirely by how long you keep the button pressed.

BULB is used for exposures longer than 30 seconds — star trails, lightning, very long light-painting sequences, or astrophotography where the required exposure time varies depending on what you are photographing. Because any vibration while pressing the shutter button will introduce camera shake, always use a remote shutter release or configure the Bulb timer (available in Shooting Menu 9, covered in Section 3.3) to set a fixed exposure duration that fires automatically without you needing to hold the button.

How to Set Shutter Speed on the R10

In Tv (Shutter Priority) mode: rotate the Main Dial clockwise to increase the shutter speed (faster, shorter exposure) and counter-clockwise to decrease it (slower, longer exposure). The shutter speed value updates on screen with each click.

In M (Manual) mode: the Main Dial controls the shutter speed. Rotate it the same way — clockwise for faster, counter-clockwise for slower.

In Fv (Flexible Priority) mode: rotate the Main Dial to change the shutter speed from AUTO to a specific value and lock it.

In all other modes (P, Av, A+, SCN), the camera sets the shutter speed automatically and it cannot be directly adjusted — you can only influence it indirectly through ISO, aperture, or exposure compensation.

7.4 Aperture

What Aperture Controls

Aperture is the adjustable opening inside the lens through which light passes on its way to the Canon EOS R10's sensor. It is controlled by a set of overlapping blades inside the lens that open and close to make the hole larger or smaller. The size of this opening is expressed as an f-stop — a ratio of the lens focal length to the diameter of the opening. A smaller f-number (f/1.4, f/1.8, f/2.8) means a larger opening. A larger f-number (f/8, f/11, f/16) means a smaller opening. This inverse relationship confuses many beginners — remembering it as small number, big hole is a reliable shorthand.

Aperture controls two things simultaneously: how much light passes through the lens to the sensor in any given moment, and the depth of field of the image — the zone of the scene that appears acceptably sharp.

Aperture Values and Their Effects

At f/1.4 and f/1.8 — the widest apertures available on fast prime lenses — a large amount of light enters the lens and the depth of field is extremely shallow. When focused on a subject at portrait distance (roughly one to three metres), the zone of sharpness extends only a few centimetres in front of and behind the exact focal plane. The subject appears razor sharp while the background melts into a smooth, heavily blurred wash. This is the quality of image associated with professional portrait and fashion photography.

At f/2.8 — the maximum aperture of most professional zoom lenses — the depth of field is still shallow and the background blur quality is good, though less extreme than at f/1.8. This is a practical working aperture for portraits and events where you need both good low-light performance and separation between subject and background.

At f/4 and f/5.6 — the maximum aperture of many consumer zoom lenses — the depth of field increases noticeably. The background blur is more modest, though still present. More of the scene in front of and behind the subject remains sharp simultaneously.

At f/8 — often called the sweet spot aperture for many lenses — the depth of field is substantial and most lenses produce their sharpest results. Both a nearby foreground element and a moderately distant background can be in focus at the same time. This is a reliable all-purpose aperture for general photography in adequate light.

At f/11 and f/16 — narrow apertures that produce a deep depth of field — the entire scene from a relatively close foreground to the far distance can appear simultaneously sharp. This is the aperture range used for landscape photography, architectural photography, group portraits, and product photography where total front-to-back sharpness is required.

At f/22 and smaller — the narrowest apertures available on most lenses — the depth of field is at its maximum, but a phenomenon called diffraction begins to reduce the overall sharpness of the image. At very small apertures, light waves bend as they pass through the narrow opening and interfere with each other, softening fine detail. On the Canon EOS R10, the diffraction correction feature in Shooting Menu 1 compensates for this automatically, but some softening at extreme apertures remains inevitable. Avoid f/22 unless total depth of field is truly necessary.

How to Set Aperture on the R10

In Av (Aperture Priority) mode: rotate the Main Dial to change the aperture. Clockwise increases the f-number (narrows the aperture). Counter-clockwise decreases the f-number (widens the aperture). The camera adjusts the shutter speed automatically in response.

In M (Manual) mode: the Quick Control Dial — the textured ring around the SET button on the back of the camera — controls the aperture. Rotate it clockwise for a narrower aperture and counter-clockwise for a wider aperture. The Main Dial controls shutter speed simultaneously.

In Fv (Flexible Priority) mode: rotate the Quick Control Dial to change the aperture from AUTO to a specific value and lock it.

In Tv (Shutter Priority), P, A+, and SCN modes: the camera sets the aperture automatically and it cannot be directly adjusted. You can influence the camera's aperture selection indirectly through exposure compensation or ISO changes.

> **Note:** *The aperture range available to you depends entirely on the lens attached. A lens with a maximum aperture of f/5.6 cannot be set wider than f/5.6, regardless of what the camera's controls would suggest. The R10 will simply limit the available range to what the attached lens physically supports.*

7.5 Exposure Compensation

What Exposure Compensation Does

Exposure compensation is an instruction you give the Canon EOS R10 to deliberately shift its automatic exposure brighter or darker than what its metering system calculates as correct. It does not override the camera's metering — it adjusts the result of that metering by the amount you specify. If the camera meters the scene at 1/125 sec and you apply plus 1 stop of exposure compensation, the camera selects a shutter speed of 1/60 sec instead — one stop slower, admitting twice as much light. The image will be one stop brighter than the camera's uncompensated automatic reading.

Exposure compensation is necessary because the Canon EOS R10's metering system, like all metering systems, is calibrated to render the average brightness of the scene it measures as a medium grey tone — approximately 18 percent reflectance. This calibration is correct for most scenes, which are composed of a mixture of light and dark tones that average out to something in the mid-range. However, for scenes that deviate significantly from this average, the camera's metering produces an incorrect result.

When to Use Positive Compensation (Brighter)

Apply positive exposure compensation — rotating the Quick Control Dial to the right, toward the plus values — in the following situations.

Photographing subjects that are predominantly white, very light, or highly reflective: snow scenes, white sandy beaches, white or cream walls, pale clothing, frosted glass, bright overcast skies. The camera sees a very bright scene and attempts to render the average as medium grey — which means pulling down the whites toward grey and producing an underexposed result where the snow looks grey rather than white. Add plus 1 to plus 2 stops of compensation to restore the whites to their actual brightness.

Photographing a person or subject backlit by a bright background — a window, the sky, a bright wall behind them. The camera meters the bright background and underexposes the subject. Add positive compensation to brighten the subject.

Any situation where the live view preview or a test shot shows an image darker than the scene appears to your eye. Trust your eye — if the image looks too dark, add positive compensation in half-stop increments until it matches reality.

When to Use Negative Compensation (Darker)

Apply negative exposure compensation — rotating the Quick Control Dial to the left, toward the minus values — in the following situations.

Photographing subjects that are predominantly dark, black, or very deep in tone: a dark-suited subject against a dark background, coal, dark wood, shadowed interior scenes, night scenes with small areas of light. The camera attempts to render these dark tones as medium grey and overexposes the result — what should be a rich, dark image is rendered flat and washed out. Apply minus 1 to minus 1.5 stops of compensation to darken the result to its intended tone.

Photographing a subject against a very dark background where the background dominates the frame. The camera meters the dark background and overexposes the subject. Apply negative compensation to pull the exposure back.

Any situation where the image appears brighter than the scene looks to your eye, or where highlights appear blown out in the image when the actual scene had detail in those areas.

How to Apply Exposure Compensation on the R10

The most direct method is to rotate the Quick Control Dial — the textured ring around the SET button on the camera back — while in any auto or semi-automatic mode (P, Tv, or Av). Rotating it to the right moves the compensation toward the plus direction (brighter). Rotating it to the left moves it toward minus (darker). The exposure indicator scale on the LCD screen and in the EVF shows the current compensation level as a marker position relative to the centre zero point.

Alternatively, press the Q button to open the Quick Control screen, navigate to the Expo. comp. panel, and rotate a dial to change the value. The range available on the R10 is minus 3 to plus 3 stops in one-third stop increments.

The compensation value is retained between shots and across power cycles — the camera remembers the last-set compensation level when you turn it back on. After using exposure compensation for a specific situation, always check the compensation value and reset it to zero when moving to a different scene. A compensation setting left at plus 1.5 from a snow scene will overexpose every subsequent shot until you clear it.

5. To reset exposure compensation to zero: rotate the Quick Control Dial back to the centre until the marker is at the zero mark on the exposure indicator. Or press the Q button, highlight the Expo. comp. panel, and press SET — a reset option may appear depending on firmware version.

Important: *Exposure compensation has no effect in fully Manual (M) mode. In Manual mode, all three exposure parameters — shutter speed, aperture, and ISO — are set by you directly. The exposure indicator shows you how your manual settings compare to the camera's metered reading, but applying exposure compensation in Manual mode does not change the actual exposure — it only shifts the zero reference point of the indicator. Use the actual shutter speed, aperture, and ISO values to adjust exposure in Manual mode.*

Tip: *A useful habit when shooting in variable lighting: check the histogram after every few shots, not just the image preview. The image preview can look different depending on screen brightness and ambient light. The histogram* *gives you objective data about whether your exposure is capturing the full tonal range of the scene, and it never lies.*

7.6 Metering Modes

Metering is the process by which the Canon EOS R10 measures the light in the scene to calculate the exposure. The camera does not measure the entire scene as a single undifferentiated reading — it divides the frame into regions, measures each one, and then combines those measurements according to a pattern defined by the selected metering mode. Different metering modes weight different parts of the frame more or less heavily, making them suited to different types of scenes and subjects.

How to Change Metering Mode

6. Press the Q button to open the Quick Control screen.
7. Use the joystick or tap the touch screen to highlight the metering mode panel. It shows the current mode as a small icon.
8. Rotate the Main Dial or Quick Control Dial to cycle between the four available modes. The icon updates with each position.
9. Half-press the shutter or press Q again to close the Q screen with the new mode active.

Metering mode can also be changed from Shooting Menu 7 via the MENU button.

Evaluative Metering

Evaluative metering is the Canon EOS R10's default and most intelligent metering mode. The camera divides the entire frame into a grid of zones — over 300 zones — and measures the brightness of each one independently. It then analyses the overall pattern of brightness distribution across the frame, identifies the position of the active autofocus point, and gives extra weight to the area around that point on the assumption that the subject is there. It applies algorithms developed from a large database of photographic scenes to make an informed decision about the exposure that will best represent the scene as a whole.

Evaluative metering handles the vast majority of photographic situations correctly without any input from you. It manages back-lit scenes better than simpler metering modes, adapts well to mixed lighting, and adjusts appropriately when the active focus point moves to different brightness regions. For general shooting, leave the camera in Evaluative metering at all times. Switch to another mode only when you have a specific reason — a very bright or very dark background that is confusing the evaluative analysis, or when you need precise, point-specific control over the exposure reading.

Partial Metering

Partial metering restricts the metering reading to a circular area in the centre of the frame covering approximately 5.5 percent of the total image area — a circle roughly one-sixth the width of the frame. Brightness outside this central circle is completely ignored in the exposure calculation.

Use Partial metering when your subject occupies the centre of the frame and is surrounded by an area that is significantly brighter or darker and would skew the Evaluative metering result. A performer in a spotlight on a dark stage — the large dark area surrounding the lit performer would cause Evaluative metering to overexpose the performer. A subject backlit by a very bright window where the window dominates the frame — Evaluative metering would underexpose the subject. In both cases, pointing the partial metering circle at the subject's face and pressing the AE Lock button (★) to lock that reading before recomposing gives you a correct exposure for the subject regardless of the surrounding brightness.

Spot Metering

Spot metering further reduces the metering area to approximately 2.5 percent of the frame — a tiny spot at the exact centre of the image. This is the most precise metering tool available on the R10, reading the light from an area small enough to isolate a single tone within a complex scene.

Spot metering is used when you need to expose specifically for a very small, precise tonal value — the shadowed side of a face in high-contrast lighting, a specific colour in a scene with extreme contrast, or any situation where you want to measure the light from a particular element of the scene without any surrounding area influencing the reading. Like Partial metering, Spot metering is most effective when combined with AE Lock: meter from the specific area you want to expose for, lock the reading with the ★ button, recompose, and shoot.

Spot metering requires a clear understanding of what you are metering. If you meter from a white area, the camera will try to render it as medium grey and underexpose the overall scene. If you meter from a black area, it will try to render it as medium grey and overexpose everything else. To use Spot metering accurately, you need to either meter from a mid-tone area or apply exposure compensation to account for the tonal deviation of whatever you are pointing the spot at.

Centre-Weighted Average Metering

Centre-weighted average metering measures brightness across the entire frame but applies approximately 75 percent of the total weighting to the central circular area, blending this with the peripheral brightness to produce a single averaged reading. The central area that receives the heavy weighting covers roughly the central quarter to third of the frame.

This is the oldest metering pattern and predates zone-based evaluative systems by decades. It produces reliable results for subjects centred in the frame against moderately uniform backgrounds, and its behaviour is highly predictable — experienced photographers who learned on earlier camera systems know intuitively how to compensate for it in different situations. It is less adaptive than Evaluative metering and more subject to error in backlit or high-contrast scenes, but its consistency makes it a preference for some photographers who want a metering pattern that behaves the same way every time without any scene-analysing intelligence that might make unexpected decisions.

> **Note:** *The metering mode you select applies to all automatic and semi-automatic modes — it determines how the camera reads the light in P, Tv, Av, and Fv modes. In Manual mode, the metering reading is used only for the exposure indicator scale — it does not change the actual exposure, which is determined entirely by your manually set values.*

7.7 AE Lock

AE Lock — Auto Exposure Lock — is a technique that allows you to separate the metering act from the recomposing act. Normally, the Canon EOS R10 meters the scene wherever the camera is pointed at the moment you half-press the shutter. If you then move the camera to recompose, the metering updates to the new framing. AE Lock prevents this update — it freezes the exposure reading at the moment you press the ★ button and holds it locked even as you move the camera.

This is distinct from simply using exposure compensation: compensation adds a fixed offset to whatever the camera meters, regardless of where the camera is pointing. AE Lock reads from a specific area and holds that exact reading. For many scenes, AE Lock is a more precise solution.

How to Use AE Lock

10. Set your metering mode. For most AE Lock situations, Evaluative or Partial metering is appropriate. Spot metering can be used for the most precise readings from a small area.
11. Point the Canon EOS R10 at the area of the scene you want to expose for. This is typically your subject — the person's face, the mid-tone area of a landscape, or any element whose brightness you want to be the reference for the exposure.
12. Half-press the shutter button to activate metering. The camera reads the scene and displays the resulting shutter speed and aperture on screen.
13. While maintaining the half-press, press the ★ button on the upper-right of the camera back with your right thumb. The asterisk symbol (*) appears on the LCD screen and in the EVF, confirming the exposure is now locked at the current reading.
14. Without releasing the half-press and without releasing the ★ lock, move the camera to your intended composition — place your subject where you want them in the frame.
15. Press the shutter fully to take the photo. The locked exposure reading is used regardless of the new framing.
16. The AE Lock releases automatically when you fully release the shutter button and the camera returns to live metering for the next shot. If you

want to take multiple shots with the same locked exposure, keep the shutter half-pressed between shots to maintain the lock.

Practical Example of When AE Lock Is Necessary

You are photographing a person standing at the entrance to a dark building, with bright sunlight behind them and a dark doorway surrounding them. When you frame the shot with the person centred in the frame, the bright sunlight and the dark doorway average together and the camera produces an exposure that leaves the person's face too dark — the bright background has pulled the metering up. You aim the centre of the frame directly at the person's face — not at the background — and press AE Lock. The camera meters only the face and locks that reading. You then recompose to the framing you want, with the person off-centre against the interesting architectural background, and take the photo. The person's face is now correctly exposed.

Tip: *AE Lock works most effectively when combined with One-Shot AF. Half-press to focus on the subject, keep the half-press to maintain focus lock, press ★ to add exposure lock on top of the focus lock, then recompose and shoot. Both focus and exposure are locked simultaneously from the subject area, giving you a correctly focused and correctly exposed image regardless of where in the frame the subject is placed.*

7.8 Reading the Histogram

What the Histogram Is

The histogram is a graph that shows the distribution of tonal values across your image — how many pixels are at each brightness level from pure black on the left edge to pure white on the right edge. It is the most objective and reliable exposure evaluation tool available on the Canon EOS R10, because it shows you quantitative data about the actual image rather than a subjective visual impression that varies depending on the brightness of the screen and the ambient light around you.

The horizontal axis of the histogram represents brightness from left to right: the far left represents pure black (zero brightness), the far right represents pure white (maximum brightness), and the middle section represents the full range of mid-tones. The vertical axis shows how many pixels exist at each brightness level — a tall peak at any position means many pixels are at that brightness; a low or absent line means few or no pixels are there.

How to Display the Histogram on the R10

To view the live histogram while shooting: press the INFO button repeatedly on the camera back until the histogram display mode appears. A small histogram graph appears in the corner of the shooting screen alongside the live view. The histogram updates in real time as you point the camera at different subjects and as the light changes. Use this real-time histogram to evaluate your exposure settings before pressing the shutter.

To view the histogram during playback: press the Playback button, then press INFO repeatedly until the histogram overlay appears on the image. This shows the histogram for the captured image, allowing you to evaluate whether the actual recorded exposure captured the full tonal range of the scene.

What Different Histogram Shapes Mean

A histogram where the graph fills most of the width from left to right, with the data peaking somewhere in the middle range and tapering off before reaching either edge, represents a well-exposed image with a full tonal range — detail in both the shadows and the highlights, and a broad range of mid-tones. This is the histogram shape to aim for in most situations.

A histogram where the graph is pressed up against the left edge — with a spike or solid mass of data at the far left and nothing in the mid or right area — indicates heavy underexposure. The image is mostly dark, the shadows have blocked up to pure black with no recoverable detail, and the highlights and mid-tones are absent. In RAW files, some shadow detail can be recovered in editing software, but the severely underexposed areas remain noisy and may not be usable.

A histogram where the graph is pressed against the right edge — with data piling up against the right wall and possibly spilling off the edge — indicates overexposure. The highlights have been clipped to pure white. Pixels at pure white contain no information — they are simply white, regardless of what colour or detail the original scene had in those areas. Blown highlights cannot be recovered in editing, in RAW or JPEG, because the information was never recorded. Any area of the histogram that touches or spills over the right edge represents permanently lost highlight detail.

A histogram where the graph is clustered only in the left half, with a gap or very low data in the right half, indicates an image that is darker than average overall — which may be correct for a predominantly dark subject, or may indicate moderate underexposure in a scene that should have more highlight information.

A histogram clustered only in the right half indicates an image that is brighter than average — correct for a scene with bright highlights (snow, a white-walled room, a subject in direct sunlight), or an indicator of overexposure in a scene that should have more shadow information.

Highlight Alert — The Blinking Overexposure Warning

In addition to the histogram, the Canon EOS R10 offers a visual overexposure warning during playback called the Highlight alert. When enabled (in the Playback menu under Highlight alert, or in the Playback information display settings), any area of the image that has been clipped to pure white blinks rapidly between black and white on the LCD screen during playback review. These blinking areas — sometimes called the blinkies by photographers — make it immediately obvious which specific parts of the image have lost highlight detail, allowing you to judge at a glance whether the blown areas are in a critical region (a face, a product, an important texture) or an unimportant one (the sky behind a building, a specular reflection on a car, a light source itself).

If the blinking areas are in critical regions, reshoot with negative exposure compensation applied — minus one-third to minus two-thirds of a stop is usually sufficient to pull the highlights back within range. If the blinking areas are only in genuinely unimportant specular highlights (the sun itself, bright reflections from glass or metal), they can be accepted without concern.

The Histogram and RAW vs JPEG

When you shoot in JPEG, the histogram displayed in playback represents the final processed image — the brightness distribution of the image exactly as it will look when you open the file. If highlights are blown in the JPEG histogram, they are blown in the file and cannot be recovered.

When you shoot in RAW, the histogram displayed in playback is generated from the embedded JPEG preview within the RAW file — not from the full RAW data itself. The full RAW file typically contains approximately one additional stop of highlight latitude beyond what the JPEG histogram suggests. This means that highlights that appear blown in the RAW histogram may in fact be recoverable when the file is processed in Canon Digital Photo Professional or another RAW editor with highlight recovery. However, this latitude is limited — do not use it as a reason to habitually overexpose. The goal remains to keep the histogram as complete and ungapped as possible, with data filling the full range without clipping at either edge.

> **Note:** *A common exposure strategy called exposing to the right involves setting the exposure so the histogram is pushed as far right as possible without the highlights actually clipping. This maximises the amount of tonal information in the brighter half of the histogram where less noise is present, particularly in RAW files. After capture, the image is darkened in post-processing to the intended final brightness. This technique is more relevant to RAW shooting in controlled conditions than to fast-moving documentary or event photography.*

PART 8 — Image Quality and Storage Settings

Every photo the Canon EOS R10 captures is written to the SD card as a file. The format, size, compression level, and processing applied to that file determine both the quality of the image and how large the file is — which in turn affects how many images fit on your card, how fast the camera can write them, and what you can do with them afterwards. This part explains how to configure these settings and what each choice means in practice.

8.1 RAW vs JPEG vs HEIF

The Canon EOS R10 can save images in three fundamentally different file formats: RAW, JPEG, and HEIF. Understanding what each format is and how it differs from the others is one of the most important foundational decisions you make as a photographer, because it determines both your creative latitude and your workflow after the shoot.

How to Set the Image Format

1. Press the MENU button on the upper-left of the camera back.
2. Rotate the Main Dial to the first red Shooting tab — Shooting Menu 1.
3. Scroll to Image quality using the Quick Control Dial and press SET.
4. The Image quality screen appears, showing two rows. The top row sets the RAW format. The bottom row sets the JPEG or HEIF format. You can select a setting in one row, both rows, or only one — if only one row is active, the camera saves only that format.
5. Use the joystick to move between the rows and rotate a dial or tap to select your preferred options. Press SET to confirm and close the screen.

JPEG

JPEG is the most universally compatible image format and the one the Canon EOS R10 produces by default out of the box. When the camera saves a JPEG, it takes the raw sensor data and processes it internally — applying the selected Picture Style, white balance, sharpening, noise reduction, and colour adjustments —

then compresses the result into a compact file. This entire process happens inside the camera in less than a second.

The advantage of JPEG is convenience. The files are small, they open immediately in any application on any device from a smartphone to a television to a professional editing suite, they can be uploaded and shared directly without any conversion step, and they look finished the moment the camera saves them. A correctly exposed, well-lit JPEG from the R10 is a complete, usable photograph that requires no further work if you are satisfied with the camera's processing decisions.

The disadvantage of JPEG is that it is a destructive, lossy format. The compression algorithm permanently discards some image data to reduce the file size. More importantly, the in-camera processing decisions — the colour rendering, the sharpening level, the noise reduction, the white balance — are baked permanently into the file. If you want a different look, a different white balance, or you need to recover highlights that were slightly clipped, you have limited ability to make those changes in editing software because the underlying data that would allow those adjustments was discarded when the file was saved.

JPEG is the right choice when you shoot in good, predictable light, when you want finished files immediately without a processing step, when storage space is a concern, or when the volume of images you shoot makes handling individual RAW files impractical.

RAW

A RAW file is not a processed image — it is a direct recording of the raw data captured by the Canon EOS R10's sensor before any of the in-camera processing has been applied. The sensor records the light values at every pixel, and those values are stored in the file exactly as measured, along with a set of metadata that records which settings were active when the shot was taken (white balance, Picture Style, noise reduction, and so on), but that metadata does not permanently alter the underlying pixel data.

The consequence of this is profound. Because the sensor data is untouched, you have complete control over how the image is processed when you open the RAW file in editing software such as Canon's own Digital Photo Professional, Adobe

Lightroom, or any other RAW-capable application. You can change the white balance entirely — from the actual captured setting to any other white balance — without any quality loss, because white balance in RAW processing is an interpretive instruction applied to the raw data rather than a destructive change to the pixels themselves. You can recover blown highlights, lift crushed shadows, change the colour rendering, apply a completely different sharpening profile, and adjust the tonal curve — all with full access to the complete sensor data that was captured at the moment of shooting.

A RAW file from the Canon EOS R10 has a file size of approximately 20 to 30 megabytes per image, depending on the complexity of the scene. This is four to eight times larger than a typical fine-quality JPEG from the same shot. On a 64 GB card, you can store approximately 2,000 to 2,500 RAW files, compared to 8,000 to 12,000 fine JPEGs.

RAW files cannot be shared directly — they must be processed and exported to a standard format (JPEG or TIFF) before use. This introduces a post-processing step into your workflow that requires both software and time. For photographers who shoot high volumes of images and do not process every frame, or who shoot in well-controlled predictable conditions, this overhead may be unnecessary. For photographers who care about image quality, creative control, or who frequently shoot in mixed or challenging lighting, RAW is the correct format.

Canon RAW files use the .CR3 file extension and are compatible with Canon Digital Photo Professional (free from Canon's website), Adobe Lightroom, Adobe Camera Raw, Capture One, and most other professional editing applications.

HEIF

HEIF (High Efficiency Image File Format) is a newer image format that uses more advanced compression mathematics than JPEG to store the same visual information at a smaller file size — or, conversely, to store more visual information at the same file size. A HEIF file from the Canon EOS R10 records 10 bits of colour per channel (compared to 8 bits in JPEG), which means it can represent a wider range of tones and colours with smoother gradations between values.

The practical advantages of HEIF over JPEG are most visible in high-contrast scenes with subtle gradations — smooth skies, skin tones in mixed lighting, sunset gradients. The 10-bit depth captures these gradations more accurately than JPEG's 8-bit recording, reducing the banding artefacts (visible steps between similar tones) that can appear in JPEG files.

HEIF is also the format required for the Canon EOS R10's HDR shooting modes to preserve the HDR PQ brightness information — a standard JPEG cannot store the extended brightness range that HDR content requires.

The disadvantage of HEIF is compatibility. While modern Apple devices (iPhone, Mac with macOS High Sierra or later), Windows 10 and 11 with the appropriate codec installed, and recent versions of major editing applications support HEIF natively, many older devices, applications, and online platforms do not. Uploading a HEIF file to a platform that does not support it may result in an error or automatic conversion to a lower-quality format. The Canon EOS R10 includes an in-camera HEIF to JPEG conversion function in the Playback menu (covered in Section 3.5) for exactly this reason.

Choose HEIF if you are shooting for an HDR-capable display workflow or if your entire pipeline — from the camera to editing software to final delivery — fully supports 10-bit HEIF files. For all other uses, JPEG or RAW remains more practical.

RAW + JPEG — Saving Both Simultaneously

The Canon EOS R10 can save a RAW file and a JPEG file simultaneously from every single shot — a combination setting available in the Image quality screen. When this is configured, each press of the shutter produces two files: a full RAW file containing the complete unprocessed sensor data, and a processed JPEG using the camera's current Picture Style and processing settings.

This gives you the immediate usability of JPEG — the files are ready to share, view on any device, and use without processing — alongside the complete editability of RAW, which you can process later whenever a particular image warrants the extra attention.

The trade-off is storage. Because every shot produces two files, the effective capacity of your SD card is roughly halved compared to shooting JPEG alone, and the write time for each shot is slightly longer because the camera must write both files. On a 64 GB card, RAW + Large Fine JPEG produces approximately 1,200 to 1,500 usable image pairs.

> **Tip:** *A practical approach for photographers who are unsure whether to shoot RAW or JPEG: shoot RAW + JPEG for a period, then review how often you actually open the RAW files versus how often the JPEG is perfectly adequate. Most photographers find they process only a small fraction of their RAW files. Once you understand your own patterns, you can simplify your storage and workflow accordingly.*

8.2 Image Size and Compression

Within the JPEG and HEIF formats, the Canon EOS R10 offers a choice of resolution (how many pixels the image contains) and compression level (how aggressively the file is compressed to reduce its size). These settings are configured in the same Image quality screen as the file format.

JPEG Size Options

The Canon EOS R10's sensor captures images at its maximum resolution of 24.2 megapixels. When saving as JPEG, you can choose to save at that full resolution or at reduced sizes. The available size options are as follows.

L (Large) saves the image at the full 24.2 megapixel resolution — approximately 6000 by 4000 pixels. This is the highest resolution option and the one you should use in almost all circumstances. The full resolution image can be printed at high quality at large sizes, cropped significantly in editing and still retain sufficient resolution for a standard print, and future-proofs your images for any use case you might later encounter. There is no situation in which deliberately reducing the resolution before saving improves the image — you can always reduce later, but you cannot recover resolution that was never recorded.

M (Medium) saves at approximately 12.4 megapixels — roughly 4000 by 2672 pixels. This is adequate for most web use and standard-sized prints up to approximately A3, but limits your cropping latitude and prevents very large print output.

S1 saves at approximately 6.1 megapixels — roughly 2880 by 1920 pixels. Sufficient for web, email, and social media, and for prints up to approximately A4. Not suitable for large prints or significant cropping.

S2 saves at approximately 3.8 megapixels — roughly 2400 by 1600 pixels. A small file suited only to web and screen use. Not recommended as a primary capture size.

> **Important:** *Reducing the JPEG size permanently reduces the resolution of the saved file. Unlike RAW, where the full 24.2 megapixel sensor data is always preserved regardless of any settings, a size-reduced JPEG records fewer pixels and that information is permanently absent from the file. Always capture at L (Large) unless you have a specific, deliberate reason for a smaller file — storage space alone is not a sufficient reason given the low cost of large SD cards.*

JPEG Compression — Fine vs Normal

In addition to resolution, each JPEG size option on the Canon EOS R10 can be saved at one of two compression levels: Fine and Normal.

Fine applies lower compression to the JPEG file — the compression algorithm discards less image data, preserving more of the fine detail, tonal gradations, and colour accuracy in the file. Fine JPEG files are larger than Normal JPEGs at the same resolution. A Large Fine JPEG from the R10 is typically between 6 and 10 megabytes per image.

Normal applies higher compression — more data is discarded to achieve a smaller file. Normal JPEGs show more compression artefacts (blockiness, smearing of fine detail, colour banding) than Fine JPEGs, particularly in areas with complex texture, high-contrast edges, or subtle tonal gradations. A Large Normal JPEG is typically between 3 and 5 megabytes.

Use Fine compression at all times. The difference in file size between Fine and Normal is relatively modest, and the difference in image quality — particularly when viewing images at full size on a high-resolution monitor or making large prints — is clearly visible. The storage saving from Normal compression does not justify the quality reduction in any practical shooting situation.

In the Image quality screen, Fine JPEG is indicated by a smooth wave icon and Normal by a rougher, more jagged wave icon next to the size letter.

RAW — Full Resolution Only

RAW files on the Canon EOS R10 are always saved at the sensor's full native resolution of 24.2 megapixels. There is no option to save a reduced-resolution RAW file. Every RAW file contains the complete data from every pixel on the sensor — approximately 6000 by 4000 pixels in the native 3:2 aspect ratio.

The only RAW-related setting that affects file size is the choice between RAW and C-RAW, described below. Both record full resolution — the difference is only in how the data is stored.

C-RAW — Compressed RAW

C-RAW (Compressed RAW) is Canon's proprietary lossily-compressed RAW format. A standard RAW file stores the full, uncompressed sensor data from each pixel individually. C-RAW applies a compression algorithm to the RAW data before saving it, reducing the file size by approximately 40 percent compared to a full RAW file from the same shot — a C-RAW file is typically between 12 and 18 megabytes, versus 20 to 30 megabytes for a standard RAW.

The compression used in C-RAW is visually lossless under normal shooting conditions — in the vast majority of images, there is no perceptible difference in quality between a RAW and a C-RAW processed side by side. The compression primarily affects the mathematical precision of the data in the shadow regions of the image, where the reduced bit-depth of the compressed data can occasionally introduce a small amount of additional noise when shadows are pushed significantly in editing. In practice, this difference is visible only under extreme shadow recovery scenarios and not in normally exposed images.

C-RAW is a practical compromise for photographers who want the editing flexibility and highlight recovery capability of RAW but need to manage storage and write speed more carefully. For everyday shooting, C-RAW is an excellent choice. For scenes where you anticipate heavy shadow recovery in editing — an underexposed image from a difficult situation, a high-contrast night scene with deep shadows that must be lifted — the full uncompressed RAW gives you a marginal additional buffer.

To select C-RAW: in the Image quality screen, look for the C-RAW option in the top row (the RAW row). It appears as a smaller icon beside the standard RAW icon. Tap or use a dial to select it.

> **Note:** *C-RAW files have the same .CR3 file extension as full RAW files and are processed identically in Canon Digital Photo Professional, Adobe Lightroom, and other compatible RAW editors. You do not need different software or different processing workflows for C-RAW versus full RAW.*

8.3 Picture Styles

Picture Style is the Canon EOS R10's system for controlling how the camera processes and presents colour, contrast, sharpness, and tone in JPEG and HEIF images. When you take a photo, the camera converts the raw sensor data into the final image using a set of processing parameters — Picture Style determines what those parameters are. Different styles produce noticeably different-looking images from the same raw data.

Think of Picture Styles as equivalent to choosing between different types of photographic film. Just as Kodak Portra film renders skin tones differently from Fujifilm Velvia, Standard Picture Style renders colour differently from Portrait or Neutral. The same scene, shot at the same exposure, looks different depending on which Picture Style is active.

How to Access and Change Picture Style

6. Press the Q button on the camera back to open the Quick Control screen.
7. Use the joystick or tap the touch screen to highlight the Picture Style panel. The current style name is shown.
8. Rotate the Main Dial or Quick Control Dial to cycle through the available styles. The live view image on screen updates in real time to show approximately how the current scene will look with each style applied.
9. To see the detailed parameters of the highlighted style — and to modify them — press SET instead of rotating. A detail screen opens showing the sharpness, fine detail, contrast, saturation, and colour tone values for that style, each adjustable with the dials.

10. Once the desired style is shown, half-press the shutter or press Q to close the Q screen with the style active.

Picture Style can also be changed from Shooting Menu 3 via the MENU button, which provides the same style list and the same parameter adjustment capability.

Auto

In the Auto Picture Style, the Canon EOS R10 analyses the scene being photographed and applies the processing parameters it determines to be most appropriate for that specific subject. For a portrait with a face present, it applies softer, skin-tone-accurate processing. For a landscape with vivid colours, it applies stronger saturation and sharpness. For a scene with mixed or neutral tones, it applies a balanced standard processing.

Auto is a useful default for photographers who do not want to think about Picture Style and are content to let the camera make the processing decision for each individual scene. However, its behaviour is not fully predictable — the style it applies may vary between similar shots if the camera's scene analysis produces different classifications. Photographers who want consistent, repeatable colour across a series of images in the same session should select a fixed style rather than Auto.

Standard

Standard is the default Picture Style for general shooting and the one the Canon EOS R10 uses when no specific style is selected. It applies moderately boosted colour saturation, moderately high sharpness, and standard contrast — parameters designed to produce pleasing, vivid images with strong colour that look finished and attractive when viewed directly without any editing. Standard JPEGs have a clean, colourful look well suited to everyday photography, social events, travel, and general shooting where the goal is a good-looking image without any processing work.

Standard is not intended as a neutral starting point for editing — its colour and sharpness processing are applied to make the image look finished as-is, not to be adjusted in post. For images that will be edited, Neutral or Faithful are better starting points.

Portrait

Portrait Picture Style is optimised specifically for images of people, with adjustments made to the three processing parameters most relevant to human subjects.

Sharpness is reduced slightly compared to Standard, softening the fine texture rendering. This softening is specifically aimed at the texture of skin — reducing the visual prominence of pores, fine lines, and other skin texture that sharpness enhancement would otherwise accentuate. The subject's eyes and hair, which have higher contrast edges, remain sharp enough to appear well-defined. A face photographed in Portrait style looks smooth and flattering without appearing artificially processed.

Colour saturation is adjusted to produce accurate, pleasing skin tones across a range of skin colours. The processing prioritises the red-orange-yellow tonal range in which skin tones fall, rendering them with warmth and accuracy rather than over-saturating them into an unnatural orange or under-saturating them into a flat grey.

Contrast is reduced slightly from Standard, producing a softer tonal range that is kinder to the face in mixed lighting — reducing the apparent harshness of shadows and the brightness of specular highlights on skin.

Use Portrait style for any image where a human face is the primary subject — individual portraits, environmental portraits, headshots, family photographs, and wedding photography. It also works well for children, where the smooth skin rendering and accurate warm tones are particularly flattering.

Landscape

Landscape Picture Style is optimised for outdoor scenes — specifically for the colours most prominent in natural outdoor photography: blues, greens, and the tonal range of natural light.

Colour saturation is boosted significantly in the blue and green channels compared to Standard — skies become deeper and more vivid, foliage becomes richer and more saturated, water takes on stronger colour. This enhancement specifically targets the colours that are most important in landscape photography while leaving other colour ranges less affected.

Sharpness is set to maximum, producing the strongest edge and texture rendering available within Picture Style processing. This maximum sharpness makes rock faces, tree bark, grass blades, architectural details, and other textured natural subjects appear highly defined and detailed in the final image.

Contrast is slightly increased from Standard, reinforcing the sense of depth and atmosphere in outdoor scenes.

Use Landscape style for natural outdoor photography — countryside, mountains, coastlines, forests, gardens — and for architecture, cityscapes, and any scene where vivid colour and maximum detail rendering are the priority. It is not suitable for portrait work — the high sharpness will accentuate skin texture unflattering, and the saturation boost may produce unnatural skin tones.

Fine Detail

Fine Detail applies the highest possible sharpness and texture rendering of any Canon Picture Style — higher than Landscape, higher than Standard, optimised specifically to make extremely fine surface detail appear as clearly defined as possible. Colour saturation and contrast are set to moderate levels to ensure that the sharpness enhancement is the dominant characteristic of the processing rather than competing with vivid colour or high contrast.

Fine Detail is suited to subjects where intricate surface texture is the primary visual content of the image: fabric weave, embroidery, engraving, architectural stonework, circuit boards, feathers, insect wings, botanical close-ups, coins and stamps, product photography of textured goods, and any macro subject where fine detail is the entire point of the photograph. It is not suitable for portraits or for scenes where sharpness enhancement would produce an unattractive, clinical look.

Neutral

Neutral Picture Style applies the minimum possible processing to the JPEG — low sharpness, low contrast, and low saturation — producing a flat, muted image that is deliberately underprocessed. The result looks dull and uninspiring when viewed directly, but that is intentional: Neutral is not a finished image style, it is a starting point for editing.

Because Neutral applies so little processing, it leaves the maximum amount of latitude for adjustments in editing software. A Neutral JPEG behaves somewhat like a very simply processed RAW — the tones are not pushed into saturation, the contrast has not been compressed, and the sharpness has not been enhanced beyond the minimum needed to render the image clearly. In editing, you can apply your own specific colour grade, contrast curve, and sharpening to produce exactly the result you want without fighting against the camera's own processing decisions.

Use Neutral when you are shooting JPEG but intend to edit every image in post-processing software and want the maximum editing headroom within the JPEG format. If you are processing images significantly in post regardless, shooting RAW provides even greater latitude than Neutral JPEG and is generally the better solution for edit-intensive work.

Faithful

Faithful Picture Style is designed for colour accuracy — producing JPEG files where the colours recorded match the colours of the original scene as closely as possible under standard 5200K daylight illumination. Unlike Standard (which boosts saturation for a pleasing look) or Portrait (which adjusts skin tones for flattery), Faithful makes no enhancement or aesthetic adjustment to colour — it simply attempts to reproduce the colours that were present in front of the lens as accurately as the JPEG format allows.

The practical use of Faithful is in work where colour accuracy matters more than colour appeal: scientific documentation, product photography where the client needs accurate colour representation, artwork reproduction, reference photography, and any context where the colour in the image must match the colour of the real-world subject with minimum deviation. When shooting under non-daylight light sources, Faithful's accuracy is dependent on the white balance being correctly set for the actual light source — without accurate white balance, the colour accuracy of the Faithful style is undermined.

Monochrome

Monochrome Picture Style converts the image to black and white at the point of capture, discarding all colour information and rendering the scene entirely in tones of grey. The Canon EOS R10 applies its full sensor resolution to the monochrome conversion, producing a detailed, clean black and white image.

Monochrome in the R10 includes two additional layers of control that allow you to customise the character of the black and white conversion.

The first control is Filter effect — a simulation of the coloured optical filters used in traditional black and white film photography. These filters change how different colours in the scene are translated to grey tones. Rotating the filter dial (accessible from the Picture Style detail screen by pressing SET on Monochrome) cycles through the options. Without any filter (N — none), all colours translate to grey tones according to their natural luminosity. The Yellow filter slightly darkens blue skies relative to white clouds, increasing the separation between sky and cloud. The Orange filter more strongly darkens blue skies, producing a dramatic increase in contrast between sky and cloud, and warms skin tones slightly in portraits. The Red filter produces the most extreme sky darkening, creating very high-contrast, dramatic landscapes with near-black skies and brilliant white clouds — a classic effect in fine art black and white landscape photography. The Green filter lightens foliage and darkens skin tones, useful for portraits with natural outdoor backgrounds where you want the greenery to appear lighter.

The second control is Toning effect — a colour tint applied uniformly across the image's grey tones to give the monochrome image a colour cast rather than a neutral grey. The available toning options are None (neutral grey), Sepia (a warm brown tone associated with aged photographic prints), Blue (a cool, cyanotype-like tint), Purple, and Green. Toning is accessible from the same Picture Style detail screen.

> **Important:** *When you shoot in Monochrome Picture Style and save only JPEG or HEIF, all colour information from the scene is permanently discarded. The file contains only grey tonal values and cannot be converted back to colour in editing. If you shoot RAW with Monochrome active, the RAW file still contains all the original colour data — the monochrome conversion is applied only to the embedded JPEG preview within the RAW file. Processing the RAW in*

editing software will produce the full-colour version of the image. To get a true monochrome RAW file, you must shoot JPEG-only in Monochrome.

User Defined 1, 2, and 3

The Canon EOS R10 provides three User Defined Picture Style slots — User Def. 1, User Def. 2, and User Def. 3 — which are blank presets you can populate and name with any combination of parameters you prefer. Each User Defined slot can be based on any of the existing styles (using its parameters as a starting point) and then modified to any values of sharpness, fine detail, contrast, saturation, colour tone, and filter/toning effects you choose.

For example, you might create a User Defined style based on Portrait but with saturation reduced further for a slightly more muted, editorial look, and contrast boosted slightly to compensate. Or a style based on Landscape but with the sharpness dialled back from maximum to a level that suits a specific lens. Or a style based on Neutral but with a specific colour tone shift toward warmth for a particular consistent look across a series of images.

11. Press MENU and navigate to Shooting Menu 3.
12. Scroll to Picture Style and press SET.
13. In the Picture Style list, scroll past the standard styles to User Def. 1 (or 2 or 3).
14. With a User Def. slot highlighted, press the INFO button. A detail screen opens showing the parameters. Scroll to Detail set. and press SET.
15. A source style selection appears — choose which existing style you want to use as the base for your User Defined style. Press SET.
16. The parameter screen now shows the selected style's values. Use the joystick to highlight each parameter — Sharpness, Fine detail, Contrast, Saturation, Colour tone — and rotate a dial to adjust it. Each adjustment shows a live preview on the image.
17. Press MENU when you have configured the parameters as desired. The User Defined slot now holds your custom settings.
18. The User Defined slot can be selected from the Q screen or Picture Style menu the same way as any standard style. Its custom parameters are applied to every JPEG or HEIF captured while it is active.

Note: *Picture Styles apply exclusively to JPEG and HEIF output. When you shoot RAW, the active Picture Style is recorded as a metadata tag in the .CR3 file and applied to the embedded JPEG preview that the camera uses for playback, but the actual RAW data is completely unaffected. When you process the RAW file in editing software, you can apply any Picture Style — or any other processing — regardless of what was active when the photo was taken. The RAW data itself is always the complete, unprocessed sensor capture.*

PART 9 — White Balance and Color

Colour accuracy is one of the most immediately noticeable qualities of a photograph. Skin that looks orange, a white shirt that appears blue, or a neutral grey wall with a green cast — these are all symptoms of incorrect white balance, and they undermine an otherwise well-exposed and sharply focused image. This part explains what white balance is, why it matters, and how to set it correctly on the Canon EOS R10 for any lighting situation you encounter.

9.1 What White Balance Is

The Problem White Balance Solves

Different light sources emit light of different colours. Sunlight on a clear day at midday produces a relatively neutral, white light. The same scene photographed in open shade — away from direct sun — is illuminated by light from the blue sky above, giving the light a distinctly blue-purple cast. On an overcast day, the light from clouds is cooler than direct midday sun, producing a slight blue-grey cast. Incandescent tungsten bulbs — the old-fashioned round household bulbs — emit a very warm, orange-yellow light. Fluorescent tube lighting produces a greenish cast. Candle flame is extremely warm, deep orange.

Your visual system — your eyes and the colour processing that happens in your brain — adapts to these different light colours automatically and almost instantly. If you walk from outside sunlight into a room lit by tungsten lamps, within a few seconds the white walls inside appear white to you, not orange, even though the light illuminating them is strongly orange. This adaptation is called chromatic adaptation and it happens below the level of conscious awareness.

The Canon EOS R10's sensor does not adapt. It records the light that reaches it according to fixed colour sensitivity characteristics. If the light is orange because the scene is lit by tungsten lamps, the sensor records orange light — and everything in the image shifts toward orange. White walls look yellow-orange. Skin looks excessively warm. A white shirt looks cream-coloured. The image does not look the way the scene appeared to your eye when you were standing in it.

White balance is the Canon EOS R10's mechanism for correcting this. It applies a mathematical colour shift to the captured image data — boosting blue and reducing red-orange for warm light sources, boosting red-orange and reducing blue for cool light sources — so that a white surface in the scene is rendered as white in the final image, regardless of the actual colour of the light illuminating it. When white is rendered correctly, all other colours in the image fall into their correct relationships relative to white, producing natural-looking, accurate colour throughout the frame.

Colour Temperature — The Kelvin Scale

The colour of light is measured on a scale called colour temperature, expressed in degrees Kelvin (K). The Kelvin scale for photographic purposes runs from approximately 2000K at the warm orange end to approximately 10000K at the cool blue end. Contrary to what you might expect, higher Kelvin numbers correspond to cooler, bluer light, and lower Kelvin numbers correspond to warmer, more orange light.

Candle flame sits at approximately 1800K to 2000K — deep, warm orange. Tungsten household bulbs are approximately 2800K to 3200K — warm yellow-orange. Sunrise and sunset light is approximately 2500K to 3500K. Household halogen bulbs sit around 3000K. Fluorescent office tubes are typically 4000K to 5000K, depending on the specific tube type. Standard daylight at midday is approximately 5200K to 5500K — the reference point for neutral, accurate colour. Overcast or cloudy sky is approximately 6000K to 7000K. Open shade (outdoors away from direct sun, illuminated by blue sky) is approximately 7000K to 8000K. Clear blue sky itself can reach 10000K or higher.

When you set the white balance on the Canon EOS R10 to a specific Kelvin value, you are telling the camera what colour the light is so it can apply the correct compensating shift to make white appear white. Setting the white balance to 3200K tells the camera the light is tungsten-warm and it should apply a blue shift to counteract the orange cast. Setting it to 7000K tells the camera the light is shade-cool and it should apply a warm shift to counteract the blue cast.

Why White Balance Matters More for JPEG Than RAW

When you shoot JPEG, the white balance setting is applied permanently to the image data at the moment the file is saved. The JPEG contains processed, colour-corrected pixels — if the white balance was wrong, the colours are wrong in the file, and correcting them in editing software means working with degraded data that has already had one incorrect colour shift applied.

When you shoot RAW, the white balance setting is recorded as a metadata tag but does not alter the underlying pixel data. The raw sensor values are stored exactly as captured. When you process the RAW file in editing software, you can change the white balance to any value — from any preset to any specific Kelvin temperature — without any quality loss, because the colour correction is applied interpretively to the unaltered data rather than baked in. For RAW shooters, white balance is therefore less critical at the time of capture and more a starting point that can be adjusted freely in post-processing. For JPEG shooters, getting the white balance right in-camera is essential.

9.2 Auto White Balance (AWB)

How AWB Works on the R10

In Auto White Balance, the Canon EOS R10 analyses the colours present in the live view image and calculates what colour the illuminating light source is likely to be, then applies a compensating white balance shift to neutralise it. This analysis happens continuously as the camera is pointed at different subjects and as the lighting changes. AWB is sophisticated enough to handle many mixed-lighting situations, gradual lighting changes as the sun moves, and moderate variations in the dominant light source.

AWB is reliable for the majority of everyday photographic situations: outdoor daylight, overcast conditions, flash photography, and mixed indoor-outdoor scenes. It falters in certain specific situations — scenes with a dominant colour that the algorithm mistakes for a coloured light source (a scene full of red flowers may confuse the AWB into over-correcting toward teal), scenes lit by light sources with unusual spectral distributions (some LED lights, sodium vapour street lights, theatrical gels), and situations where deliberate colour preservation is important (described below).

AWB Ambience Priority vs AWB White Priority

The Canon EOS R10 offers two AWB sub-modes that determine how the auto white balance handles warm artificial light sources such as tungsten bulbs, candles, and warm LED lights.

AWB Ambience priority is the default AWB setting and the one most photographers should use. In this mode, when the camera detects that the scene is lit by warm artificial light, it corrects the white balance enough to make the image look natural and accurate, but deliberately retains some of the warmth of the light source. Under a tungsten lamp, AWB Ambience priority will shift the image away from the extreme orange of uncorrected tungsten, but will leave a noticeable warm quality that conveys the character of the light — the ambience of the scene. A portrait taken by candlelight in AWB Ambience priority will look warm and intimate, as the scene actually appeared, rather than clinically neutral. This is the right choice whenever the colour of the light is part of the mood you are trying to capture.

AWB White priority fully corrects the warm cast of artificial light sources toward neutral white, regardless of how warm the original light was. Under the same tungsten lamp, AWB White priority will produce an image where white surfaces are neutral white and skin tones are accurate, as if the room were lit by daylight. This is the right choice when colour accuracy is more important than preserving the character of the light — product photography, documentary work, or any context where you need consistent, neutral colour regardless of the light source.

How to Set AWB and Choose Priority on the R10

1. Press the Q button on the camera back to open the Quick Control screen.

2. Use the joystick or tap the touch screen to highlight the White Balance panel. The current white balance setting is shown as a name or icon.
3. Rotate the Main Dial or Quick Control Dial until AWB is displayed.
4. Press SET to open the AWB detail screen. Two options appear: AWB (Ambience priority) and AWB W (White priority).
5. Highlight your preferred option and press SET to confirm it.
6. Half-press the shutter or press Q to close the Q screen. AWB is now active with the selected priority.

AWB can also be set from Shooting Menu 3 via the MENU button, which provides access to the same AWB priority option.

> **Note:** *AWB Ambience priority and AWB White priority both adapt continuously to changes in the scene. The distinction between them is not which one corrects the white balance — both do — but how much warmth they preserve after correcting it. In scenes lit by standard daylight, both options produce virtually identical results because there is no artificial warmth to either preserve or remove.*

9.3 Manual White Balance Presets

The Canon EOS R10 provides seven fixed white balance presets, each calibrated for a specific, common light source. When you know the type of light illuminating your scene, selecting the matching preset gives you a consistent, predictable colour result that does not shift between shots the way Auto White Balance can. This consistency is particularly valuable when shooting a series of images in a controlled environment where the light is constant — a studio, a venue under fixed artificial lighting, or a sunny outdoor scene where the light quality is stable.

How to Select a Preset

7. Press the Q button on the camera back to open the Quick Control screen.
8. Highlight the White Balance panel using the joystick or touch screen.
9. Rotate the Main Dial or Quick Control Dial to scroll through the available presets. Each preset shows its icon and name as you rotate.

10. When the correct preset for your lighting is displayed, half-press the shutter or press Q to close the Q screen with the preset active.

Alternatively, press MENU and navigate to Shooting Menu 3, then select White balance to access the full preset list.

Daylight

Daylight preset is calibrated for direct sunlight at typical daylight hours — morning through mid-afternoon on a clear day. Its calibration point is approximately 5200K, which is the internationally recognised standard for neutral daylight colour. Use Daylight when shooting outdoors in direct sun with no significant cloud cover and no shade influence on the subject. Under these conditions, Daylight preset produces accurate, neutral colours with no perceptible cast.

Do not use Daylight preset indoors under artificial lighting or in overcast or shaded conditions — the colour temperature of those light sources is significantly different from 5200K and the result will have a visible colour cast.

Shade

Shade preset is calibrated for open shade — outdoor environments where the subject is not in direct sunlight but is illuminated by reflected light from the blue sky above. This is the condition that exists under a tree canopy, on the shaded side of a building, under an overhang, or anywhere the sun is blocked but the sky overhead is open and blue. In shade, the light is cooler (higher Kelvin temperature, more blue) than direct sunlight. The Shade preset applies a strong warm shift — approximately equivalent to setting the camera to 7000K — to neutralise this blue cast and render the scene with natural, accurate colours.

Without the Shade preset (or an equivalent correction), photos taken in open shade have a noticeably cool, blue-purple cast — particularly visible in skin tones and white surfaces. Shade preset eliminates this cast entirely. Use it any time your subject is in shade outdoors on a clear day with blue sky visible overhead.

Cloudy

Cloudy preset is calibrated for overcast conditions — days when the sky is covered with thin to moderately thick cloud that diffuses the sunlight but does not block it entirely. Overcast light is cooler than direct sunlight but warmer than open shade, sitting at approximately 6000K to 6500K. The Cloudy preset applies a moderate warm shift to neutralise this slight cool cast.

Overcast light is actually among the most flattering and even for portrait photography because the cloud acts as a giant natural diffuser, eliminating harsh shadows. Using the Cloudy preset ensures the soft, attractive quality of overcast light is reproduced with accurate colour rather than a slight blue-grey cast. Use Cloudy on any overcast or heavily cloudy day, outdoors, where the light comes primarily from the cloud-covered sky above.

Tungsten Light

Tungsten preset is calibrated for incandescent tungsten light bulbs — the traditional round glass bulbs with a glowing filament inside that were the standard in homes and buildings before LED and compact fluorescent lamps became widespread. Tungsten light has a colour temperature of approximately 2800K to 3200K and emits a strongly warm, orange-yellow light. Without white balance correction, images under tungsten light are heavily orange.

The Tungsten preset applies the strongest cool shift of any standard preset — a large blue correction to counteract the deep orange of the tungsten source. The result is a neutral, accurate colour rendering with white surfaces appearing white and skin tones appearing natural.

Tungsten preset is calibrated specifically for traditional incandescent bulbs. Warm-white LED bulbs and halogen bulbs also produce warm light but at slightly different colour temperatures. In these cases the Tungsten preset may produce a slightly cool result — a minor overcorrection. If this happens, use the Colour temperature setting (described below) to dial in a more precise value, or use Custom White Balance to capture an exact reading from your specific light source.

White Fluorescent Light

White Fluorescent preset is calibrated for standard fluorescent tube lights — the long, linear white tubes used in offices, schools, supermarkets, warehouses, and many commercial buildings. Standard cool-white fluorescent tubes produce light at approximately 4000K with an additional greenish spectral peak that the Kelvin scale alone does not fully capture. This green cast is what gives fluorescent-lit environments their characteristic slightly sickly look in unprocessed photographs.

The White Fluorescent preset applies both a warm shift (to compensate for the lower colour temperature relative to daylight) and a magenta shift (to counteract the green spectral peak) to produce a more neutral colour result. Use this preset indoors in any environment lit primarily by traditional fluorescent tubes.

Modern LED panel lights, which are now common in offices and commercial buildings, produce very different spectral characteristics from traditional fluorescent tubes. The White Fluorescent preset may not correct them accurately. If you are shooting under modern LED panels and the fluorescent preset is not producing accurate colour, use Custom White Balance to capture an exact correction for your specific lights.

Flash

Flash preset is calibrated for the colour temperature of Canon Speedlite flash units, which produce light at approximately 5500K to 6000K — slightly cooler and more neutral than midday daylight. The Flash preset applies a very subtle warm shift relative to Daylight to ensure accurate colour when the primary light source is an electronic flash.

Use this preset when shooting with an external Speedlite as the dominant or sole light source. In mixed situations — where flash is providing fill light alongside ambient daylight — Auto White Balance often handles the mixture more accurately than either the Flash or Daylight preset, because AWB can balance the combination of the two sources. Use the Flash preset in pure flash-only environments, particularly indoors where there is no daylight contribution to the exposure.

Colour Temperature — Manual Kelvin Entry

The Colour temperature setting allows you to specify a precise colour temperature value in Kelvin rather than relying on one of the named presets. The available range on the Canon EOS R10 is 2500K to 10000K in increments of 100K.

This is the most precise and flexible manual white balance option. It is particularly useful when you know the exact colour temperature of your light source — for example, a studio strobe rated at 5600K, a specific LED panel rated at 4500K, or when you want to deliberately set an off-neutral white balance for a specific visual effect.

11. Press the Q button and highlight the White Balance panel.
12. Rotate the dial until the Colour temperature option appears — it is shown as a Kelvin value (for example, 5200K) with a thermometer icon.
13. Press SET to open the Kelvin entry screen.
14. Rotate the Main Dial to change the Kelvin value. Rotating right increases the value (cooler, bluer correction). Rotating left decreases the value (warmer, more orange correction).
15. Press SET to confirm the value and return to the shooting screen.

As a practical reference: values below 5200K apply a cooling effect to the image (used to counteract warm light sources or to add deliberate coolness). Values above 5200K apply a warming effect (used to counteract cool light sources such as shade or overcast, or to add deliberate warmth). If you deliberately set a Kelvin value higher than the actual colour temperature of your light source — setting 7000K when shooting in daylight at 5200K, for example — the image will appear warm with an amber-orange cast. Setting a lower value than the actual colour temperature will add a cool blue cast.

> **Tip:** *Colour temperature control is useful for creative white balance shifts. Setting the Kelvin value to 3200K when shooting outdoors in daylight gives the image a strong blue cast — used deliberately in certain advertising and fashion contexts for a cold, clinical aesthetic. Setting it to 8000K in daylight produces a deep golden warmth — useful for creating the feeling of golden-hour light even at midday. These are deliberate creative choices, not corrections.*

9.4 Custom White Balance

When to Use Custom White Balance

The white balance presets and the Auto White Balance system cover the most common lighting situations accurately. However, there are situations where neither approach gives you the precise accuracy you need. Mixed artificial lighting — a combination of tungsten and fluorescent, or different brands of LED panels with different colour temperatures — may not match any single preset. Unusual or theatrical light sources — coloured gels, sodium vapour, mercury vapour, or specialised studio lights with unusual spectral characteristics — fall outside the calibration range of the standard presets. In any of these situations, Custom White Balance allows you to capture an exact, measured white balance reading from your specific light in your specific environment, producing a correction that is perfectly tailored to your conditions rather than approximated from a generic preset.

Custom White Balance is also the professional standard for critical colour work — product photography, catalogue shooting, fashion, and commercial work where colour accuracy must be consistent and verifiable. By capturing a custom white balance at the beginning of a session, every subsequent image in that session will have identical, accurate colour without any variation between frames.

What You Need

To set a Custom White Balance you need a white balance reference — a surface that is known to be neutral. The most reliable options are a dedicated photographic grey card (which reflects exactly 18 percent of the light hitting it and has a completely neutral colour), or a commercially available white balance card or white balance disc. A sheet of plain white printer paper can work in a pinch but is not as reliable because paper often has a slight optical brightener applied that can skew the reading in UV-rich outdoor light. The reference surface must be large enough to fill the centre of the frame when you photograph it.

Step-by-Step: Setting Custom White Balance on the R10

16. Set up your scene and turn on all the lights that will be illuminating the subject during the shoot. The custom white balance reading must be taken under the actual lighting conditions you will be shooting in — if you change or add lights afterwards, repeat the process.
17. Hold the white balance card or grey card so that it is illuminated by the same light that will illuminate your subject. If you are shooting a person, have them hold the card in front of their face at the shooting position so the card is lit from the same angle and by the same sources as the subject will be.

18. On the Canon EOS R10, set the image format to JPEG temporarily if you are normally shooting RAW — the Custom White Balance capture function reads from a JPEG image. If you are already shooting JPEG, proceed.
19. Point the camera at the white or grey card so that it fills the centre portion of the frame. It does not need to fill the entire frame, but the centre area — where the camera takes its reading — should show only the card with no other colours visible.
20. Set the white balance to any setting (AWB or a preset) and take a photograph of the card. The card photograph does not need to be perfectly exposed — slightly over or under by one stop is acceptable. What matters is that it is a clear, in-focus image of the neutral card under your specific lighting.
21. Press the MENU button and rotate the Main Dial to Shooting Menu 3.
22. Scroll to Custom White Balance and press SET.
23. The screen displays your most recently captured image. If the card photograph is visible, it is already selected. If not, rotate the Main Dial to scroll to the card photograph.
24. With the card photograph selected, press SET. A confirmation message appears asking whether to use the white balance data from this image. Scroll to OK and press SET to confirm.
25. The camera has now extracted the colour information from the card photograph and stored it as the custom white balance value. Return to the White Balance setting — via Q or MENU → Shooting Menu 3 → White balance — and select the Custom White Balance option, shown as a square icon with small dots or lines around it. Press SET to confirm.
26. All subsequent shots will now use the custom white balance reading taken from the card. The colours in every image will be corrected specifically to the light in your environment.

Verifying the Custom White Balance

After setting the Custom White Balance and selecting it, take a test shot of something you know the colour of — a white wall, a white piece of paper, the white balance card itself. Review the image on the LCD screen. White surfaces should appear neutral white with no perceptible colour cast. Skin tones on any person in the scene should look natural and accurate. If there is a residual cast, check whether the light has changed since you took the card photograph — even a cloud passing overhead or a door opening to let in daylight can shift the colour temperature enough to affect the result. Repeat the card capture and the Custom White Balance setup if the light conditions have changed.

White Balance Correction — Fine-Tuning Any Preset

In addition to the main white balance settings, the Canon EOS R10 provides a White Balance Correction function that allows you to apply a persistent colour shift on top of any white balance preset — including AWB and Custom White Balance. This is used for fine-tuning: if you find that a particular preset is consistently producing a result that is slightly too warm, slightly too cool, slightly too green, or slightly too magenta, you can offset it without switching to a different setting.

27. Press MENU and navigate to Shooting Menu 3.
28. Scroll to White balance correction and press SET.
29. A colour grid appears with two axes: a blue-to-amber axis running horizontally (B on the left, A on the right) and a green-to-magenta axis running vertically (G at the bottom, M at the top). A small square marker sits at the centre of the grid, indicating no correction is applied.
30. Use the joystick to move the marker away from centre in the direction of the colour shift you want to apply. Moving toward A (amber) adds warmth. Moving toward B (blue) adds coolness. Moving toward M (magenta) adds a pink-purple shift. Moving toward G (green) adds a green shift.
31. Each unit of movement represents one unit of correction in that direction. Apply corrections in small amounts — one to two units in most cases is sufficient.
32. Press SET to confirm the correction. The white balance correction icon appears in the EVF and on the LCD shooting screen as a reminder that a correction is active.

Important: *White Balance Correction remains active persistently — it applies to every shot taken after it is set, including across power cycles. When you are finished with the session that required the correction, return to this setting and move the marker back to centre to clear it. Leaving an unintended correction active will affect the colour of every subsequent image until it is cleared.*

Note: *White Balance Correction does not replace the main white balance setting — it shifts the result of whatever setting is active. If you set both AWB and a correction, the correction is applied on top of AWB's automatic reading. If you then switch to a Daylight preset, the same correction is applied on top of Daylight. The correction is a global offset that follows you across all white balance modes until you clear it.*

Tip: *For photographers who shoot JPEG in controlled studio or event lighting over long sessions, Custom White Balance combined with a small White Balance Correction fine-tune is the most reliable path to consistent colour across an entire shoot. Set the Custom White Balance at the start, review a test shot, and apply a minor correction if needed. Every image from that point on will be colour-consistent without any further attention to white balance during shooting.*

PART 10 — Flash

Flash photography adds a controlled burst of artificial light to a scene, either to illuminate a subject in low-light conditions, to balance a subject against a bright background, or to add a specific quality of light that the ambient environment does not provide. This part explains how flash works on the Canon EOS R10, how to attach and use an external Speedlite, how to control the flash output level, and the technical constraint of flash synchronisation and how to exceed it when needed.

10.1 The R10 Has No Built-In Flash

The Canon EOS R10 does not have a built-in flash unit of any kind. There is no pop-up flash, no embedded front-facing flash window, and no flash that rises from the camera body. The top panel of the R10 is completely flat above the lens mount — the hot shoe is present, but the camera itself produces no flash output independently.

This is a deliberate design decision. Eliminating the built-in flash allows the camera body to be made more compact and robust, removes a mechanical component that adds complexity and failure risk, and forces the use of an external Speedlite that is significantly more powerful, more flexible, and capable of being angled, bounced, and positioned in ways that a fixed built-in flash cannot match. A built-in flash fires directly at the subject from a point very close to the lens axis, producing flat, harsh, shadowless light that is generally unflattering. An external Speedlite mounted on the hot shoe can be tilted upward to bounce off a ceiling, rotated to bounce off a side wall, or removed from the camera entirely and placed at any position for off-camera flash arrangements.

If you want to use flash with the Canon EOS R10, you must attach a compatible external Speedlite. Canon's RF and EF-compatible Speedlite range includes units at various power levels and feature sets — from the compact Speedlite 270EX II to the professional Speedlite 600EX II-RT. Any Canon Speedlite that supports E-TTL II metering is fully compatible with the R10's automatic flash exposure system.

Note: *Third-party flash units from manufacturers such as Godox, Nissin, Profoto, and others are also compatible with the Canon EOS R10 hot shoe, provided they support Canon's E-TTL II protocol. Units that only support manual flash operation or a different manufacturer's TTL protocol will fire at a fixed power level and will not communicate with the camera's automatic flash metering system.*

10.2 Using an External Speedlite

Attaching the Speedlite to the Hot Shoe

The hot shoe is the rectangular metal bracket on the top of the Canon EOS R10, positioned between the Mode Dial and the EVF eyepiece. It has four electrical contact pins inside it — a central large contact for the main sync signal and three smaller contacts along the rear for the multi-pin communication between camera and Speedlite.

1. Hold the Speedlite with its mounting foot pointing downward and its head facing the same direction as the camera lens.
2. Align the foot of the Speedlite with the hot shoe slot. The foot slides in from the rear — position the back edge of the foot at the front of the hot shoe and slide it forward until it is fully seated.
3. Rotate the locking ring on the base of the Speedlite's mounting foot clockwise — toward the lock symbol — until it is firm. The Speedlite is now physically secured to the camera and electrically connected through the hot shoe contacts.
4. Power on the Speedlite using its own on/off switch. The Canon EOS R10 detects the Speedlite automatically within a second of it being powered on, and a lightning bolt icon appears on the camera's LCD screen and in the EVF to indicate that a flash unit is ready.

How Flash Fires in Different Shooting Modes

The Canon EOS R10 handles flash differently depending on which shooting mode is active when the Speedlite is attached and powered on.

In Scene Intelligent Auto (A+), the camera decides automatically whether the flash is needed based on its analysis of the scene brightness. In adequately lit conditions the flash does not fire. In low light the camera activates the Speedlite to fire for each shot. You have no direct control over this decision in A+ mode — the camera makes the judgement entirely.

In Program AE (P), Tv, Av, and Fv modes, the Speedlite is ready but does not fire automatically unless you explicitly activate it. To fire the flash, press the flash activation button on the Speedlite itself — typically a button on the back of the unit labelled with a lightning bolt symbol. On most Canon Speedlites this button raises and activates the flash head. Once activated, the flash fires with every subsequent shot until you deactivate it by pressing the button again or powering the Speedlite off. The camera's E-TTL II system manages the flash exposure automatically in these modes.

In Manual mode (M), the Speedlite fires with every shot when it is active. Flash exposure is still controlled by E-TTL II automatically unless you switch the Speedlite itself to manual power control, in which case you set the flash output level on the Speedlite directly.

How E-TTL II Automatic Flash Metering Works

When the Canon EOS R10 fires the shutter with a Speedlite attached, the process happens in two stages rather than one. Immediately before the main exposure, the camera instructs the Speedlite to fire a brief, low-power pre-flash. This pre-flash illuminates the scene for a fraction of a second — too brief to register as a visible flash to people in the scene — and the camera's metering system measures how much of that light bounces back through the lens from the subject. Based on this measurement, the camera calculates precisely how much power the Speedlite needs to output during the actual main flash to correctly expose the subject. It then fires the main flash at that calculated power level simultaneously with the shutter opening.

This system — Evaluative Through-The-Lens metering, or E-TTL II — gives the camera the information it needs to expose the subject correctly regardless of the subject's distance, the reflectivity of their clothing, or the ambient light level. It adjusts the flash power independently for each shot, so if the subject steps closer or moves to a darker background, the flash compensates automatically.

The E-TTL II calculation also gives extra weighting to the area around the active autofocus point, assuming that is where the subject is located. This makes flash exposure more accurate when the subject is positioned away from the centre of the frame — the system bases its power calculation on the subject's actual position rather than just the centre of the image.

Bouncing the Flash

Most Canon Speedlites have a head that tilts upward and rotates left and right. Pointing the Speedlite head directly at the subject — the default position with the head facing straight forward — produces a direct, relatively harsh light from above and slightly in front of the subject, creating strong shadows beneath the nose and chin and a flat-looking result in portraits.

Bouncing the flash changes this significantly. Tilt the Speedlite head upward so it points at the ceiling above the scene, and the flash fires upward, hits the ceiling, and scatters back down onto the subject as a large, soft, diffuse light source — the ceiling effectively becomes a giant soft box. The light is flattering, shadow-free, and much more natural-looking than direct flash. The E-TTL II system compensates for the additional distance the light must travel (up to the ceiling and back down) by increasing the flash power automatically.

For the bounce to work correctly the ceiling must be white or very light in colour. Bouncing off a coloured ceiling will tint the light — a yellow ceiling produces yellow-tinted portraits, a pink ceiling produces pink-tinted portraits. In rooms with dark or coloured ceilings, rotate the Speedlite head to bounce off a white side wall instead, or use the flash with a diffuser attachment.

> **Note:** *When the Speedlite head is tilted or rotated, the camera's LCD screen and EVF will show a small indicator warning that the flash head is not in the direct-forward position. This is a reminder, not an error — the flash will still fire correctly at the tilted angle.*

10.3 Flash Exposure Compensation

What Flash Exposure Compensation Does

Flash Exposure Compensation (FEC) adjusts the power output of the attached Speedlite brighter or darker than the E-TTL II system's automatically calculated level, without changing any other aspect of the camera's exposure. It is the flash equivalent of the exposure compensation used for ambient light — a plus value instructs the camera to tell the Speedlite to output more power than the automatic reading, and a minus value instructs it to output less.

The most common use of flash exposure compensation is to reduce the flash output. E-TTL II is calibrated to produce a technically correct exposure — meaning the subject is correctly exposed at the metered level. In many portrait situations, particularly close-range or indoor portraits, this technically correct level produces a flash-lit result that looks artificial — the subject is too brightly and evenly lit, the light is clearly from a flash, and the image lacks the natural interplay of light and shadow that makes a portrait look real. Reducing the flash output by minus 1 to minus 2 stops softens the flash contribution, allowing more ambient light to contribute to the overall exposure and producing a result that looks natural and appropriate rather than flash-dominated.

How to Set Flash Exposure Compensation

There are two ways to set Flash Exposure Compensation on the Canon EOS R10.

The first way is through the Quick Control screen. Press the Q button on the camera back. When a Speedlite is attached and active, the Flash exp. comp. panel appears in the Q grid alongside the other settings. Use the joystick or tap it to highlight this panel, then rotate the Main Dial or Quick Control Dial to change the value. The available range is minus 3 to plus 3 stops in one-third stop increments. The current value is shown as a position on a scale. Set it and close the Q screen by half-pressing the shutter or pressing Q again.

The second way is through the menu. Press MENU, rotate the Main Dial to Shooting Menu 8, scroll to Flash control, press SET, then scroll to Flash exposure comp. and press SET again. A scale appears — rotate a dial to set the compensation level and press SET to confirm.

Practical Flash Exposure Compensation Settings

A flash exposure compensation of zero — the default — produces the E-TTL II automatically calculated output, which is technically correct but may look artificial in portraits at close range.

Minus two-thirds of a stop (–0.7 on the scale) is a subtle reduction that takes the edge off overly bright flash without dramatically reducing the flash contribution. This is a good starting point if the auto flash result looks just slightly too bright.

Minus one stop (–1) noticeably reduces the flash brightness, creating a more balanced blend of flash and ambient light. This is the most commonly used setting for indoor portrait work where the goal is natural-looking flash.

Minus one and two-thirds stops (–1.7) or minus two stops (–2) produces a very subtle flash contribution — the flash is still firing and contributing to the exposure, but its effect is barely perceptible. The ambient light dominates the overall look of the image. This level of reduction is used when you want the flash to provide fill light only — just enough to lift the shadows and reduce the contrast ratio, without the image appearing flash-lit at all.

Plus one-third (plus 0.3) or plus two-thirds (plus 0.7) is used when the flash is slightly underpowering the subject — the subject appears darker than the background or darker than a test shot indicates is correct. A small positive adjustment increases the output while keeping the exposure balanced.

Plus one stop (plus 1) and higher is used for longer flash distances or highly reflective environments where the E-TTL II reading is underestimating the required output, or where the Speedlite is bouncing off a very large or distant surface and losing power in transit.

> **Important:** *Flash Exposure Compensation on the Canon EOS R10 stacks on top of any flash exposure compensation set on the Speedlite itself. If you set minus 1 stop on the camera and minus 1 stop on the Speedlite simultaneously, the total reduction is minus 2 stops. Always check both the camera's FEC setting and the Speedlite's own FEC setting when diagnosing unexpected flash brightness — it is easy to accumulate unintended compensation from both sources.*

> **Tip:** *After any shooting session that required flash exposure compensation, reset the value to zero before your next shoot. Flash exposure compensation persists across power cycles on the R10 — the value you set today will still be active the next time you turn the camera on. A residual compensation of*

minus 1.5 from a portrait session will significantly underpower the flash in your next situation without any obvious indication of why.

10.4 Flash Sync Speed

What Flash Sync Speed Is

The Canon EOS R10 uses a mechanical shutter — a pair of metal curtains that move across the sensor to control the exposure. The first curtain moves across the sensor to begin the exposure and the second curtain follows to end it. At moderate shutter speeds, the first curtain completes its travel across the entire sensor before the second curtain begins to follow. During the interval between the two curtain movements, the entire sensor is exposed simultaneously — there is a moment where the full sensor area is open to light at the same time. The electronic flash fires during this moment of full exposure, illuminating the entire frame evenly.

As the shutter speed increases beyond a certain threshold, the first curtain has not finished crossing the sensor before the second curtain begins to follow. This means the two curtains travel together with a narrow gap between them — essentially a slit that moves across the sensor. At any given moment, only the portion of the sensor within the gap between the curtains is exposed to light. The flash, which fires instantaneously, can only illuminate the portion of the sensor that happens to be within the gap at the precise microsecond it fires. The rest of the frame, which is either already covered by the second curtain or not yet uncovered by the first curtain, receives no flash illumination. The result is a dark band across the image — part of the frame is flash-lit and part is not.

The fastest shutter speed at which the entire sensor is simultaneously open — and therefore at which the flash can illuminate the entire frame — is called the maximum flash synchronisation speed, or the sync speed. On the Canon EOS R10 with the mechanical or electronic first-curtain shutter, the maximum flash sync speed is 1/250 sec.

What Happens When You Exceed the Sync Speed

If you set the shutter speed to 1/500 sec, 1/1000 sec, or any value faster than 1/250 sec while using flash with the mechanical shutter, a dark band will appear in the image — typically across the bottom of the frame, though its position depends on the exact timing of the flash firing relative to the curtain movement. The band represents the area of the sensor that was covered by the second curtain when the flash fired.

The Canon EOS R10 protects against this in automatic modes by preventing the shutter speed from exceeding 1/250 sec when a Speedlite is attached and active. In Tv mode and Manual mode, however, you can manually set a shutter speed faster than 1/250 sec — and if the flash fires at that speed, the dark band will appear. The camera does not prevent you from making this setting, so it is important to understand the limit and work within it.

5. To check your current shutter speed when a Speedlite is attached: look at the shutter speed display on the LCD screen or in the EVF. If it shows a value faster than 1/250, either reduce the shutter speed to 1/250 or slower, or enable High-Speed Sync as described below.

High-Speed Sync (HSS) — Exceeding the Sync Limit

High-Speed Sync is a feature available on compatible Canon Speedlites — including the Speedlite 430EX III-RT, 470EX-AI, 600EX II-RT, and others — that allows flash photography at any shutter speed the camera supports, including up to 1/4000 sec with the mechanical shutter and up to 1/8000 sec with the electronic shutter on the R10.

HSS works by pulsing the flash many times per second rather than firing a single full burst. As the narrow slit formed by the two curtains moves across the sensor, the HSS Speedlite pulses rapidly to illuminate each part of the sensor as the gap passes over it. Because the flash illuminates each section of the sensor as the gap reaches it, the entire frame is evenly lit even though the sensor was never fully open at any single moment. This is fundamentally different from normal single-burst flash.

The trade-off is flash power. Pulsing the flash many times per second to simulate continuous illumination requires far more energy than a single burst, and the total light delivered to any one point on the sensor is much less than a standard full-power flash burst. As a result, HSS flash is significantly less powerful than standard flash at the same distance. At 1/2000 sec HSS, the effective range of the flash is dramatically reduced compared to 1/250 sec standard sync.

How to Enable High-Speed Sync on the R10

6. Confirm that your Speedlite supports HSS. Check the Speedlite's manual or Canon's website — HSS is listed as a feature specification. Speedlites without HSS capability cannot perform this function regardless of the camera setting.
7. Press MENU on the Canon EOS R10 and rotate the Main Dial to Shooting Menu 8.
8. Scroll to Flash control and press SET.
9. Scroll to Flash sync speed in Av mode and press SET. This setting controls how the camera manages sync speed in Aperture Priority mode specifically. For Tv and Manual mode, the sync speed is simply set by your shutter speed selection.
10. On the Speedlite itself, access the flash unit's menu system and enable the HSS (High Speed Sync) or FP (Focal Plane) setting — the exact name and method vary by Speedlite model; refer to your Speedlite's instruction manual.
11. Once HSS is enabled on the Speedlite, a small HSS indicator icon appears in the camera's shooting display when a shutter speed faster than 1/250 sec is selected. This icon confirms that HSS is active and the flash will illuminate the entire frame at the selected fast shutter speed.
12. Set your shutter speed to the value needed for your shot. In bright daylight for outdoor portraiture with a wide aperture, this may be 1/1000 sec or faster. Take your shot — the Speedlite will pulse automatically to illuminate the full frame.

When to Use High-Speed Sync

HSS is most valuable in two specific situations.

The first is outdoor portraiture in bright sun where you want to use a wide aperture — f/1.8 or f/2.8 — to blur the background, but the bright ambient light forces a shutter speed faster than 1/250 sec to avoid overexposure. Without HSS, you would have to use a neutral density filter to reduce the light and bring the shutter speed back within the sync limit. With HSS, you can shoot at whatever fast shutter speed the ambient light requires while still firing the Speedlite to provide fill flash on the subject's face — filling in the shadows created by harsh sunlight and ensuring the subject is well-exposed against the bright background.

The second is any situation where you want to use flash at a fast shutter speed to freeze motion while also illuminating the subject — for example, freezing a moving subject outdoors in daylight while providing flash fill, or shooting a sport or action subject with fill flash faster than the 1/250 sec sync limit.

> **Note:** *HSS is only effective within a limited distance range that decreases as the shutter speed increases. At 1/2000 sec HSS, the usable flash range may be only one to two metres for a mid-range Speedlite, compared to five to seven metres at standard sync speed. Position the Speedlite as close to the subject as practical when using HSS at very fast shutter speeds.*

> **Tip:** *For outdoor portrait work, a practical HSS setup on the R10 is: Av mode, aperture at f/1.8 or f/2.8, HSS enabled on the Speedlite, Flash sync speed in Av mode set to Auto in Shooting Menu 8, Flash exposure compensation at minus 1 stop. The camera will select the shutter speed automatically to expose the background correctly, the Speedlite will pulse at whatever speed is needed to sync, and the minus 1 FEC keeps the flash subtle enough to look like natural light rather than obvious flash fill.*

PART 11 — Drive Modes and Burst Shooting

Drive mode controls how the Canon EOS R10 behaves each time you press the shutter button — whether it takes one photo and waits, fires a rapid sequence of photos for as long as the button is held, or delays the shot by a set countdown. Choosing the right drive mode for your subject and situation is as important as choosing the right focus mode. This part explains every drive mode available on the R10, what each one does, and when to use it.

11.1 Selecting a Drive Mode

The drive mode setting persists across power cycles — the camera remembers the last-used drive mode when it is turned back on. Before each shooting session, check that the active drive mode is appropriate for the subject you are about to photograph.

Via the Quick Control Screen

1. Press the Q button on the back of the camera to open the Quick Control screen.
2. Use the joystick or tap the touch screen to highlight the Drive mode panel. The current mode is shown as an icon — a single rectangle for Single shooting, overlapping rectangles for continuous modes, or a clock symbol for self-timer modes.
3. Rotate the Main Dial or Quick Control Dial to cycle through the available drive modes. The icon and name update with each position.
4. Half-press the shutter or press Q to close the Q screen with the selected drive mode active.

Via the M-Fn Button Shortcut

Drive mode is one of the settings accessible through the M-Fn button shortcut. Press and hold the M-Fn button on the top of the camera with your left hand, then rotate the Main Dial with your right index finger to cycle through the M-Fn function options until Drive mode is shown on screen. Release the M-Fn button, then rotate the Main Dial again to change between drive modes directly. This method allows you to change drive modes without taking your eye away from the viewfinder.

Via the Menu

5. Press MENU and rotate the Main Dial to Shooting Menu 7.
6. Scroll to Drive mode using the Quick Control Dial and press SET.
7. The drive mode options appear as a list. Scroll to the desired mode and press SET to confirm.

11.2 Drive Mode Options

Single Shooting

Single shooting is the default drive mode and the correct choice for most photographic situations. In this mode, one photograph is taken each time the shutter button is pressed fully. After the shot is captured and written to the SD card, the camera returns to standby and waits for the next press. You have complete, deliberate control over every individual frame — nothing fires without an intentional full press of the shutter button.

Use Single shooting for portraits, landscapes, architecture, still life, street photography, food photography, and any subject that is stationary or moving slowly enough that you do not need multiple frames per second to capture it. In Single shooting, you are not relying on volume — you are making a considered decision with each press of the shutter.

Single shooting is also the most storage-efficient and battery-efficient drive mode, since the camera processes and writes only one file per deliberate press rather than running the buffer and write system continuously during a burst.

High-Speed Continuous Plus (Electronic Shutter)

High-Speed Continuous Plus is the fastest drive mode available on the Canon EOS R10, reaching up to 15 frames per second. It uses the electronic shutter exclusively — no physical curtains move during the exposure. Because there are no mechanical parts to move, reset, and move again between frames, the camera can sustain an extremely high capture rate. At 15 fps, you are capturing a frame every 66 milliseconds — faster than most subjects can change position perceptibly between frames.

To use this mode: select High-Speed Continuous Plus from the drive mode list, press the shutter button fully, and hold it down. The camera fires continuously at its maximum sustained rate for as long as you hold the button and as long as the buffer and card write speed allow. Release the button to stop the burst. During the burst the camera applies Servo AF continuously, tracking the subject and adjusting focus between frames.

The Electronic Shutter — Advantages and Limitations

The electronic shutter eliminates all mechanical shutter sound and vibration. In High-Speed Continuous Plus mode, the camera operates in complete silence. This is a genuine advantage in environments where shutter noise would be disruptive — wildlife photography from a hide, sports events where camera sounds are prohibited, theatre and concert photography, and documentary work where you want to remain unobtrusive.

The electronic shutter also eliminates shutter shock — the subtle vibration that a mechanical curtain introduces at the moment it begins to travel across the sensor. At high magnification or long telephoto focal lengths, shutter shock can introduce a slight softening of the image. The electronic shutter removes this variable entirely.

However, the electronic shutter has two significant limitations that determine when it should and should not be used.

The first limitation is rolling shutter distortion. Unlike a physical shutter that exposes the entire sensor simultaneously, the electronic shutter reads out the sensor line by line from top to bottom. This readout takes a finite amount of time — on the Canon EOS R10, approximately 1/30 of a second for a full sensor readout. During this readout window, any fast horizontal motion in the scene shifts position between the time the top of the frame is read and the time the bottom is read. The result is a visible skewing or bending of vertical lines in fast-moving subjects — a vertical goalpost photographed during a fast pan becomes a slanted line, a fast-moving vehicle appears stretched or tilted, a spinning propeller appears warped. For subjects with fast lateral motion, the mechanical shutter avoids this distortion entirely.

The second limitation is banding under artificial light. Fluorescent tubes, many LED panels, and other discharge-type artificial light sources cycle between bright and dim at a frequency determined by the AC power supply — typically 50 or 100 times per second in 50Hz regions (Europe, Australia) and 60 or 120 times per second in 60Hz regions (Americas, Japan). A mechanical shutter exposes the entire sensor simultaneously, so if the light happens to be at a dim phase when the shutter fires, the whole frame is slightly darker — this is what the Anti-flicker shooting setting in Shooting Menu 7 addresses. But the electronic shutter reads out line by line across the full readout time, so the sensor scans through multiple light cycles during a single exposure. Different rows of the sensor are read at different phases of the light cycle — some rows during a bright phase, some during a dim phase. The result is visible horizontal bands of alternating brightness across the image. This banding is often subtle at moderate shutter speeds but can become strongly visible at fast speeds under certain artificial lights.

> **Important:** *Do not use the electronic shutter or High-Speed Continuous Plus mode when photographing fast lateral motion such as racing vehicles, swinging bats, or fast-moving machinery, or when shooting under fluorescent or certain LED artificial light sources. Use the mechanical shutter in both of these situations to avoid rolling shutter distortion and banding artefacts.*

High-Speed Continuous (Mechanical or Electronic First-Curtain Shutter)

High-Speed Continuous mode also reaches up to 15 frames per second but uses either the mechanical shutter or the electronic first-curtain shutter rather than the fully electronic shutter. You select which shutter mechanism is active via the Shutter mode setting in Shooting Menu 7 — setting it to Mechanical or Electronic first-curtain shutter while in the High-Speed Continuous drive mode uses those mechanisms respectively.

With the mechanical shutter, both the opening and closing curtains physically travel across the sensor for each frame. The mechanical shutter produces the characteristic shutter sound and a small amount of vibration with each frame. Its advantage is compatibility with all light sources and immunity to rolling shutter distortion, making it the reliable choice for sports and action under artificial lighting.

With electronic first-curtain shutter, the first curtain (the opening of the exposure) is simulated electronically by resetting the sensor charge uniformly across all rows simultaneously. Only the closing curtain is mechanical. This reduces shutter shock compared to full mechanical shutter because half of the curtain movement is eliminated, and it is slightly quieter — the closing curtain still makes a sound, but the opening is silent. At fast shutter speeds in telephoto shooting where shutter shock is a concern, electronic first-curtain is preferable to full mechanical. It is still subject to minor rolling shutter effects in extreme circumstances but significantly less so than the fully electronic shutter.

In practice, for the majority of action, sports, and wildlife shooting, High-Speed Continuous with the mechanical or electronic first-curtain shutter is the recommended configuration — it gives you the maximum burst rate without the compromises of the fully electronic shutter.

Buffer and Card Write Speed in Continuous Mode

When you hold the shutter in any continuous drive mode, the Canon EOS R10 captures frames faster than it can write them to the SD card. The camera manages this by storing frames in an internal buffer — a fast electronic memory — as they are captured, then writing them to the card progressively as space allows. The buffer has a limited capacity. Once it fills, the camera must wait for space to be written out to the card before accepting new frames, and the effective burst rate drops.

The number of frames the buffer can hold before it fills depends on the image format — RAW files are larger than JPEGs and fill the buffer more quickly. At 15 fps shooting in full RAW, the buffer typically sustains approximately 25 to 35 frames before filling. In Large Fine JPEG, the buffer holds considerably more frames and may sustain the burst for longer periods.

The speed at which the buffer empties into the card is determined by the write speed of the SD card. A faster card — rated UHS Speed Class 3 (U3) or Video Speed Class 30 (V30) or higher — empties the buffer more quickly, allowing the camera to resume full burst rate sooner after the buffer has filled. For serious burst shooting, using the fastest card available is the most practical way to extend usable burst length.

> **Tip:** *When shooting a burst sequence, do not release the shutter button immediately after the peak action. Keep the button held for an extra half second — the best frame in any action sequence is often just after the apparent peak, not at it. The R10 at 15 fps gives you 7 or 8 additional frames in that half second, any one of which may be the sharper, better-timed image.*

Low-Speed Continuous

Low-Speed Continuous fires at approximately 4 frames per second — roughly one frame every 250 milliseconds — rather than the maximum 15 fps available in the high-speed modes. The shutter mode used is whichever is selected in the Shutter mode setting in Shooting Menu 7.

Use Low-Speed Continuous when you need to capture a sequence of frames from a moving subject but do not need the maximum burst rate. Walking subjects, cyclists at moderate pace, children moving around a playground, animals walking rather than running, vehicles at low speed — these subjects move slowly enough that 4 fps captures the action at sufficient temporal resolution to get a usable frame, without generating the large volume of files that a 15 fps burst produces. Managing and selecting from 60 frames in a 4-second burst is far more practical than working through 225 frames from the same 4-second burst at 15 fps.

Low-Speed Continuous is also less demanding on the buffer and card, meaning the camera can sustain the burst for longer without hitting the buffer limit.

Self-Timer: 10 Seconds

In 10-second self-timer mode, pressing the shutter button fully starts a countdown. The AF-assist beam and self-timer lamp on the front of the camera blink slowly during the first eight seconds, then blink rapidly during the final two seconds, and the shutter fires at the end of the countdown — ten seconds after you pressed the button.

The ten-second delay gives you enough time to walk around to the front of the camera and join a group photo, to set down the camera and step into position, or to move away from the camera before a tripod-mounted shot where your presence near the camera would disturb the composition.

8. Rotate the drive mode to Self-timer: 10 sec via the Q screen or M-Fn shortcut.
9. Frame the shot and confirm focus on the area where the subject will be standing.
10. Press the shutter button fully. The countdown begins. You have ten seconds to move to your position in the scene.

11. Stand still for the final two seconds (rapid blink phase) to avoid motion blur.
12. The shutter fires. The camera returns to standby after the shot.

Note: *In self-timer mode, the camera locks focus at the moment you press the shutter button rather than at the moment the shutter fires. If the subject moves between the button press and the shutter firing, the focus may not be on the subject in the final image. In Auto modes, the camera may re-evaluate focus using subject detection during the countdown. For best results with group shots, place focus at the correct distance before starting the timer — use a stand-in or focus on an object at the same distance as where you will stand.*

Self-Timer: 2 Seconds

In 2-second self-timer mode, pressing the shutter button starts a two-second countdown before the shutter fires. The self-timer lamp blinks rapidly for both seconds and then fires.

The primary use of the 2-second self-timer is to eliminate camera shake on a tripod when pressing the shutter button would introduce vibration. Even a light touch on the shutter button causes a small tremor in the camera body that takes approximately one to two seconds to dissipate completely. At long shutter speeds — anything slower than about 1/60 sec — this tremor is visible in the image as a slight blur or softness, even though the camera is mounted on a tripod. The 2-second delay allows the camera to settle completely after you press the button, ensuring the shutter fires into a perfectly still camera.

Use the 2-second self-timer for landscape photography, long-exposure night photography, macro photography on a tripod, and any other tripod-mounted situation where you cannot use a remote shutter release. It is a simple, effective solution to shutter-induced camera shake with no additional accessories required.

Tip: *For the absolute maximum sharpness in tripod-mounted long-exposure photography, combine the 2-second self-timer with the electronic shutter (set via Shutter mode in Shooting Menu 7). The electronic shutter eliminates all mechanical curtain vibration, and the 2-second delay eliminates the button-*

press vibration. The result is an exposure with zero mechanical disturbance from either source.

Self-Timer: Continuous

Self-Timer Continuous mode combines the countdown delay of the self-timer with continuous multi-shot capture. After the countdown elapses, the camera fires a preset number of frames in rapid succession — between 2 and 10 frames — before stopping. The interval between the frames in the burst uses the current continuous shooting rate.

The number of shots in the sequence is configured within the drive mode settings. To set it:

13. Select Self-timer: Continuous from the drive mode list via the Q screen or menu.
14. Press SET to open the detail settings for this mode, or look for the shot count option that appears alongside the Self-timer Continuous icon on the Q screen.
15. A number appears showing the current shot count — typically shown as 2 or 10. Rotate a dial to change the count to your preferred number of frames (2 through 10).
16. Press SET to confirm.

When you press the shutter button with Self-timer Continuous active, the camera counts down the full timer duration (10 seconds if 10-second self-timer is the base, or 2 seconds if 2-second self-timer is selected), then fires the configured number of frames automatically.

Self-timer Continuous is particularly useful for self-portraiture and group photography where you want multiple shots to choose from in a single sequence — you press the button, walk into position, and the camera fires several frames automatically, giving you multiple options from the same pose or arrangement. It is also useful for time-critical tripod shots where you want both the vibration-free delay of the self-timer and the safety net of multiple frames in case one is slightly blurred or mistimed.

After the full sequence is complete, the camera returns to standby. If you want another sequence, press the shutter button again to start another countdown.

Note: *Self-timer Continuous uses whichever base self-timer duration was most recently selected — either the 2-second or 10-second timer. The base duration is shared between Self-timer: 10 sec, Self-timer: 2 sec, and Self-timer: Continuous in the drive mode selection cycle. Check the countdown duration shown on screen before pressing the shutter to confirm the timer is set to the length you expect.*

PART 12 — Video Recording

The Canon EOS R10 is a capable video camera as well as a stills camera. Its sensor records 4K video at up to 30 frames per second and Full HD video at up to 120 frames per second, with manual exposure control, continuous autofocus, optical and electronic image stabilisation, and external microphone support. This part covers everything you need to know to begin recording video — from switching the camera into video mode through to controlling exposure, audio, stabilisation, and the time-lapse function.

12.1 Switching to Video Mode

Activating Video Mode

The Canon EOS R10 has a dedicated video mode position on the Mode Dial, separate from all still photography modes. Rotating to this position reconfigures the camera specifically for video recording: the live view display changes to a video-specific layout, the menu system shows video-relevant settings, the autofocus system switches to Movie Servo AF behaviour, and the drive mode no longer controls burst shooting.

1. Hold the camera and locate the Mode Dial on the top-left of the body.
2. Rotate the Mode Dial clockwise past the Creative Filters icon until you reach the video camera icon — a small symbol showing a film camera or video recorder outline, at the far clockwise end of the dial.
3. The LCD screen switches to the video live view. In the corners and along the edges of the screen you will see the recording format — for example 4K 25p ALL-I — along with the current recording time available on the card, battery level, audio level meters, and other video-specific indicators.

Starting and Stopping Recording

4. Frame your shot and confirm the subject is in focus. The camera focuses continuously in video mode using Movie Servo AF when it is enabled.
5. Press the Movie Record button to begin recording. The Movie Record button is the small button with the red ring surrounding it, located on the top of the camera just to the left of the shutter button. Press it once firmly.

6. A red REC indicator appears on the LCD screen and in the EVF, and a timecode counter begins counting upward from zero, showing the duration of the current clip in hours, minutes, seconds, and frames.
7. Record your scene. The camera writes video data continuously to the SD card while recording.
8. Press the Movie Record button again once to stop recording. The REC indicator disappears, the timecode counter stops, and the camera writes the final data and closes the file. The clip is saved automatically — there is no separate save step required.

Recording from Still Photography Modes

The Movie Record button is also active from most still photography shooting modes — you do not have to be in the dedicated video mode position to record video. If you are in P, Av, Tv, M, or Fv mode and press the Movie Record button, the Canon EOS R10 immediately begins recording at the last-used video settings. This is useful for capturing a spontaneous video moment without rotating the Mode Dial away from your current still photography configuration.

However, recording from a still photography mode limits your access to video-specific settings — the Movie menu settings are only fully accessible when the Mode Dial is in the video position. For any video work beyond a quick clip, rotate the Mode Dial to video mode first to have full access to all video controls.

> **Important:** *The Canon EOS R10 has a 29 minutes and 59 seconds recording limit per individual video clip. This is a standard limitation of many consumer cameras and is related to customs and tax classifications. At the limit, the camera stops recording automatically and saves the file. If you need to continue recording, press the Movie Record button immediately to begin a new clip. The new clip is a separate file from the previous one.*

12.2 Video Resolution and Frame Rates

Accessing Movie Recording Quality Settings

9. Rotate the Mode Dial to the video camera icon to enter video mode.
10. Press MENU and confirm the menu opens on the pink Movie tab — it should open here automatically when in video mode.

11. Scroll to Movie rec quality and press SET. A list of available resolution and frame rate combinations appears.
12. Scroll through the options and press SET on your chosen combination to confirm it.

4K Resolution (3840 x 2160)

4K video records at 3840 by 2160 pixels — four times the number of pixels as Full HD (1920 by 1080). The additional resolution captures significantly more fine detail, which is particularly visible in wide shots with complex scenes, architectural subjects, or any footage that will be displayed on a 4K television or monitor. 4K files are also more forgiving of minor cropping or stabilisation in post-production, because the extra pixel data provides headroom to reframe without losing full HD quality in the final output.

On the Canon EOS R10, 4K video is available at the following frame rates, depending on whether the Video system setting in the Setup menu is set to NTSC or PAL.

Under NTSC (Americas, Japan): 23.98 fps and 29.97 fps are available at 4K. Under PAL (Europe, Australia, most of Asia and Africa): 25 fps is available at 4K. These frame rates produce standard motion quality suitable for normal playback.

4K video files are substantially larger than Full HD — a minute of 4K at 25 fps in the ALL-I compression format occupies approximately 1.5 to 2 GB of card space. A 64 GB card holds approximately 30 to 40 minutes of 4K ALL-I footage. IPB compression reduces this by roughly half, at the cost of reduced per-frame image data.

4K with Sensor Crop

The Canon EOS R10 records full-width 4K — using the majority of the sensor area — at 23.98 and 25 fps. At 29.97 fps in 4K, the camera applies a crop to the sensor, using a smaller central portion of the sensor area to read out at the required speed. This crop multiplies the effective focal length of the attached lens by approximately 1.56 times compared to the full-width 4K modes. A 50mm lens records 4K at 29.97 fps as if it were approximately a 78mm lens. A 24mm wide-angle lens becomes approximately a 37mm standard lens.

This crop is important to be aware of when choosing a lens for 4K video shooting — a lens that provides a wide field of view at full-width 4K will become noticeably less wide at the cropped 4K frame rate. For the widest possible 4K field of view, use 23.98 fps (NTSC) or 25 fps (PAL), which record without the crop.

Full HD Resolution (1920 x 1080)

Full HD video records at 1920 by 1080 pixels and is the standard resolution for web video, social media, streaming, broadcast television, and most consumer playback devices. Full HD files are significantly smaller than 4K — a minute of Full HD at 25 fps in IPB compression is typically 200 to 400 MB. On a 64 GB card you can record several hours of Full HD footage.

Full HD is also the resolution that enables the highest frame rates on the R10. Under NTSC, Full HD is available at 29.97 fps and 59.94 fps for standard motion and slow-motion capture. Under PAL, Full HD is available at 25 fps and 50 fps. The High Frame Rate mode (120 fps) is exclusively available in Full HD — see the High Frame Rate section below.

For video intended for web sharing, social media, YouTube, or Vimeo, Full HD at 25 or 29.97 fps in IPB compression is the most practical setting — it produces excellent image quality for screen viewing at a manageable file size and processes quickly.

Frame Rates and What They Determine

Frame rate — the number of individual frames recorded per second — determines both the compatibility of your video with different regional broadcast standards and the motion quality of the footage.

23.98 fps (often rounded to 24 fps) is the traditional cinema frame rate, associated with the motion quality and aesthetic of theatrical film. Footage at this frame rate has a slightly staccato quality of motion that the human eye associates with cinematic storytelling. It is used for narrative film, documentary features, and any video intended to have a cinematic look. Under NTSC, 23.98 fps is the primary cinema frame rate on the R10.

25 fps is the standard broadcast television frame rate for PAL regions — Europe, Australia, China, India, and most of Africa and Asia. It produces smooth motion for everyday video and is the default for any video produced for broadcast or

streaming in those regions. It also provides a 2x slow-motion capability when 50 fps footage is played back at 25 fps in editing software.

29.97 fps is the standard broadcast frame rate for NTSC regions — the Americas and Japan. It produces smooth motion comparable to 25 fps and is the default for video production in those regions. When 59.94 fps footage is played back at 29.97 fps, it produces smooth 2x slow motion.

50 fps (PAL regions) and 59.94 fps (NTSC regions) record at twice the standard frame rate, capturing twice as many individual frames per second as standard footage. When played back at the standard 25 or 29.97 fps in editing software or on a playback device, the footage is slowed to exactly half speed — a smooth, fluid 2x slow-motion effect. This slow-motion capability is particularly effective for capturing fast action — sports, running water, a subject turning quickly — and revealing details of motion that are invisible at normal speed.

120 fps is available exclusively in Full HD via High Frame Rate mode. When played back at 25 fps, 120 fps footage is slowed to one fifth of real-time speed — 4.8x slow motion. When played back at 29.97 fps, it is slowed to approximately 4x real-time speed. This extreme slow-motion capability reveals motion details that are imperceptible at standard speeds — the individual frames of a golf swing, water droplet splash impacts, the precise mechanics of athletic movement. See the High Frame Rate section below.

High Frame Rate Mode — 120fps Slow Motion

High Frame Rate mode enables recording at 119.88 fps (under NTSC) or 100 fps (under PAL) in Full HD resolution. This is the R10's maximum frame rate and produces footage suitable for extreme slow-motion playback in post-production.

13. In video mode, press MENU and navigate to the pink Movie tab.
14. Scroll to Movie rec quality and press SET.
15. Look for the High Frame Rate option in the list — it is typically labelled with the fps value (119.88 or 100) alongside the Full HD resolution indicator. Select it and press SET.
16. A warning will appear noting that audio is not recorded during High Frame Rate shooting — the files are video-only with no audio track. Press OK to confirm.

17. Record your footage as normal. The camera records at the high frame rate internally, but the timecode and display still reference the output frame rate (29.97 or 25 fps), so one second of camera time becomes approximately four seconds of footage in the final video.

High Frame Rate files are significantly larger than standard frame rate footage of the same duration because more frames are captured per second. Monitor your remaining card space during a High Frame Rate session as it depletes faster than standard recording.

In post-production, import the High Frame Rate footage into your editing software and set the clip's playback speed to match the ratio of recording frame rate to output frame rate. At 120 fps recording and 29.97 fps playback, set the clip to approximately 25 percent speed for smooth 4x slow motion. At 100 fps and 25 fps playback, set the clip to 25 percent speed for 4x slow motion.

> **Note:** *Audio is not recorded during High Frame Rate shooting. If your scene requires both slow-motion footage and audio from the same angle, record two clips — one at the high frame rate for the slow-motion footage and one at a standard frame rate to capture the audio. Sync and layer them in editing.*

12.3 Video Exposure Control

Why Video Exposure Is Different from Still Photography

In still photography, you can set the shutter speed to any value from 1/8000 sec to 30 sec based purely on your creative and technical needs, and each shot is an independent exposure decision. In video, the shutter speed is constrained by a different rule — the 180-degree shutter rule — because video is a sequence of frames that creates the illusion of continuous motion when played back. The relationship between shutter speed and frame rate determines whether that motion looks natural or artificial.

The 180-degree shutter rule states that the shutter speed for natural-looking motion in video should be approximately double the frame rate. At 25 fps, the ideal shutter speed is 1/50 sec. At 29.97 fps, it is 1/60 sec. At 50 fps, it is 1/100 sec. At 23.98 fps, it is 1/48 sec — in practice 1/50 sec is the closest available value.

At these shutter speeds, each frame captures a small amount of motion blur — the slight blurring of moving subjects between frames — that the human eye is accustomed to seeing in cinema and television. This motion blur makes movement look fluid and natural during playback. If you use a much faster shutter speed — 1/1000 sec at 25 fps, for example — each frame is razor sharp with no motion blur, and when played back the motion appears staccato, choppy, and unnaturally sharp, similar to footage shot on an early digital video camera. If you use a much slower shutter speed than double the frame rate — 1/25 sec at 25 fps — too much motion blur accumulates per frame and motion smears excessively.

Auto Exposure in Video Mode

When the Canon EOS R10 is in video mode with Auto exposure active, the camera automatically sets the ISO, shutter speed, and aperture to produce a correctly exposed video. The shutter speed and ISO adjust continuously as the light changes during recording, which can cause visible exposure changes within a clip — a noticeable brightening or darkening as the camera adjusts to a change in scene brightness.

Auto exposure is the most convenient starting point and works acceptably for casual video in stable lighting. For any serious video work, manual exposure gives you more control and produces a more professional result.

To use Auto exposure in Aperture Priority video mode — where you set the aperture and the camera adjusts ISO and shutter speed automatically — rotate the Mode Dial to video mode and then press Q to open the Quick Control screen. Set the aperture to your preferred value. Set ISO to Auto. The camera will manage the shutter speed, keeping it close to the double-frame-rate ideal if the exposure smoothing setting is configured appropriately.

Manual Exposure in Video Mode

Manual video exposure gives you complete control over shutter speed, aperture, and ISO independently, ensuring the exposure does not change between shots or during a clip. This is the standard approach for professional video production.

18. Rotate the Mode Dial to the video camera icon.
19. Press the Q button to open the Quick Control screen.

20. Highlight the ISO panel and rotate a dial to set the ISO to a specific value rather than Auto.
21. Highlight the shutter speed panel and set it to the double-frame-rate value for your recording format — 1/50 sec for 25 fps, 1/60 sec for 29.97 fps, 1/100 sec for 50 fps, or 1/120 sec for 59.94 fps. This is the starting point recommended by the 180-degree shutter rule. Adjust ISO and aperture to achieve correct exposure at this shutter speed.
22. Highlight the aperture panel and set it to the aperture appropriate for your depth of field intent.
23. Evaluate the exposure using the on-screen exposure indicator. Adjust ISO first — raise it to brighten, lower it to darken — to achieve correct exposure while keeping the shutter speed at the double-frame-rate value and the aperture at your intended setting.

In video, aperture controls both depth of field and exposure simultaneously. A wide aperture (low f-number) gives a shallow depth of field with blurred background and admits more light, reducing the ISO required. A narrow aperture (high f-number) gives deep depth of field and requires more ISO or a slower shutter speed to compensate for the reduced light.

Controlling Exposure in Bright Conditions — ND Filters

The 180-degree shutter rule fixes the shutter speed close to a value that is often too slow for bright daylight conditions — 1/50 sec in bright sun requires a very narrow aperture (f/16 or smaller) to avoid overexposure, which eliminates background blur and may introduce diffraction softening. The practical solution is a neutral density (ND) filter, which attaches to the front of the lens and reduces the incoming light without affecting colour, allowing you to maintain the correct shutter speed and a wide aperture simultaneously in bright conditions. ND filters are rated by their light reduction — a 3-stop ND filter reduces the light by the equivalent of 3 stops of aperture. For bright outdoor video with a wide aperture at 1/50 sec, a 3-stop or 6-stop ND filter is typically required.

Tip: *If you find that the image is slightly too bright or too dark when using manual exposure in video mode, always adjust the ISO first before changing the shutter speed. Keeping the shutter speed at double the frame rate preserves the motion rendering quality. Let ISO carry the exposure* *compensation burden — the R10's sensor handles ISO 1600 to 3200 well in video, producing acceptable results for most screen-viewing purposes.*

12.4 Audio Settings

The Canon EOS R10 records stereo audio using its built-in microphones — two small holes on the front face of the camera and two on the top panel. All audio settings for video recording are located in a single sub-menu within the pink Movie tab.

Accessing Audio Settings

24. Rotate the Mode Dial to video mode.
25. Press MENU and navigate to the pink Movie tab.
26. Scroll to Audio and press SET. The Audio sub-menu opens, showing all audio-related settings in one location.

Recording — Enable or Disable Audio

The Recording setting is the master switch for audio. It is set to Enable by default. Set it to Disable only when you specifically do not want any audio track in the video file — for silent clips intended to be used with music or voice-over added in editing, or to reduce file size slightly when audio is genuinely irrelevant. When set to Disable, no audio data is written to the file and the audio meters on the shooting screen disappear.

Recording Level — Setting the Microphone Input Sensitivity

The Recording level setting controls how sensitive the microphone is — how loudly it captures the sound in the scene. The scale runs from 1 (minimum sensitivity) to 64 (maximum sensitivity). This setting is not a volume knob for the final audio — it controls the input level at which sound is captured and encoded. Setting it too high causes the audio to distort and clip on loud sounds. Setting it too low produces quiet, difficult-to-hear audio that requires amplification in editing, which also amplifies background noise.

Two audio level meters are visible on the shooting screen while in video mode — horizontal bars that move in response to the sound level. The left bar shows the left channel and the right bar shows the right channel. Watch these meters as you speak or as the ambient sound at the shooting location reaches its typical level.

The target is to have the meters peaking in the upper portion of the scale during normal sound levels, without touching the red zone at the far right. The red zone indicates that the audio signal is at or near the maximum the system can handle — any further increase in sound level will cause clipping, which sounds like harsh crackling or distortion in the recorded audio. Clipping is permanent and cannot be corrected in editing.

27. In the Audio sub-menu, select Recording level and press SET.
28. The recording level scale appears with a numerical value and the live audio meters visible.
29. Rotate a dial to increase or decrease the level while watching the meters respond. The meters update in real time as you speak or the ambient sound plays.
30. Aim to set a level where normal speech or ambient sound peaks around halfway to two-thirds of the meter scale, leaving headroom for louder unexpected sounds to peak in the upper range without entering the red zone.
31. Press SET or MENU to confirm and close the recording level screen.

Wind Filter

The Wind filter setting applies a high-pass filter to the built-in microphones that cuts the low-frequency rumble produced by wind blowing across the microphone openings. Wind noise is one of the most common problems in outdoor video recording and is extremely difficult to remove cleanly in post-production once it has been recorded.

Press SET on Wind filter and choose Enable to activate it. The filter removes frequencies below approximately 200 Hz, which is where wind noise is most concentrated. Speech and most ambient sound occur above this frequency and are largely unaffected by the filter — voices remain clear, camera sounds are still captured, and the overall audio character does not change noticeably in windless conditions. In windy conditions, the filter significantly reduces the rumble without silencing the recording.

Disable the Wind filter in completely windless indoor environments if you need to capture the full low-frequency content of the audio — deep bass in music recording, for example, or the low-frequency character of a voice. In any outdoor or semi-outdoor setting where wind is possible, leave the Wind filter enabled.

Attenuator

The Attenuator automatically reduces the microphone input level by 12 dB at the moment a sound exceeds the safe recording level, preventing it from distorting. It then restores the level after the loud sound passes. Think of it as an automatic safety gate that prevents sudden loud sounds from destroying a recording.

Press SET on Attenuator and choose Enable in environments where unexpected loud sounds are possible — live events, outdoor shooting near traffic, sports, busy public spaces, or any situation where you cannot continuously monitor and manually adjust the recording level in real time. The attenuator prevents a sudden shout, horn blast, or burst of applause from producing a distorted audio spike in what would otherwise be a clean recording.

Disable the Attenuator in controlled recording environments where you have set the level carefully and the sound will be consistent — a studio interview, a controlled voice-over, or any setting where the audio level will not change unexpectedly. In these cases the attenuator is not needed and its momentary level reduction, though brief, is an unnecessary alteration of the audio.

Using an External Microphone

The built-in microphones on the Canon EOS R10, while functional, have two inherent limitations. They pick up mechanical noise from the camera itself — autofocus motor sounds, button presses, zoom ring rotation, and general handling vibration. They are also omnidirectional, meaning they capture sound from all directions equally rather than focusing on the sound in front of the lens.

An external microphone solves both of these problems. Plugging a microphone into the 3.5mm external microphone terminal on the left side of the camera — behind the rubber protective flap, at the bottom of the port cluster — automatically disables the built-in microphones and routes all audio through the external microphone instead.

32. Open the rubber protective flap on the left side of the camera by pulling it gently toward you.
33. Insert the 3.5mm stereo mini-jack plug of the external microphone into the microphone port — the port closest to the bottom of the flap opening.
34. The camera detects the external microphone automatically. The audio meters on the shooting screen now reflect the input from the external microphone rather than the built-in mics.
35. Set the Recording level appropriately for the external microphone's output level — different microphones have different output sensitivities and the level may need to be adjusted from the built-in mic setting.

The most effective external microphones for the Canon EOS R10 are directional shotgun microphones that mount on the hot shoe and connect to the camera via a short 3.5mm cable. These microphones capture sound primarily from the direction the lens is pointing and reject sound from the sides and rear, dramatically reducing background noise and focusing the recording on the intended source. Models such as the Rode VideoMicro, Rode VideoMic GO, or Canon DM-E1D are compact and well-matched to the R10.

> **Note:** *The Canon EOS R10 does not have a dedicated headphone output port. To monitor audio during recording, you need a USB-C to 3.5mm headphone adapter and headphones connected to the USB-C port. The headphone volume level is adjustable in the Setup menu under Headphone volume. Real-time audio monitoring during recording allows you to hear exactly what is being recorded, making it possible to detect problems — wind noise, handling noise, distortion — as they occur rather than discovering them after the fact.*

12.5 Movie Digital IS

What Movie Digital IS Does

The Canon EOS R10 does not have In-Body Image Stabilisation — the sensor does not physically shift to counteract camera movement. Stabilisation comes from the lens (for lenses equipped with optical IS) or from the Movie Digital IS system in the camera's processing software. Movie Digital IS applies electronic image stabilisation: the camera crops slightly into the sensor area and uses the surrounding pixel margin as a buffer, shifting the recorded region of the sensor electronically to counteract camera shake frame by frame. The result is smoother, less shaky video footage than would be produced without it.

How to Access and Set Movie Digital IS

36. Rotate the Mode Dial to video mode.
37. Press MENU and navigate to the pink Movie tab.
38. Scroll to Movie digital IS and press SET.
39. Three options appear: Off, Enable, and Enhanced. Highlight your choice and press SET to confirm.

Off

When Movie Digital IS is set to Off, no electronic stabilisation is applied to the video. Only the optical IS of the attached lens provides stabilisation, if the lens is IS-equipped. The full sensor area is used for the recording — no crop is applied beyond the standard recording crop for the chosen resolution.

Use Off when the camera is mounted on a tripod, a gimbal, or any other mechanical stabilisation system where the camera shake has already been eliminated externally. Electronic stabilisation on a perfectly stable camera would produce no improvement and would unnecessarily crop the frame. Also use Off when shooting with a non-IS lens on a stable support, or when you specifically need the widest possible field of view without any additional crop.

Enable

Enable activates a moderate level of electronic stabilisation. The camera applies a small crop to the sensor area — approximately 10 to 15 percent narrower on each side than the Off setting — and uses the cropped margin as movement buffer. Within this buffer, the camera tracks camera shake and shifts the recorded area electronically to counteract it. The result is noticeably smoother video for handheld shooting than with no stabilisation.

Use Enable for handheld shooting from a stationary position — standing still while holding the camera and recording, or sitting in a vehicle that is stationary. The level of stabilisation is effective for the typical minor tremor of holding a camera, though it does not fully counteract large deliberate movements such as walking.

Enable works most effectively when combined with an IS-equipped lens. The lens IS handles the lower-frequency, larger oscillations of the camera movement, and Movie Digital IS handles the higher-frequency, finer micro-tremors that optical IS may not fully suppress. The combination of optical and electronic IS produces smoother results than either alone.

Enhanced

Enhanced applies the strongest level of electronic stabilisation, using a larger crop — approximately 25 to 30 percent narrower than the Off setting — to create a larger movement buffer. This stronger crop allows the camera to counteract significantly greater camera shake, making it effective for walking shots and other high-movement handheld recording situations.

The trade-off of Enhanced is the more aggressive crop to the sensor area. The effective field of view in Enhanced mode is noticeably narrower than Off or Enable. A 24mm wide-angle lens will no longer deliver a wide-angle perspective — it will appear closer to a 32mm or 35mm equivalent. If you are shooting with a wide lens specifically to capture a broad field of view, Enhanced will compromise that significantly.

Use Enhanced for walking shots — moving the camera while recording, either walking with the camera or panning while walking — where the regular Enable level is insufficient to smooth out the footfall vibration. Accept the additional field-of-view crop as the cost of usable stabilisation in those conditions.

> **Note:** *Movie Digital IS works best in combination with an IS-equipped lens. With a non-IS lens, Movie Digital IS alone provides useful but more limited stabilisation compared to the combined optical-plus-electronic approach. When choosing a lens for serious video work on the R10, an IS-equipped lens is a meaningful advantage for handheld recording.*

> **Tip:** *A practical stabilisation hierarchy for the Canon EOS R10: for tripod or gimbal shooting, use Off and let the mechanical support eliminate shake. For stationary handheld shooting, use Enable with an IS lens for the smoothest result. For walking shots, use Enhanced with an IS lens and walk with a*

deliberate heel-to-toe gait — a smooth, low-impact walking technique reduces the footfall shock that stabilisation must counteract.

12.6 Time-Lapse Video

What Time-Lapse Does

Time-lapse video compresses long periods of time into short video clips by photographing a scene at regular intervals — for example, one frame every five seconds — and then assembling those frames into a video where each frame represents five seconds of real time. When played back at 25 or 29.97 frames per second, the compressed motion becomes visible: clouds race across the sky, shadows sweep across a landscape, flowers open and close, traffic flows like a river of light, construction progresses visibly. Events that take hours appear compressed into seconds of video.

The Canon EOS R10 handles the entire time-lapse process internally — it shoots each frame automatically at the set interval, assembles the frames, and delivers a finished MP4 video file without any external software or manual frame assembly required.

Equipment Requirements

A sturdy tripod is essential. Any camera movement between frames — even the slight drift of a flimsy tripod leg — will produce a jarring jump in the final video. The tripod must remain completely stationary for the entire duration of the time-lapse sequence. Do not touch the camera or tripod during recording.

A fully charged battery or USB power supply is also required for longer sequences. A time-lapse shooting 600 frames at 10-second intervals runs for 100 minutes. The Canon EOS R10's battery is sufficient for shorter sequences, but for anything over 60 minutes, connect USB power via the USB-C port to avoid the time-lapse being interrupted by a depleted battery.

A memory card with sufficient space for the chosen sequence is also required. Time-lapse mode saves the individual frames as internal still images before assembling the video — ensure the card has adequate space for both the frames and the assembled video file.

Setting Up a Time-Lapse on the R10

40. Mount the Canon EOS R10 securely on a tripod and frame the scene. Compose carefully — you will not be adjusting the frame during the sequence.
41. Set focus manually or use One-Shot AF to lock focus on the primary subject. Switch to manual focus (MF) after locking to prevent the camera from re-evaluating focus between frames. Time-lapse shooting with autofocus can produce small focus variations between frames that create flicker in the finished video.
42. Set the exposure manually. Use Manual mode (M) on the Mode Dial and set a specific shutter speed, aperture, and ISO. Consistent exposure across every frame is essential — any variation in brightness between frames produces a flickering effect in the final video. Do not use Auto ISO or auto shutter in time-lapse mode.
43. Rotate the Mode Dial to video mode.
44. Press MENU and navigate to the pink Movie tab.
45. Scroll to Time-lapse movie and press SET.
46. The Time-lapse configuration screen opens. The first setting is Time-lapse — set it to Enable.
47. Set the Interval — the time between each frame. Rotate a dial to change the value in seconds. For fast-moving subjects like clouds, an interval of 2 to 5 seconds is effective. For slow subjects like flowers opening or shadows moving across a scene, 10 to 30 seconds produces better compression. For very slow subjects like building construction, intervals of several minutes may be appropriate.
48. Set the Number of shots — how many frames the sequence will contain. The camera calculates and displays the total shooting duration (how long the sequence will take to complete) and the video duration (how long the finished video will be at the output frame rate) based on your interval and shot count. Adjust both values until the estimated video duration matches your intent. For a 10-second finished video clip at 25 fps, you need 250 frames.
49. Set the Movie rec quality to your preferred resolution for the output video.
50. Select Start and press SET to begin the sequence. The camera shows a countdown to the first frame, then fires the first shot and counts

down to the next. A progress indicator shows how many frames have been captured and how many remain.

51. When all frames are captured, the camera assembles them into a finished MP4 video file and saves it to the card automatically. This assembly takes a moment — do not power off the camera until it completes.

Avoiding Flicker in Time-Lapse

Flicker — the visible pulsing or variation in brightness between frames in the finished time-lapse video — is the most common problem in time-lapse photography and is caused by any exposure variation between frames. The most effective way to prevent it is to shoot with fully manual exposure (manual shutter speed, manual aperture, manual ISO) so that every frame is recorded at exactly the same settings. Do not rely on Auto ISO, auto aperture, or any automatic exposure mode during a time-lapse sequence.

Under artificial lighting, the Anti-flicker shooting setting in Shooting Menu 7 can also help by timing each frame capture to the peak phase of the light cycle, reducing the variation caused by the cycling of artificial light sources. Enable this setting when shooting time-lapse indoors under fluorescent or LED lighting.

Important: *Do not open the SD card door, change the battery (unless using USB power), or turn off the camera during a time-lapse sequence in progress. Any interruption will terminate the sequence and the assembled video will contain only the frames captured up to the interruption — or the assembly may fail entirely. Plan the sequence duration so it completes within your available battery capacity, or connect USB power before starting.*

Tip: *For a visually compelling time-lapse, look for scenes with multiple layers of motion at different speeds — clouds moving fast overhead, slower-moving shadows on the ground, and static foreground elements. The contrast between moving and still elements gives the finished video visual depth and makes the motion compression more impactful. Dawn and dusk transitions, with the light changing rapidly in colour and intensity, are among the most dramatic subjects for time-lapse on the R10.*

PART 13 — Image Stabilization

Image stabilisation compensates for the natural tremor of holding a camera by hand — the small, involuntary movements of your hands, arms, and body that cause the image to shift slightly during the exposure. Without stabilisation, these movements produce a diffuse, overall softness in the image, most visible at slow shutter speeds and long focal lengths. With stabilisation active, the sharpness of handheld images at moderate shutter speeds improves significantly. This part explains how stabilisation works on the Canon EOS R10 specifically, what the different IS modes do, and when to disable it.

13.1 How IS Works on the R10

Lens-Only Stabilisation — No IBIS

Many mirrorless cameras from Canon and other manufacturers include In-Body Image Stabilisation — a mechanism inside the camera body that physically shifts the sensor to counteract camera movement. The Canon EOS R10 does not have this. There is no sensor-shifting stabilisation mechanism inside the R10's body. The body itself contributes no optical stabilisation to any attached lens.

This means that whether a given lens-and-camera combination is stabilised or unstabilised depends entirely on the lens. If the lens is IS-equipped — meaning it contains internal optical image stabilisation elements that move to counteract camera shake — you have stabilisation. If the lens is not IS-equipped, you have no optical stabilisation at all, regardless of any menu settings on the camera body.

When you attach an IS-equipped RF or EF lens to the Canon EOS R10, the camera and lens communicate via the electrical contacts in the mount. The camera sends shooting information — shutter speed, focal length setting on zoom lenses, and exposure status — to the lens's IS system, which uses this information to apply the correct level and type of stabilisation for the current shooting conditions. The IS system in the lens contains a gyroscope that detects rotational movement, a microprocessor that calculates how much the image-forming elements need to shift, and a small electromagnetic mechanism that moves the stabilising element group within the lens accordingly — all within the fraction of a second between you half-pressing the shutter and the image being captured.

What Stabilisation Corrects — and What It Cannot

Optical IS in Canon RF and EF lenses corrects for the handshake-type movement of the camera — the small, irregular oscillations produced by holding the camera in your hands. This type of movement is angular rather than linear — the camera rotates slightly around the photographer's grip point, shifting the image in the viewfinder. IS detects and counteracts these rotational movements effectively, typically allowing sharp handheld images at shutter speeds two to four stops slower than would be possible without IS. A lens rated for four stops of stabilisation allows you to shoot at 1/15 sec as confidently as an unstabilised lens allows at 1/250 sec.

IS does not correct for subject motion. If your subject is moving during the exposure, IS cannot prevent that subject from blurring — it only stabilises the camera's own movement. A stationary building is sharper with IS active. A running child is not sharper with IS active unless you also use a fast enough shutter speed to freeze the motion.

IS also does not correct for large deliberate movements — panning, tilting, walking, or any motion faster or larger than the handshake tremor the system is designed to handle. It cannot stabilise a camera that is being moved intentionally.

Identifying Whether Your Lens Has IS

Canon RF and EF lenses that include image stabilisation are marked with the letters IS in their name — for example, RF 24-105mm F4 L IS USM, or EF 70-300mm f/4-5.6 IS II USM. The IS designation in the lens name is the reliable indicator. You can also look for a physical IS switch on the lens barrel — most IS-equipped lenses have a small two-position switch labelled IS ON and IS OFF.

Canon's RF prime lenses and compact RF zoom lenses do not all include IS — some are designed for use on cameras with IBIS, which the R10 does not have. When choosing an RF lens for use specifically on the R10 for handheld photography, confirming that the lens is IS-equipped is particularly important, as there is no camera-body stabilisation to compensate for its absence.

> **Note:** *When no IS-equipped lens is attached, the Image stabilizer setting in Shooting Menu 9 is greyed out and inaccessible — the camera recognises that there is no IS system to configure. If you navigate to this setting and find it unavailable, it confirms that the attached lens does not have IS.*

13.2 IS Modes on Lenses

IS-equipped Canon RF and EF lenses offer between one and three IS modes depending on the lens design. Not all lenses offer all three modes — some have only Mode 1, some have Mode 1 and Mode 2, and others support all three. Check the specifications of your specific lens to confirm which modes are available. The IS mode is selected using a physical switch on the lens barrel itself, or in some cases through the camera's Image stabilizer setting in Shooting Menu 9 when the lens supports camera-controlled mode switching.

Mode 1 — All-Direction Stabilisation

Mode 1 is the standard IS setting and the one you should use for the majority of handheld photography. In Mode 1, the IS system corrects for angular movement in all directions simultaneously — up, down, left, right, and diagonal. The stabilising element group inside the lens moves in any direction needed to counteract whatever handshake the gyroscope detects. You can see Mode 1 at work by half-pressing the shutter button while looking through the EVF or at the LCD screen — the live image will settle and stop drifting as the IS system locks in and compensates for hand movement.

Mode 1 is appropriate for all stationary or moderately moving subjects where you are holding the camera still and the subject is the source of any motion in the frame. Portraits, architecture, street photography, nature photography, still life — any situation where you are not deliberately moving the camera — benefit from Mode 1 active.

Mode 2 — Panning Mode

Mode 2 switches the IS system to correct only vertical movement, deliberately allowing horizontal movement to pass through uncorrected. This configuration is specifically designed for panning photography — the technique of following a moving subject by rotating the camera horizontally while pressing the shutter, so that the subject remains sharp against a blurred background that conveys speed and motion.

When panning, you are intentionally moving the camera horizontally to track a moving subject. If Mode 1 were active during a panning shot, the IS system would attempt to counteract your deliberate horizontal movement — fighting against your pan and producing an inconsistent, erratic result. Mode 2 recognises the sustained horizontal movement as intentional panning and disables horizontal correction, while continuing to correct the vertical component of any unintentional hand tremor that would otherwise appear as vertical blur in the panned image.

The result in Mode 2 is that the background blurs horizontally (from the pan) while the subject, tracked by the camera, remains relatively sharp — with any vertical jitter removed by the IS system. This is the defining visual quality of successful panning photography: a sharp, frozen subject against a streaked, motion-blurred background.

1. Locate the IS mode switch on the lens barrel — a small two-position or three-position switch labelled with mode numbers or icons.
2. Slide the switch to Mode 2.
3. Set the drive mode to continuous shooting (High-speed or Low-speed continuous) so multiple frames are captured during each pan.
4. Set the shutter speed to between 1/30 sec and 1/125 sec — slow enough to blur the background during the pan but fast enough to keep the subject relatively sharp. The ideal shutter speed depends on the speed of the subject and the focal length of the lens.
5. Track the subject before it reaches your frame, press the shutter and continue tracking smoothly through the shot. Keep the horizontal pan movement as consistent as possible throughout the burst.

> **Note:** *Mode 2 must be selected before you begin panning. Selecting it mid-shot has no effect on that exposure. Switch back to Mode 1 when the panning session is complete to restore full all-direction stabilisation for subsequent general shooting.*

Mode 3 — Active Stabilisation at Exposure Only

Mode 3 is the most specialised IS mode and is available on relatively few Canon lenses. In Mode 3, the IS system is completely inactive while you are composing and framing the shot — the live view image drifts with your hand movement as if no IS were present. At the exact moment the shutter fires — when the image is actually being captured — the IS system activates for the duration of the exposure, counteracting movement only during the actual moment of capture rather than continuously throughout the shooting session.

The purpose of this design is to handle subjects with extremely erratic, unpredictable movement — the kind of rapid, multi-directional movement that causes a continuously active IS system to chase the movement rather than smooth it, and to potentially introduce its own artefacts as it tries to keep up. By activating only at the moment of exposure, Mode 3 avoids this chasing behaviour and applies a single, clean correction at the critical moment.

Mode 3 is rarely needed in everyday photography. It is most applicable to wildlife photography at very close range where a subject is moving rapidly and unpredictably, or in certain sports contexts where the subject's movement pattern cannot be smoothly tracked by a continuously active IS system. For most photographers, Mode 1 is the correct choice for virtually all handheld shooting, and Mode 2 specifically for panning. Mode 3 should be selected only if Mode 1 is producing worse results than expected due to an erratic subject interaction with the continuous IS correction.

13.3 When to Turn IS Off

Tripod Use — The Primary Reason to Disable IS

Image stabilisation is designed to detect and counteract the movement of a handheld camera. When the camera is mounted on a tripod, the tripod's rigid structure eliminates the large-scale handshake that IS is designed to correct. However, a very high-quality IS system can also detect the extremely small vibrations transmitted through the tripod — vibrations from the ground (traffic, footsteps, nearby machinery), vibrations from the tripod head or leg joints, or even the resonance of wind against the tripod legs. When an IS system detects these micro-vibrations on a tripod, it may respond by introducing counter-movement that, rather than cancelling the vibration, adds its own movement on top of it. The result can be images that are marginally less sharp than images taken without IS active — the IS system is creating a problem by trying to solve one that the tripod has already solved.

The practical solution is to disable IS whenever the camera is on a tripod. With the tripod doing the stabilisation work, the IS system is not needed and should be switched off to remove any possibility of it interfering.

6. If your lens has a physical IS switch on the barrel: slide it to the OFF or IS OFF position. This immediately disables the IS system in the lens.
7. If you prefer to control IS from the camera body: press MENU, rotate the Main Dial to Shooting Menu 9, scroll to Image stabilizer and press SET. From the IS settings, select IS mode and choose Off or Disable. This instructs the lens to deactivate its IS system from the camera side.

Lenses That Detect Tripod Use Automatically

Some Canon IS lenses — particularly newer RF lenses and higher-tier EF lenses — include a tripod detection feature that senses when the camera has been mounted on a stable support and automatically reduces or disables the IS correction accordingly. When the gyroscope in the lens detects that no significant movement is occurring — indicating the camera is on a stable surface — the IS system enters a lower-activity state or switches off independently, without any input from you.

Whether your specific lens has this automatic tripod detection is stated in the lens's instruction manual. If you are uncertain, the safest practice is to manually disable IS via the lens switch or the camera menu whenever the camera is tripod-mounted, regardless of whether the lens claims to detect tripod use. The cost of manually disabling IS when it would have disabled itself automatically is zero —

the cost of leaving IS active when it introduces vibration on a tripod could be a series of slightly soft images.

Other Situations Where IS Should Be Disabled

Beyond tripod use, there are two further situations where disabling IS is appropriate.

When using a remote shutter release, a cable release, or a timed self-timer release on a tripod at very long exposures — particularly in the BULB mode range of several seconds or more — the IS system should be off. At exposure durations longer than approximately one to two seconds, the IS mechanism may produce low-frequency oscillations that are visible in the image as a slow, rhythmic blur. At short shutter speeds the correction applies and releases quickly enough that this is not a problem, but at very long exposures the IS has time to settle into a slow oscillation cycle. Disabling IS before any exposure longer than about two seconds on a tripod prevents this.

When shooting at the fastest available shutter speeds — 1/2000 sec and faster — IS provides no practical benefit. The shutter opens and closes so quickly that no amount of hand movement during that fraction of a second can produce visible blur. Keeping IS active at these speeds is not harmful, but it does consume a small amount of battery power from the lens unnecessarily. In a shooting session where battery conservation is a concern — wildlife photography at the end of a long day, for example — disabling IS when shooting consistently at very fast shutter speeds is a reasonable battery conservation measure.

IS in Video Mode

For video recording, the IS mode guidance is somewhat different from stills. When recording video on a tripod or gimbal, disable the lens IS and ensure Movie Digital IS in the Movie menu is set to Off, as both optical and electronic IS can introduce subtle floating or drifting movement into a locked-off shot — a quality that is invisible in stills but clearly visible in the continuous motion of video.

For handheld video recording, leave the lens IS active in Mode 1, and enable Movie Digital IS as covered in Section 12.5. The combination of optical IS (handling larger, lower-frequency movements) and electronic IS (handling finer, higher-frequency tremors) produces the smoothest possible handheld video from the R10 without additional stabilisation hardware.

> **Tip:** *A useful practice when switching from handheld to tripod shooting is to make IS a deliberate part of your tripod setup checklist: mount the camera, frame the shot, lock the head, then disable IS via the lens switch before taking the shot. Making it a fixed step in the setup routine prevents the common situation of forgetting to disable IS on a tripod and spending time trying to diagnose why tripod shots are slightly less sharp than expected.*

PART 14 — Playback and Review

The Canon EOS R10 has a full set of tools for reviewing your images after they have been captured — evaluating sharpness, checking exposure, protecting important files, deleting unwanted ones, and even processing RAW files into JPEGs without a computer. This part explains how to navigate and use all of the playback functions available on the R10.

14.1 Viewing Photos and Videos

Entering Playback Mode

The Canon EOS R10 can enter playback mode at any time the camera is powered on, regardless of which shooting mode is active or whether the lens is attached.

1. Press the Playback button on the back of the camera. It is marked with a white triangle pointing to the right — the universal play icon — and is located on the right side of the camera back below the Q button. The shooting screen is replaced by the most recently captured image, displayed at full size on the LCD.
2. If you are using the EVF at the moment you press Playback, the display switches to the LCD screen automatically for playback — the EVF is not used for image review.

Navigating Between Images

Once an image is displayed, moving between images is straightforward.

Rotate the Main Dial — the textured wheel just behind the shutter button on top of the camera — clockwise to advance to the next image (the one taken after the displayed image) and counter-clockwise to go back to the previous image (taken before it). Each click of the dial moves one image in the selected direction.

On the touch screen, swipe your finger horizontally across the LCD — swipe left to advance to the next image, swipe right to go back to the previous image. The transition is smooth and immediate.

To jump through images more quickly rather than moving one at a time, the Main Dial can be configured to jump by larger increments — by date, folder, rating, or a set number of images — using the Image jump with dial setting in the Playback menu (covered in Section 3.5). When a jump function is configured, the Quick

Control Dial continues to move one image at a time while the Main Dial performs the jump.

Viewing Videos During Playback

Video files are included in the playback sequence alongside still images. When a video clip is displayed, a play triangle icon and the clip duration are shown on the screen. To play the video:

3. Navigate to the video clip using the Main Dial or by swiping until the video appears on screen.
4. Press SET to begin playback. The clip plays on the LCD screen with audio through the camera's speaker. An audio volume indicator and a progress bar appear on screen.
5. To adjust the playback volume during video review, rotate the Quick Control Dial. Rotating it clockwise increases the volume; rotating it counter-clockwise decreases it.
6. Press SET again to pause playback. Press it once more to resume.
7. To exit video playback and return to the single-image display, press MENU or rotate the Main Dial.

Returning to Shooting Mode

To close playback and return to the live view shooting screen, press the Playback button again, or half-press the shutter button. Half-pressing the shutter is the faster method because it simultaneously returns to shooting mode and activates autofocus, placing the camera in a ready state immediately.

> **Note:** *The camera's auto power-off timer is active during playback. If you are reviewing images and stop pressing buttons, the camera will power down after the Auto power off duration set in the Setup menu — typically one or two minutes by default. Press any button to wake the camera from auto power off without losing your place in the image sequence.*

14.2 Checking Sharpness by Zooming In

Why Zooming In During Playback Is Essential

The LCD screen on the Canon EOS R10 is three inches diagonally. At the standard single-image playback view, a 24.2 megapixel image is displayed at a very small fraction of its actual resolution — each pixel on the screen represents dozens of image pixels. An image that is significantly out of focus can look acceptable, even sharp, at this small playback size. An image that is sharp at the critical focus point and soft elsewhere can look uniformly sharp. You cannot make reliable judgements about focus quality from the standard playback view.

To evaluate focus accurately, you must zoom in to the area of the image where critical sharpness matters — typically a subject's eye in a portrait, the stamens of a flower in a macro shot, the detail of a bird's feather in a wildlife photo, or the fine texture of stone in an architectural image. Only at high magnification — 5x or 10x — can you confirm that focus landed precisely where you intended, that the autofocus system selected the correct point, and that no camera or subject movement blurred the image at the pixel level.

Making this review a habit after every important series of shots prevents the situation of returning home and discovering on a large monitor that a session's best images are unusably soft.

How to Zoom In During Playback

8. With the image you want to review displayed on screen, press the Magnify button on the back of the camera. It is marked with a magnifying glass and a plus sign (+), located near the upper area of the camera back. Each press increases the magnification by one step.
9. Continue pressing the Magnify button to zoom further. The available magnification steps are approximately 1.5x, 2.5x, 5x, 7.5x, and 10x. A small thumbnail of the full image appears in a corner of the screen, with a white rectangle indicating which portion of the image is currently displayed.
10. Use the joystick to navigate to the area of the image you want to inspect. Push it in the direction you want to move — up to move toward the top of the image, right to move toward the right edge, and so on. The view pans smoothly in the pushed direction.
11. Evaluate the sharpness at the area of interest. At 10x magnification, the difference between a sharp eye and a slightly soft eye is clearly visible. Look for clean, defined edges rather than fuzzy or smeared detail.

12. To zoom back out one step at a time, press the Reduce button (-), marked with a magnifying glass and a minus sign. Pressing it repeatedly reduces magnification in reverse order back to the standard single-image view.

13. Pressing SET while zoomed in also returns to the standard single-image view in one step, without going through intermediate magnification levels.

Using the Default Magnification Setting

By default, the first press of the Magnify button during playback zooms to a moderate magnification — approximately 1.5x to 2x — which is useful for checking composition and general exposure but is insufficient for evaluating critical focus. To immediately jump to high magnification on the first press rather than stepping up from a low level, change the Magnification setting in the Playback menu.

14. Press MENU during playback or from the shooting screen.

15. Navigate to the blue Playback tab.

16. Scroll to Magnification (approx.) and press SET.

17. Choose 10x — this sets the first press of the Magnify button to immediately zoom to 10x magnification, centred on the active AF point used when the photo was taken. Subsequent presses reduce magnification rather than increase it.

18. Press SET to confirm. From this point, pressing the Magnify button during playback immediately shows the image at 10x, positioned at the focus point — the fastest possible route to checking critical sharpness.

Tip: *When reviewing a burst sequence for sharpness, zoom to 10x on the first frame and then use the Main Dial to step through the remaining frames of the burst at the same magnification level. The camera maintains the zoom and position as you advance through images, allowing you to quickly compare sharpness across multiple frames at the same area of interest without re-zooming for each one.*

14.3 Playback Information Display

Cycling Through Information Overlays

During playback, pressing the INFO button on the camera back cycles through different information overlays that appear on the LCD screen alongside the displayed image. Each press advances to the next display mode. The cycle runs continuously — after the last mode, the next press returns to the first.

The specific overlays available during playback depend on which items are enabled in the Playback information display setting in the Playback menu (covered in Section 3.5). By default, the following modes are available.

Basic Display

The first INFO mode shows the image with minimal information overlaid — typically only the file number, the image protection status (a lock icon if the image is protected), and a small battery indicator. This is a clean view that allows you to evaluate the image with minimal distraction.

Shooting Data Display

The second INFO mode adds a panel of shooting information to the display. This panel lists the settings that were active when the photo was taken: the shooting mode, shutter speed, aperture, ISO sensitivity, exposure compensation level, metering mode, white balance setting, the lens focal length at the time of capture (for zoom lenses), the image quality and file format, the shooting date and time, and the file size. This data is drawn from the EXIF metadata stored in the image file and provides a complete record of how the photo was taken. Reviewing the shooting data alongside an image you are unhappy with is a diagnostic tool — it tells you exactly what settings produced the result and points toward which setting to change in future.

Histogram Display

The third INFO mode overlays the image's histogram on the playback screen. The histogram shows the distribution of tonal values in the image from black on the left to white on the right, exactly as described in Part 7.8 of this guide. In playback, the histogram is generated from the actual captured image data, giving you an accurate picture of how the exposure turned out in the final file.

Use the histogram in playback to verify that the exposure you intended was actually recorded. If the histogram shows a gap between the data and the right edge, there was room to expose further right for a brighter image with less noise.

If the histogram is pressed against the right edge with data spilling off, highlights were clipped in the final file — evaluate whether the clipped area was important (a face, a product, a key detail) or acceptable (a light source, a specular reflection).

When the Highlight alert setting is enabled in the Playback menu, this display mode also shows the blinking overexposure warning — any areas of the image that are clipped to pure white blink between black and white, overlaid on the image. The combination of the histogram and the blinking alert gives you simultaneous quantitative and visual feedback about the exposure.

GPS Information Display

If GPS location data was recorded with the image — either via a connected Canon GPS receiver or through the Bluetooth GPS logging feature of the Canon Camera Connect smartphone app — a GPS information panel is available in the INFO cycle. This panel displays the latitude, longitude, altitude, and the direction the camera was pointed (bearing) at the moment of capture. This information is also stored in the image's EXIF metadata and can be read by mapping applications and photo management software. If no GPS data was recorded, this display mode does not appear in the cycle.

No Information Display

The final mode in the INFO cycle shows the image filling the entire screen with no overlaid text, icons, or data. This clean view is useful when evaluating the visual qualities of an image — composition, colour, tonal balance, and overall impact — without any graphical elements competing for attention.

> **Note:** *You can customise which information overlays appear in the playback INFO cycle by going to MENU, navigating to the Playback menu (blue tab), selecting Playback information display, and enabling or disabling individual overlay items. Removing overlays you do not use shortens the INFO cycle so you reach the display you want more quickly.*

14.4 Protecting Images

What Protection Does

Protecting an image marks it with a lock that prevents it from being deleted by the Delete button or by the Erase images function in the Playback menu. A small key icon appears on the image during playback to indicate that it is protected. Protection is a safety measure for images you want to keep regardless of any accidental button presses or bulk deletion operations.

Protection does not prevent an image from being erased when the SD card is formatted. The Format card function in the Setup menu erases all data on the card regardless of protection status. Protection is only effective against the dedicated deletion functions.

Protecting a Single Image

19. Navigate to the image you want to protect using the Playback button and the Main Dial.
20. Press MENU to open the menu while the image is displayed.
21. Navigate to the blue Playback tab using the Main Dial.
22. Scroll to Protect images and press SET.
23. Select images is shown — press SET. The current image is displayed with a tick box.
24. Press SET to toggle the protection on. A key icon appears on the image, confirming it is now protected.
25. Press MENU to return to the menu, then press MENU again or half-press the shutter to return to playback.

Protecting Multiple Images

26. Press MENU from the shooting screen or during playback.
27. Navigate to the blue Playback tab and select Protect images, then press SET.
28. From the options, select Select images. The image browser opens showing all images on the card.
29. Use the Main Dial to navigate to each image you want to protect. Press SET to toggle protection on each selected image — a key icon appears on each protected image.
30. After marking all the images you want to protect, press the Q button to apply the protection to all marked images at once.

31. A confirmation screen may appear — select OK and press SET to confirm.

Protecting All Images in a Folder or on the Card

32. Press MENU, navigate to the Playback tab, and select Protect images.
33. Choose All images in folder to protect every image in the currently active folder, or All images on card to protect every image on the entire SD card.
34. Press SET and confirm with OK. The protection is applied immediately to all images in the chosen scope.

Removing Protection

To remove protection from an image, follow the same steps used to apply it. Navigate to the protected image, open Protect images from the Playback menu, and press SET on the image — the key icon disappears and the image is no longer protected. The Unprotect all in folder and Unprotect all on card options are also available from the same Protect images screen to remove protection from all images at once.

> **Tip:** *Protect your very best images — or any images you specifically need to keep — immediately after a burst or session, before reviewing or editing anything. This gives you a safety net if you accidentally press the Delete button while scrolling through images or if you later run a bulk deletion of unneeded frames.*

14.5 Deleting Images

> **Important:** *Deleted images cannot be recovered from within the camera. Once deletion is confirmed, the image data is gone from the card. If you delete an image by mistake, stop using the card immediately and use data recovery software on a computer — new data written to the card can overwrite the deleted file and make recovery impossible.*

Deleting a Single Image

35. Navigate to the image you want to delete during playback using the Playback button and the Main Dial.

36. Press the Delete button on the back of the camera. It is marked with a trash can icon, located below the Playback button on the right side of the camera back.

37. A confirmation screen appears with two options: Cancel and Delete. The camera waits for your confirmation before deleting — a single press of the Delete button does not delete the image.

38. Press the Delete button a second time, or use the Quick Control Dial to highlight Delete and press SET, to confirm. The image is deleted immediately and the camera displays the next image in the sequence.

Note: *Protected images are ignored by the Delete button. Pressing Delete on a protected image shows the protection icon and does nothing — the image is safe. To delete a protected image, you must remove the protection first via the Protect images function in the Playback menu.*

Deleting Multiple Selected Images

39. Press MENU from the shooting screen or during playback.

40. Navigate to the blue Playback tab using the Main Dial.

41. Scroll to Erase images and press SET.

42. From the options, select Select and erase images and press SET. The image browser opens.

43. Use the Main Dial to navigate to each image you want to delete. Press SET to mark it for deletion — a tick mark appears on the image. Navigate to the next image and repeat.

44. To review an image more closely before marking it, press the Magnify button to zoom in and confirm you are marking the correct image, then press the Reduce button to return to the browser view.

45. After marking all images for deletion, press the Q button. A confirmation screen shows the number of images selected for deletion.

46. Highlight OK and press SET to confirm. All marked images are deleted simultaneously.

Deleting All Images in a Folder or on the Card

47. Press MENU, navigate to the Playback tab, and select Erase images.

48. Choose All images in folder to erase every unprotected image in the current folder, or All images on card to erase every unprotected image on the entire card.

49. A confirmation screen shows the number of images that will be deleted. Highlight OK and press SET to confirm. Protected images in the selected scope are skipped and remain on the card.

Important: *All images in folder and All images on card are irreversible bulk deletions. Ensure you have backed up any images you want to keep before using these options. Protected images are preserved — all others are permanently deleted.*

14.6 In-Camera RAW Processing

What In-Camera RAW Processing Does

When you shoot in RAW format, the image file contains unprocessed sensor data that must be converted to a standard format — JPEG, TIFF, or another viewable format — before it can be shared, printed, or displayed on most devices. Normally this conversion is done on a computer using dedicated software such as Canon Digital Photo Professional, Adobe Lightroom, or another RAW processor. However, the Canon EOS R10 includes a RAW processing function that performs this conversion internally, allowing you to produce a processed JPEG directly from a RAW file without any computer required.

The in-camera RAW processing function gives you a meaningful set of adjustable parameters — not just the Picture Style applied at the time of capture, but a range of adjustments that let you intentionally change the look of the final JPEG. You can correct a white balance error, apply a different Picture Style, increase or decrease the brightness, adjust the noise reduction level, and more. The original RAW file is not altered in any way — the function creates a new JPEG as a separate file, leaving the RAW intact.

This is particularly useful when you are away from your computer and need a processed, shareable JPEG from a RAW file — to send to a client, share on social media, or transfer to a phone for review — without returning to a workstation.

How to Process a RAW File In-Camera

50. Press the Playback button to enter playback mode.
51. Navigate to the RAW image you want to process using the Main Dial or by swiping. Only RAW files can be processed with this function —

JPEG files are not listed. RAW files are identified in playback by the RAW or CRAW badge shown on the image.

52. With the RAW image displayed, press MENU to open the menu.
53. Navigate to the blue Playback tab using the Main Dial.
54. Scroll to RAW processing and press SET. The RAW processing screen opens, showing the current image with a panel of adjustable settings.
55. The adjustable parameters are listed on screen. Use the joystick or Quick Control Dial to highlight each parameter, then press SET to open the individual adjustment control for that parameter. Rotate a dial to adjust the value and press SET to confirm it. The image preview updates in real time as you adjust each parameter, showing approximately how the final JPEG will look with the current settings.

Adjustable Parameters in RAW Processing

The following settings can be adjusted individually before saving the JPEG. Each operates independently — changing one does not affect the others.

Brightness adjusts the overall exposure of the output JPEG — equivalent to applying exposure compensation to the RAW conversion. The range is approximately minus 2 to plus 2 stops. Use this to brighten a slightly underexposed RAW or darken a slightly overexposed one.

White balance allows you to change the white balance applied to the output JPEG independently of what was recorded at the time of shooting. You can select any of the standard white balance presets, the Custom White Balance if one is stored, or a specific Kelvin value. This is one of the most valuable adjustments in RAW processing — if the white balance was wrong at capture, you can correct it here without any quality loss, because white balance in RAW processing is an interpretive instruction to the unaltered pixel data rather than a destructive colour change.

Picture Style applies any of the available Picture Styles to the output JPEG — Standard, Portrait, Landscape, Fine Detail, Neutral, Faithful, Monochrome, Auto, or User Defined. The Preview on screen updates immediately to show how each style changes the colour, contrast, and sharpness of the image. You can apply a Picture Style that was not active when the shot was taken, or apply the

Monochrome style to produce a black and white JPEG from a full-colour RAW without affecting the colour data in the original RAW file.

Auto Lighting Optimizer applies the same shadow-lifting brightness optimisation described in Section 3.3. Enable it to automatically brighten dark shadow areas in the output JPEG.

High ISO speed NR adjusts the luminance noise reduction applied during the RAW-to-JPEG conversion. Choose from Standard, Low, High, or Disable. If the RAW was shot at high ISO and shows visible grain in the preview, increase the noise reduction level to smooth it in the output JPEG.

Lens aberration correction enables or disables the automatic lens correction options — peripheral illumination correction, distortion correction, digital lens optimizer, chromatic aberration correction, and diffraction correction. These are the same corrections described in Shooting Menu 1 in Section 3.3.

Clarity adjusts the mid-tone contrast enhancement from minus 4 to plus 4, exactly as described in Section 3.3. Increasing it adds definition and texture to the output JPEG.

Cropping opens the in-camera crop tool, allowing you to define a crop area that will be applied to the saved JPEG. The original RAW is uncropped — only the new JPEG is saved with the crop applied.

Saving the Processed JPEG

56. After adjusting all the parameters to your preference, use the joystick or Quick Control Dial to navigate to the Save option at the bottom of the parameter list and press SET.
57. A confirmation screen appears showing the file name that will be assigned to the new JPEG. Press SET or OK to confirm.
58. The camera processes the RAW file using all your adjustments and saves the output as a new JPEG file to the SD card. This takes a moment — a progress indicator shows the processing status.
59. When complete, the camera returns to the playback display showing the newly created JPEG. The original RAW file remains on the card, unchanged.

Note: *The JPEG created by in-camera RAW processing is saved at the Large Fine quality setting regardless of what is currently configured in the Image quality menu. It is always a full-resolution, high-quality JPEG. The file is numbered sequentially after the last file on the card.*

Tip: *In-camera RAW processing is also accessible directly during playback without going through the menu. Display the RAW image, press the Q button to open the Quick Control screen, and look for the RAW processing option in the Q grid — pressing it takes you directly to the processing screen for the displayed image. This is faster than navigating through MENU to the Playback tab when you want to process a specific image quickly.*

PART 15 — Wireless and Connectivity

The Canon EOS R10 includes Wi-Fi and Bluetooth connectivity, a USB-C port, and an HDMI mini output — giving you multiple ways to transfer images, control the camera remotely, display images on a larger screen, and connect to other devices. This part explains each connection method step by step.

15.1 Connecting to the Canon Camera Connect App

What the Connection Allows

Canon Camera Connect is a free application for iOS and Android that establishes a wireless connection between the Canon EOS R10 and your smartphone. Once connected, you can browse all images stored on the camera's SD card directly from your phone, download selected images to your phone's camera roll without removing the card, control the camera shutter remotely to take photos from a distance, adjust certain camera settings from the app, view a live view feed on your phone screen, and enable automatic image transfer as you shoot.

The connection uses both Wi-Fi and Bluetooth. Bluetooth maintains a low-power persistent background link between the phone and camera so they can find each other quickly. Wi-Fi carries the actual image data when you are browsing or downloading images. The first-time setup pairs the devices permanently — subsequent connections are faster because the pairing information is saved on both devices.

Step 1 — Install Canon Camera Connect on Your Phone

1. On your iPhone, open the App Store. On an Android phone, open the Google Play Store.
2. Search for Canon Camera Connect. The app is published by Canon Inc. — confirm the developer name before downloading to ensure you have the official app.
3. Download and install the app. Open it once to accept any permissions it requests — Camera Connect requires access to your phone's local network, Bluetooth, and photo library to function correctly.
4. Leave the app open or in the background while you proceed to the camera setup.

Step 2 — Initiate the Connection from the Camera

5. On the Canon EOS R10, press the MENU button.
6. Rotate the Main Dial to navigate to the yellow Setup tab — the tab with the wrench icon.
7. Scroll down using the Quick Control Dial to find Wi-Fi/Bluetooth connection and press SET.
8. A connection type selection screen appears. Scroll to Connect to smartphone and press SET.
9. The camera asks whether to add a new device or connect to a registered device. Select Add device to connect to and press SET — this is for first-time pairing.
10. The camera activates its Bluetooth transmitter and searches for nearby devices. A screen appears showing a QR code and a Bluetooth pairing code. Leave this screen visible on the camera.

Step 3 — Complete the Pairing on Your Phone

11. On your phone, open the Canon Camera Connect app if it is not already open.
12. The app should detect the Canon EOS R10 automatically via Bluetooth and display it as an available camera. Tap its name or serial number to initiate pairing.
13. If the app does not detect the camera automatically, tap the plus icon or Add Camera within the app, then point your phone's camera at the QR code shown on the R10's screen. The app reads the QR code and initiates the connection automatically.
14. A pairing confirmation prompt appears on both the phone and the camera. On the camera, select OK and press SET to confirm. On the phone, tap Pair or Allow when prompted.
15. The camera and phone exchange pairing credentials. Once pairing is complete, the R10 connects to the phone via both Bluetooth and Wi-Fi. The camera screen shows a connection confirmation and the Canon Camera Connect home screen appears on your phone.

Step 4 — Reconnecting After the First Pairing

Once the initial pairing is complete, reconnecting on subsequent occasions is significantly faster and does not require repeating the full pairing process. Simply ensure Bluetooth is enabled on your phone, open the Canon Camera Connect app, and the app will detect the R10 automatically if the camera is powered on and within Bluetooth range. Tap the camera name to reconnect — the full Wi-Fi connection establishes itself within a few seconds.

If the connection does not establish automatically, return to MENU → Setup → Wi-Fi/Bluetooth connection → Connect to smartphone and select the registered device name rather than Add device to connect to. The camera initiates the connection from its side.

Managing and Resetting Wireless Settings

To view or remove registered smartphone pairings: press MENU → Setup tab → Wi-Fi settings → and navigate to the paired device list. From here you can disconnect a specific device or remove it from the registered list entirely. To reset all wireless settings — including all pairings, access point data, and network configurations — press MENU → Setup tab → Wi-Fi settings → Clear settings and confirm. After a full reset, all devices must be re-paired from scratch.

> Note: *The Canon EOS R10 can store connection settings for multiple smartphones simultaneously. If you use both a personal phone and a work phone with the camera, or if multiple photographers in a team use the same camera, each device can be registered and reconnected independently without clearing the other pairings.*

15.2 Transferring Images to a Phone

Browsing and Downloading Selected Images

Once the Canon EOS R10 is connected to your phone via Camera Connect, transferring images is straightforward. The app gives you a direct view of the SD card contents over the Wi-Fi connection, allowing you to browse and selectively download exactly the images you want without transferring the entire card.

16. With the camera connected via Camera Connect, tap Images on device in the app's home screen. The app displays a thumbnail grid of all images currently on the camera's SD card.
17. Scroll through the thumbnails to find the images you want to transfer. Tap any thumbnail once to view it at a larger preview size. The preview

loads over the Wi-Fi connection and may take a moment depending on signal strength and image file size.

18. To select images for download, tap the select icon (typically a checkmark or tick icon within the app). Tap each image you want to download — a tick mark or highlight appears on selected images.

19. When your selection is complete, tap the download icon or Download button. The selected images transfer from the camera's SD card to your phone's camera roll over the Wi-Fi connection. A progress indicator shows the transfer status. Transfer speed depends on the file size — RAW files take noticeably longer than JPEGs.

20. When the transfer completes, the images are available in your phone's default photo library — the Photos app on iPhone or the Gallery on Android. They can be shared, edited, or uploaded immediately from your phone.

Automatic Image Transfer While Shooting

Canon Camera Connect can be configured to transfer images automatically to your phone as you shoot them, without any manual selection step. Each new image is transferred to the phone wirelessly within seconds of being captured.

21. In the Camera Connect app, access the settings or preferences for the connected camera.

22. Find the Auto transfer or Auto send images option and enable it.

23. Return to shooting. Each image you capture is automatically queued and transferred to your phone over the Wi-Fi connection. A small indicator may appear on the camera screen confirming each image has been sent.

Auto transfer is particularly useful at events, press situations, or client shoots where images need to reach a recipient quickly. The images arrive on the phone in real time and can be shared or uploaded immediately while shooting continues.

Auto transfer requires the Wi-Fi connection to remain active, which draws battery power from both the camera and the phone. For extended sessions, ensure both devices have adequate battery charge, or charge the camera via USB during the session.

Remote Shooting via the App

Camera Connect also allows you to trigger the shutter on the Canon EOS R10 remotely from your phone. This is useful for self-portraits, wildlife photography from a distance, group photos where you need to be in the frame, or any situation where physically pressing the shutter would be impractical.

24. With the camera connected, tap Remote Live View shooting in the Camera Connect home screen.
25. A live view feed from the camera appears on your phone screen — you are seeing what the camera's sensor is seeing in real time, with a short delay of approximately half a second.
26. Tap anywhere on the live view image on your phone screen to set the autofocus point for the next shot.
27. Tap the shutter icon on the app to take the photo. The camera fires immediately and the captured image appears briefly on your phone screen.
28. To zoom in on the live view feed, use the standard pinch-to-zoom gesture on the phone screen.

In Remote Live View shooting mode you can also adjust certain camera settings from the app — typically ISO, white balance, and drive mode — depending on the current shooting mode and app version. The range of remotely adjustable settings is more limited than direct camera control but covers the most frequently needed parameters for remote shooting.

> **Note:** *The live view feed in Remote Live View shooting updates at a reduced frame rate compared to the camera's native live view — typically around 10 to 15 frames per second depending on your Wi-Fi signal strength. This is sufficient for general remote shooting but may be slightly choppy for fast-moving subjects. Position the phone and camera within a reasonable Wi-Fi range — a crowded environment with many competing Wi-Fi networks may slow the feed.*

15.3 Connecting to a Computer via USB

What the USB Connection Allows

Connecting the Canon EOS R10 to a computer via the included USB-C cable enables two different types of interaction depending on how the connection is configured: direct file transfer from the camera's SD card to the computer, and camera control from the computer using Canon's EOS Utility software. The camera can also be powered via USB during the connection, which keeps the battery from draining during extended tethered shooting or transfer sessions.

Connecting the Cable

29. Locate the USB-C port on the left side of the Canon EOS R10. Open the rubber protective flap by pulling it gently toward you — it is hinged and swings open to reveal the port cluster.
30. Insert the USB-C end of the included Interface Cable IFC-600PCU into the USB-C port on the camera. The USB-C connector is symmetrical — it inserts in either orientation.
31. Insert the other end of the cable (the standard USB-A connector) into a USB port on your computer. If your computer has only USB-C ports, you will need a USB-C to USB-C cable or a USB-C to USB-A adapter — the included cable has USB-A on the computer end.
32. Turn the Canon EOS R10 on by sliding the ON/OFF switch to ON. The camera detects the USB connection and a communication mode selection screen may appear on the camera's LCD screen.

Using the Camera as a Removable Drive

The simplest way to transfer images via USB is to use the camera as a standard removable storage device. In this mode the computer recognises the camera's SD card as an external drive and you can browse, copy, and move files using your computer's file manager — Windows Explorer on PC, or Finder on Mac.

33. If a communication mode prompt appears on the camera screen, select Mass storage or Connect to computer (the exact wording depends on your firmware version) and press SET.
34. The computer detects the camera's SD card as a removable drive. On Windows, it appears in This PC as a removable device. On Mac, it appears on the desktop and in Finder under Locations.
35. Open the drive and navigate to the DCIM folder inside it. Your image files are organised in numbered sub-folders within DCIM — for example, 100CANON or 101CANON. Each folder contains up to 9999 image files.

36. Copy image files from the camera folders to your chosen location on the computer by dragging them or using copy and paste. The files transfer at the speed of the USB connection and the card's read speed.
37. When the transfer is complete, safely eject the camera before disconnecting the cable. On Windows, use the Safely Remove Hardware option in the system tray. On Mac, drag the camera drive to the Bin, or right-click and select Eject. Disconnecting the cable without ejecting can interrupt a write operation if images are still being transferred.

Using Canon EOS Utility for Import and Tethered Shooting

Canon EOS Utility is a free software application available from Canon's website (canon.com) that provides a more capable interface for working with the Canon EOS R10 via USB. It offers a guided import wizard, tethered shooting control, remote camera adjustment, and live view display on the computer screen.

38. Download Canon EOS Utility from Canon's official website. Search for EOS Utility and select the version for the R10. Install it on your computer following the on-screen instructions.
39. Connect the camera to the computer via the USB-C cable as described above and power the camera on.
40. Open EOS Utility on the computer. It should detect the connected R10 automatically within a few seconds and display the main interface.
41. To import images, click the Import images and movies option in EOS Utility. A window shows all images on the card. Select which images to import and choose a destination folder on your computer. EOS Utility copies the files and can optionally delete them from the card after transfer.
42. To use tethered shooting — where each shot is captured directly to the computer rather than to the SD card — click Remote shooting in EOS Utility. A live view window appears on the computer screen and you can trigger the shutter from the software, adjust camera settings, and see each captured image appear on the computer immediately after it is taken.

Tethered shooting via EOS Utility is the standard workflow for studio photography and product photography where clients or art directors need to review each image on a large screen immediately after capture. It allows the captured images to go directly into the computer's filing system rather than to the SD card, eliminating the card-reading step from the workflow.

> **Note:** *The Canon EOS R10 can also be powered through the USB-C port during a computer connection using a compatible USB power source. If the camera's battery is low during a long tethered session, connect a USB power adapter to the camera's USB-C port using a second cable while the computer cable is connected — the camera draws power from the USB source and the battery charge is maintained. Confirm that your USB power adapter is capable of providing sufficient current to power the camera (at least 9V/2A output is recommended for stable operation during tethered shooting).*

15.4 HDMI Output

What HDMI Output Allows

The HDMI mini output port on the left side of the Canon EOS R10 allows the camera's video signal to be sent to any device with a standard HDMI input — televisions, computer monitors, video recorders, and field monitors. Both the live view shooting display and playback review are output over HDMI, so whatever appears on the camera's LCD screen also appears on the connected external display, usually at a larger size and higher resolution than the camera's own 3-inch LCD.

HDMI output is used in several distinct contexts: displaying finished images on a large screen for client review or group presentation, monitoring the live view on a field monitor during video production, outputting a clean video signal to an external recorder for capture at higher bit rates than the camera records internally, and connecting to a capture card for live streaming or video conferencing.

Connecting via HDMI

43. You need an HDMI cable with a mini HDMI (Type C) connector on one end and a standard HDMI (Type A) connector on the other. This cable is not included with the Canon EOS R10 and must be purchased separately. Confirm the cable is labelled as Mini HDMI to HDMI or Type C to Type A HDMI.

44. Locate the HDMI mini port on the left side of the camera, in the port cluster behind the rubber flap. It is the smaller of the two ports in that cluster — above the USB-C port.
45. Open the rubber flap and insert the mini HDMI connector into this port. It inserts in only one orientation — align the connector carefully and push it in gently until it seats.
46. Connect the standard HDMI end of the cable to the HDMI input port on your television, monitor, or recording device.
47. Turn on the external display and set it to the HDMI input the camera is connected to. On most televisions this means selecting the HDMI source from the input menu using the TV remote.
48. Power on the Canon EOS R10. The camera detects the HDMI connection and begins outputting its display signal to the external device. The camera's LCD screen may dim or turn off depending on the HDMI display setting configured in the Setup menu.

Controlling What Appears on the HDMI Output

The HDMI display setting in the Setup menu determines how the camera manages its output when HDMI is connected. To access it: press MENU, navigate to the yellow Setup tab, scroll to HDMI display, and press SET.

When set to Display On, both the camera's rear LCD screen and the external HDMI display are active simultaneously. The camera's LCD continues to show its normal shooting or playback information while the external display mirrors the output. Use this setting when you need to see both your own camera display and the external monitor simultaneously — for example, when the external monitor is positioned for a client while you continue to operate the camera normally.

When set to Display Off, the camera's LCD screen turns off as soon as an HDMI device is detected, and the signal is sent only to the external display. Use this setting for video production where the external monitor or recorder is your primary display, and you want to save camera battery power by not driving the internal LCD simultaneously.

Clean HDMI Output for External Recording

When recording video for professional productions, external video recorders are frequently used to capture footage at higher bit rates or in better quality formats than the camera records to the SD card internally. The Canon EOS R10 outputs a video signal over HDMI that external recorders can capture — the HDMI signal carries the live video from the sensor in real time.

For clean external recording, the HDMI output can be configured to show a clean signal — without the on-screen text, icons, and camera information overlays that appear in the normal shooting display. To produce a clean HDMI output: press MENU → Setup tab → HDMI display, and ensure the shooting information overlays are removed from the HDMI output. On the shooting screen, press INFO to cycle to the no-information display mode — this removes most overlays from both the LCD and HDMI output simultaneously.

The HDMI output resolution and frame rate match the selected video recording quality in the Movie menu. If you are recording 4K at 25 fps to the SD card, the HDMI output also carries a 4K 25 fps signal. External recorders must be configured to accept the matching input format — check that your recorder's input setting matches the camera's output resolution and frame rate before recording.

> **Important:** *Do not connect or disconnect the HDMI cable while the camera is recording video to the SD card. The camera may stop recording or produce a file write error if the HDMI connection is disturbed mid-recording. Connect the HDMI cable before pressing the Movie Record button and leave it connected for the duration of the recording session.*

Using HDMI for Image Playback and Client Review

For presenting captured images to clients, colleagues, or a group — at a portfolio review, on a shoot, or at an event — HDMI output provides the simplest and highest-quality way to display images on a large screen directly from the camera without involving a computer.

49. Connect the camera to a television or large monitor via the HDMI mini cable as described above.
50. Power on both the camera and the external display, and confirm the display is set to the correct HDMI input.
51. Press the Playback button on the camera back. The most recently captured image appears on both the camera's LCD and the external display.

52. Use the Main Dial or swipe the touch screen to move between images. Each image appears on the external display at full resolution, filling the screen.
53. Press INFO on the camera to add or remove data overlays — for client presentations, pressing INFO to remove all overlays produces the cleanest, most professional display with the image filling the screen without any text or icons.
54. Press the Magnify button to zoom into an image on the external display — useful for showing fine detail or discussing sharpness with a client.

Tip: *For event photographers showing same-day images to clients on site, a battery-powered portable monitor with HDMI input allows HDMI playback anywhere without needing access to a television or power outlet. Connect the R10 to the portable monitor via the HDMI mini cable and use it as a dedicated review screen while continuing to shoot with the camera. The camera's LCD can remain active for your own shooting while the external monitor shows the client their images.*

PART 16 — Custom Settings and Personalization

The Canon EOS R10 is configurable well beyond its factory defaults. Custom Controls let you reassign physical buttons to functions that better match your shooting style. My Menu creates a personal shortcut panel for your most frequently accessed settings. Custom Functions modify how the camera's core systems behave at a deeper level than the standard menu options allow. This part explains each of these systems and how to use them to configure the R10 to work the way you work.

16.1 Custom Controls — Reassigning Buttons

What Custom Controls Does

By default, every button on the Canon EOS R10 performs a factory-assigned function. The AF-ON button activates autofocus. The ★ button locks exposure. The M-Fn button cycles through ISO, white balance, drive mode, AF operation, and flash compensation. The SET button confirms menu selections. These defaults are well-considered, but they reflect Canon's assumptions about how a typical photographer works — not necessarily how you work.

Custom Controls allows you to reassign many of these buttons to different functions that better suit your shooting style or subject matter. You can swap the functions of two buttons, assign a rarely used button to something you access constantly, remove a function from a button you keep accidentally pressing, or configure a button to perform multiple actions depending on whether it is pressed or pressed and held.

The changes you make in Custom Controls affect only the shooting screen — buttons behave as normal within the menu system regardless of any custom assignments.

How to Access Custom Controls

1. Press MENU on the upper-left of the camera back.
2. Rotate the Main Dial to navigate to the yellow Setup tab — the wrench icon.
3. Scroll down using the Quick Control Dial until Custom controls (shooting) is highlighted. Press SET.
4. A schematic diagram of the Canon EOS R10 appears on screen, showing the camera body from the back and top with labelled indicators over each assignable button and control. The currently assigned function for each button is shown as text beside its indicator.

Selecting a Button and Changing Its Function

5. Use the joystick to move the selection highlight to the button you want to reassign, or tap the button's indicator directly on the touch screen. The selected button is highlighted and its current function is shown.
6. Press SET to open the function assignment screen for that button. A list of all functions that can be assigned to that button appears. Different buttons support different lists of assignable functions — not every function is available for every button.
7. Scroll through the list using the Quick Control Dial and highlight the function you want to assign. A brief description of the highlighted function appears below the list.
8. Press SET to confirm the assignment. The camera diagram updates to show the new function beside the reassigned button.

9. Repeat for any other buttons you want to reassign.
10. Press MENU to close the Custom Controls screen when you are finished. The new assignments take effect immediately and remain active until you change them again.

Assignable Buttons and Their Default Functions

The following buttons can be reassigned on the Canon EOS R10. Their factory default functions are shown alongside each button name.

Shutter button (half-press): The half-press of the shutter button default function is Metering and AF start — activating both the exposure metering system and the autofocus simultaneously. This can be changed to Metering start only (removing AF from the half-press, used in conjunction with back-button focus on AF-ON), or to AE lock (locking the exposure on half-press rather than metering continuously).

AF-ON button: Default function is Metering and AF start — identical to the shutter half-press, giving you a second route to focus activation. This is the button most commonly reassigned as part of the back-button focus setup, where it becomes the sole AF activation control (and the shutter half-press is set to Metering only). It can also be assigned to subject detection switching, One-Touch image quality change, or other functions.

AE Lock button (★): Default function is AE lock (hold) — pressing and holding it locks the exposure. Common alternatives include AF stop (pressing it pauses Servo AF tracking without losing the last acquired focus point), FE lock (for flash exposure lock), switching the AF area mode momentarily, or enabling a preset AF point position.

M-Fn button: Default function is the M-Fn shortcut cycle — pressing and holding while rotating the Main Dial cycles through ISO, white balance, drive mode, AF operation, and flash compensation. It can alternatively be assigned to IS mode switching, RAW quality switching for a single shot, exposure compensation, or other frequently needed single-step functions.

SET button: Default function on the shooting screen is No function assigned — pressing SET while on the shooting screen does nothing by default (it is active only within menus and the Quick Control screen). It can be assigned to open the

Quick Control screen directly, activate AF, start recording video, switch IS modes, or many other functions. Assigning it to Quick Control screen access is particularly useful.

Control ring (on RF lenses): Default function is Exposure compensation in auto and semi-auto modes, and ISO in Manual mode. It can be reassigned to aperture, shutter speed, ISO, or sensitivity only, or set to Disabled to prevent accidental rotation from affecting any setting.

Movie Record button (in still shooting modes): By default, pressing the Movie Record button from a still shooting mode begins video recording. This can be changed if you want to prevent accidental video recording from still modes.

Practical Custom Control Configurations

The most widely used Custom Controls configuration on the Canon EOS R10 is back-button focus setup — reassigning AF activation away from the shutter half-press and exclusively to the AF-ON button. To set this up: in the Custom Controls screen, set the Shutter button (half-press) to Metering start only, and confirm the AF-ON button is set to Metering and AF start. From this point, the shutter button only meters and shoots — it never activates AF — and the AF-ON button is the sole control for all autofocus. This configuration is covered in detail in Section 4.4.

Another useful configuration is assigning the SET button to open the Quick Control screen. By default the SET button does nothing in the shooting screen, making the Q button the only way to open Quick Control. Assigning SET to Quick Control screen access gives you a second, more centrally placed route to the Q screen.

Assigning the ★ button to AF stop is valuable for wildlife and sports photographers using Servo AF. When tracking a subject with Servo AF active, pressing AF stop pauses the focus tracking at the current distance — useful for holding focus on a specific subject at a specific distance while another subject passes closer to the camera, then releasing the button to resume tracking when the nearer subject has passed.

> **Important:** *Custom Controls assignments are saved in the camera's settings and are not reset by the camera's standard power cycle. However, performing*

a Clear all camera settings from the Setup menu will return all Custom Controls assignments to their factory defaults. If you have configured an elaborate Custom Controls setup, back it up by saving the camera settings to an SD card using Camera user settings in the Setup menu before performing any settings reset.

16.2 My Menu — Setup

My Menu is a blank menu tab on the Canon EOS R10 that you populate yourself with up to six settings drawn from anywhere in the menu system. Instead of navigating to the correct coloured tab, scrolling through a list, and drilling down to a setting every time you need it, My Menu gives you direct access to your most-used settings in a single location that can be set to open first whenever you press the MENU button.

My Menu was covered in full in Section 3.7, including the step-by-step procedures for adding items, reordering them, deleting them, and configuring the camera to open My Menu first. Refer to that section for the complete directional guide. This section provides guidance on what to put in My Menu based on common shooting workflows.

Choosing What to Put in My Menu

The six items you add to My Menu should be settings that you access regularly but that are buried deep enough in the menu system that reaching them takes multiple steps. Settings that are already quickly accessible via the Q screen, the M-Fn button, or a physical button assignment do not need to be in My Menu — they are already fast enough. My Menu earns its value for settings that sit two or three levels deep in specific menu tabs.

Suggested My Menu items for general photography include: Custom White Balance (in Shooting Menu 3, requires four menu steps to reach without My Menu), Long exp. noise reduction (in Shooting Menu 4), High ISO speed NR (in Shooting Menu 4), Dust Delete Data (in Shooting Menu 4), Anti-flicker shooting (in Shooting Menu 7), and Firmware (in the last Setup tab, useful for checking the version quickly without navigating the full Setup menu).

For portrait photographers: Custom White Balance, Picture Style (if you prefer menu access over the Q screen), Copyright information (if you update it regularly), and MF peaking settings if you frequently switch between optical and manual focus work.

For video shooters: Movie rec quality, Audio (the full audio sub-menu), Canon Log settings, Movie digital IS, and Time-lapse movie are all multiple steps deep in the Movie tab and benefit from My Menu shortcuts.

For travel photographers who frequently board flights or cross borders: the Wireless communication settings, GPS device settings, and Date/Time/Zone are all worth adding to My Menu if you regularly adjust them.

Display from My Menu — Opening My Menu First

The most significant productivity improvement My Menu offers is the option to make it the first screen that appears every time you press the MENU button, regardless of which tab you were on last. To enable this: navigate to the green My Menu tab (star icon), scroll to Display from My Menu at the bottom of the tab, press SET, and select Enable. Confirm with SET.

With this enabled, every press of MENU takes you directly to your six-item shortcut list rather than to the last-used tab. The other menu tabs are still fully accessible by rotating the Main Dial left from My Menu. For photographers who access the same small set of settings repeatedly during a session, this configuration reduces every menu navigation to a single press of MENU followed by a short scroll.

> **Tip:** *Review your My Menu items periodically — after a month of shooting, you will have a clear picture of which items you actually access repeatedly versus which ones you added speculatively. Replace infrequently used items with the settings you find yourself navigating to manually, so your My Menu stays genuinely useful rather than a collection of settings you thought you might need.*

16.3 Custom Functions (C.Fn)

What Custom Functions Are

Custom Functions are a set of advanced configuration options on the Canon EOS R10 that modify how the camera's core systems behave at a level below the standard menu settings. While the standard menu settings control what settings are applied, Custom Functions control how the controls and systems work — the increment size of exposure adjustments, what happens when you half-press the shutter, how the AF point moves across the frame, and similar low-level operational behaviours.

Most photographers will use the Custom Functions settings infrequently — once configured to suit a preferred working style, they rarely need changing. They are not day-to-day adjustments but permanent configurations of how the camera operates.

How to Access Custom Functions

11. Press MENU and rotate the Main Dial to the yellow Setup tab.
12. Scroll down to Custom Functions (C.Fn) and press SET.
13. The Custom Functions list appears. Scroll through the numbered functions using the Quick Control Dial.
14. To change a function, highlight it and press SET. The available options for that function appear. Scroll to the desired option and press SET to confirm.
15. Press MENU when finished. All changes take effect immediately.

Custom Functions Available on the R10

C.Fn 1 **Exposure level increments** — Sets the size of each increment when you rotate a dial to change shutter speed, aperture, or exposure compensation. The default is 1/3 stop — each click of the Main Dial or Quick Control Dial changes the value by one third of a stop. Setting this to 1/2 stop makes each increment half a stop, meaning fewer dial clicks to move between common exposure values but less fine-grained control between them. Most photographers leave this at 1/3 stop for the finest available control. Switch to 1/2 stop if you find the 1/3-stop increments too granular for your workflow and prefer the coarser but faster 1/2-stop steps.

C.Fn 2 **ISO speed setting increments** — Sets the increment size specifically for ISO adjustments, independently of the general exposure increment in C.Fn 1. The default is 1/3 stop, matching the general increment. Setting it to 1 stop means the ISO dial clicks through whole stops only — ISO 100, 200, 400, 800, 1600, 3200 — rather than the intermediate values between them. Whole-stop ISO increments are simpler to reason about when you are calculating exposure mentally, but they reduce your ability to fine-tune the ISO for precise exposure balance.

C.Fn 3 **Bracketing auto cancel** — Controls whether Auto Exposure Bracketing (AEB) resets after the camera has fired the full bracket sequence. When set to Enable (the default), after the three-frame bracket sequence completes — one underexposed, one at the metered level, one overexposed — the AEB setting automatically resets to zero and the camera returns to single-shot mode. When set to Disable, the AEB setting persists after the sequence and the camera continues shooting in three-shot brackets with every subsequent press of the shutter until you manually clear it. Disable is preferred by photographers who regularly shoot extensive bracketed sequences and do not want to re-enable AEB after every three-shot set. Enable is safer for occasional use, where forgetting that AEB is still active could result in unexpectedly shooting three-shot sequences when you intend single shots.

C.Fn 4 **Shutter button / AF-ON** — This is the Custom Function most directly related to the back-button focus technique described in Section 4.4. It controls what the half-press of the shutter button does in relation to autofocus. The default setting (0: Metering and AF start) makes the shutter half-press activate both metering and autofocus simultaneously, which is the standard operation. Setting this to 1: Metering start (AF disabled) removes autofocus from the shutter half-press entirely — the shutter half-press only activates metering. Setting it to 3: AE lock / AF start reverses the roles of the shutter button and AE lock button, with the shutter half-press locking exposure and the AE lock button activating AF. Note that this Custom Function provides a global change to the shutter half-press behaviour, while the Custom Controls screen (Section 16.1) provides per-button assignment of individual functions — both tools affect the same behaviours but at different levels of granularity.

C.Fn 5 **AF point selection movement** — Controls what happens when you push the joystick to move the active AF point and it reaches the edge of the available AF area. When set to Stops at AF area edges (the default), the AF point stops at the boundary and cannot be moved further in that direction — it is bounded. When set to Continuous, the AF point wraps around: pushing right from the rightmost point causes the point to reappear at the leftmost edge, and vice versa. Continuous wrap is useful for photographers who frequently need to move the AF point across the full width or height of the frame quickly — wrapping saves the time of crossing the entire frame one step at a time. Stops at edges is more intuitive for photographers who prefer the AF point to stay where it is without jumping unexpectedly.

C.Fn 6 **Add image verification data** — Appends a digital verification signature to each image file that can be used to confirm the image has not been altered since it left the camera. When enabled, Canon's Original Data Security Kit software can verify whether a given image file matches the signature embedded at capture. This function is relevant in legal, journalistic, and evidentiary photography contexts where proving an image is unaltered is important. For general photography, this function has no practical effect and can be left at its default off setting.

C.Fn 7 **Magnification (approx.)** — Sets the default zoom level that the camera displays when you use the Magnify button to zoom into the AF point area during manual focus live view. The options are 1x (no magnification — shows the full frame when the magnify button is pressed), 5x, and 10x. Setting the default to 10x means the first press of the Magnify button during manual focus zooms immediately to full pixel-level magnification, allowing precise focus evaluation without requiring multiple button presses to reach maximum zoom. For photographers who regularly use manual focus with MF magnification as part of their workflow, setting the default to 10x saves time on every shot.

C.Fn 8 **AF during BULB** — Controls whether the Canon EOS R10's autofocus system operates during BULB exposures. BULB mode keeps the shutter open for as long as the button is held, and is used for very long exposures — typically seconds to minutes. The default setting is Disable, which prevents AF from operating during a BULB exposure. This is appropriate for most BULB shooting situations (astrophotography, long-exposure night scenes, light painting) where the subject is static and there is insufficient light for AF to operate usefully anyway. Setting to Enable allows AF to operate during BULB exposures for situations where the subject may move during a long exposure and you want the camera to attempt to maintain focus — though in practice, the low light levels typical of BULB shooting usually prevent AF from operating effectively regardless of this setting.

Resetting Custom Functions

To return all Custom Functions to their factory default values without affecting any other camera settings: from within the Custom Functions list screen, scroll to the bottom of the list and look for the Clear all C.Fn option. Press SET and confirm with OK. All Custom Functions reset to their defaults immediately.

Alternatively, performing a full Clear all camera settings from the Setup menu resets all settings including Custom Functions, but also resets every other camera configuration simultaneously — date, time, Wi-Fi pairings, My Menu, Custom Controls, and all shooting settings. Use Clear all C.Fn specifically when you want to reset only the Custom Functions without disturbing the rest of your setup.

Note: *Custom Functions settings are included when you save camera settings to an SD card using Camera user settings in the Setup menu. This means that if you configure a complete camera setup — Custom Controls, My Menu, and Custom Functions all configured for your workflow — you can save the entire configuration to a card and restore it later on the same camera after a reset, or load it onto a second R10 body to maintain a consistent setup across multiple bodies.*

Tip: *New to Custom Functions and not sure where to start? The three changes that have the most practical impact on everyday shooting are: setting C.Fn 4 to Metering start (AF disabled) if you want to set up back-button focus via Custom Controls, setting C.Fn 7 to 10x magnification if you use manual focus regularly, and leaving everything else at the default until a specific operational need arises that one of the other functions addresses. Making too many changes simultaneously makes it difficult to evaluate which change produced which result — adjust one function, shoot for a session, and assess before changing another.*

PART 17 — Maintenance and Care

The Canon EOS R10 is a precision optical instrument and electronic device. Treating it well extends its working life, protects the quality of your images, and prevents avoidable failures in the field. This part covers sensor cleaning, physical protection, battery care, and keeping the camera's firmware up to date — the four maintenance tasks that every R10 owner should understand and perform regularly.

17.1 Sensor Cleaning

How Dust Gets onto the Sensor

The Canon EOS R10's image sensor is located at the back of the lens mount, behind a thin protective glass layer. When you change lenses, the lens mount is exposed to the surrounding air — and airborne dust particles can enter through the mount opening and settle on the sensor's protective glass. Even with careful technique, some dust transfer is inevitable over time, particularly if you change lenses frequently outdoors, in dusty or sandy environments, or in any location with elevated particulate matter in the air.

Dust on the sensor does not affect the camera's mechanical function, but it does appear in your images. Dust particles cast small shadows onto the sensor surface during the exposure, appearing as dark spots or blobs in the image — most visible in out-of-focus areas and at small apertures where the increased depth of field makes the shadow sharper and more defined. A single large dust particle at f/16 can produce a clearly visible dark circle in a plain sky or other smooth tonal area. Multiple particles produce multiple spots across the image, which become time-consuming to remove in editing software if present on every frame.

The Automatic Sensor Cleaning System

The Canon EOS R10 has a built-in automatic sensor cleaning mechanism that activates by default each time the camera is powered on and each time it is powered off. The system vibrates the sensor's protective glass at ultrasonic frequency for a few seconds, shaking loose any dust particles that have settled on the surface. The dislodged particles fall away from the sensor into a collection area at the bottom of the chamber where they cannot affect the image.

The automatic cleaning is invisible and silent — you will not see or hear it operating. The only evidence is a brief delay of approximately one to two seconds when powering on and off while the cleaning cycle completes. This delay is normal and not a fault.

You can configure when automatic cleaning occurs by going to MENU → Setup tab → Sensor cleaning → Auto cleaning. The options are Enable (cleans on power on and power off — the default), Clean on start-up only, Clean on shutdown only, or Disable. The default Enable setting is appropriate for most users. Disable it only in situations where the startup and shutdown delay is unacceptable — professional run-and-gun video work, for example — and re-enable it for normal shooting.

Triggering a Manual Cleaning Cycle

If you notice dust spots in your images and want to run the vibration cleaning cycle without powering the camera off and on, you can trigger it manually at any time.

1. Press MENU and navigate to the yellow Setup tab.
2. Scroll to Sensor cleaning and press SET.
3. The Sensor cleaning sub-menu opens showing three options: Auto cleaning, Clean now, and Manual cleaning.
4. Select Clean now and press SET.
5. The camera runs the ultrasonic vibration cleaning cycle immediately. The process takes a few seconds. The camera displays a cleaning indicator on screen while it operates.
6. When the cycle is complete, the camera returns to the Sensor cleaning menu. Press MENU to close it and return to shooting.

Run a manual cleaning cycle after any lens change in a dusty environment, after bringing the camera in from very cold to very warm conditions (condensation can attract dust), and any time you notice new spots appearing in images that were not there previously.

Checking for Dust Spots

To check whether your sensor has dust that needs addressing, photograph a plain, evenly lit surface — a white wall, a clear blue sky, or a piece of white paper

— at a small aperture (f/11 or f/16) with the camera slightly out of focus. Any dust spots will appear as clearly visible dark circles in the flat-toned image. Note their positions. After running a cleaning cycle, photograph the same surface at the same settings and compare — spots that have disappeared were removed by the cleaning. Spots that remain are more stubborn particles that were not dislodged.

Dust Delete Data — Software Removal

For dust spots that survive multiple automatic cleaning cycles, the Canon EOS R10 offers a supplementary tool called Dust Delete Data. This function photographs a white reference surface and records the precise position of any remaining dust spots on the sensor. When you open RAW files captured after the Dust Delete Data was taken in Canon's Digital Photo Professional software, the software automatically removes the corresponding dark spots from each image using the recorded position data.

7. Press MENU and navigate to Shooting Menu 4.
8. Scroll to Dust Delete Data and press SET.
9. A prompt explains the procedure. Press OK to continue.
10. The camera instructs you to photograph a plain white surface at approximately 20 to 30 centimetres distance. Use a white wall, a sheet of white paper, or any plain light-coloured surface with no pattern or texture. The surface should fill the entire frame.
11. Set the camera to Av mode and the widest available aperture on the attached lens. Do not worry about precise focus — the test shot is used for dust position mapping, not image quality.
12. Point the camera at the white surface and press the shutter fully. The camera photographs the surface and automatically analyses the image to identify dust spot positions.
13. The Dust Delete Data is stored in the camera and embedded into the EXIF metadata of every RAW file captured from this point forward, until you update the data by repeating the process.

Update the Dust Delete Data whenever you notice new dust spots appearing after a cleaning cycle has failed to remove them, or after any manual sensor cleaning.

Manual Sensor Cleaning — When Automatic Methods Fail

If the automatic ultrasonic cleaning system and the Dust Delete Data workaround are insufficient for your needs — for example, if a stubborn particle is producing a very visible spot in the centre of the frame and you need it physically removed — manual sensor cleaning is possible but requires careful consideration.

To place the mirror in the locked-up position for sensor cleaning access: press MENU → Setup tab → Sensor cleaning → Manual cleaning and press SET. The camera raises the shutter and locks it in the open position, exposing the sensor surface. The camera must remain powered on during manual cleaning — the shutter drops immediately when the camera powers off.

> **Important:** *Manual sensor cleaning carries a genuine risk of damage to the sensor if performed incorrectly. The sensor surface is extremely delicate — contact with an incorrect tool, excessive pressure, or contaminated cleaning materials can cause permanent scratches or coating damage that cannot be repaired without professional sensor replacement. If you have never cleaned a mirrorless sensor before, take the camera to an authorised Canon service centre for professional cleaning. If you are experienced with sensor cleaning and choose to do it yourself, use only purpose-made sensor cleaning swabs of the correct size for APS-C sensors and Eclipse-type sensor cleaning fluid. Never use compressed air canisters directly on the sensor surface — the propellant can freeze on contact with the sensor coating and leave residue. Never touch the sensor with anything not designed explicitly for sensor cleaning.*

> **Tip:** *The single most effective way to reduce sensor dust accumulation is to change lenses as infrequently as possible, in the cleanest available environment, with the camera pointing downward so that falling particles do not land on the exposed sensor. When you must change lenses outdoors, turn your back to the wind, shield the camera with your body, keep the lens cap and body cap close at hand, and complete the change quickly. Fewer lens changes in dirty environments means fewer dust problems over the life of the camera.*

17.2 Protecting the Camera

Weather Sealing — What the R10 Has and Does Not Have

The Canon EOS R10 is not weather-sealed. It does not have the dust-resistant and moisture-resistant gaskets around the buttons, dials, ports, and seams that weather-sealed Canon bodies (such as the R7, R5, or professional 1-series bodies) incorporate. This means the R10 has no built-in resistance to rain, splashing water, dust infiltration through gaps in the body, or sand ingress.

Exposing the R10 to rain without protection risks water entering through the mode dial, the port flaps, the battery door seam, or the SD card door. Even moderate rain exposure over a short period can introduce moisture into the camera body that causes corrosion of electrical contacts, shorts in circuit boards, or fungal growth on internal optical elements — any of which can cause permanent damage. Sand is similarly damaging — individual grains that work their way into the dial mechanisms or button gaps can cause abrasion and mechanical failure.

This does not mean the R10 cannot be used outdoors or in imperfect conditions — many photographers use it in the field without problems. It means you must actively protect it when conditions deteriorate, rather than assuming the camera can tolerate the exposure.

Protection in the Field

In light rain or fine mist: cover the camera with a rain sleeve — an inexpensive transparent plastic bag with an elastic opening designed to slip over the camera and lens while still allowing operation through the material. These are available from camera accessory retailers and collapse to almost nothing in a bag when not needed. Alternatively, use your camera bag's rain cover over the bag when you are not actively shooting, and retrieve the camera only during dry intervals.

In heavy rain: do not use the R10 without a weather housing — a rigid underwater-rated housing that fully encapsulates the camera and provides direct control of all buttons through sealed external controls. Weather housings are available from manufacturers such as Ikelite and others for the R10 specifically.

In sand or dust: keep the camera in the bag or case when not shooting. Check that the rubber port flaps on the left side are fully closed before exposure to dusty air. Avoid changing lenses in sandy environments — any sand that enters the lens mount can travel to the sensor during the exposure of the mount opening. If sand does get onto the body exterior, use a soft brush to sweep it away before opening any doors or moving any dials, to prevent grinding it into the mechanism.

In extreme cold: protect the camera from rapid temperature changes. Bringing a cold camera into a warm humid environment causes condensation — moisture from the warm air condenses on the cold metal and glass surfaces inside and outside the camera. Place the camera in a sealed plastic bag before bringing it indoors from cold conditions, and leave it in the bag for 30 to 60 minutes while it gradually warms to room temperature. The condensation forms on the outside of the bag rather than on the camera surfaces. Remove the camera from the bag only after it has reached or is close to room temperature.

Storage and Transport

Never store the Canon EOS R10 without a body cap or lens attached. The lens mount opening is a direct path for dust and insects to reach the sensor chamber. Attach the body cap — the white plastic cap that came in the box — whenever removing a lens for transport or storage. Keep a spare body cap in your camera bag.

Store the camera in a dry environment. High humidity encourages fungal growth inside the lens and on the sensor's protective glass — a problem that is expensive to remediate and may require professional service. In humid climates, store the camera in an airtight container with silica gel desiccant packets that absorb moisture from the enclosed air. Rechargeable silica gel containers, which can be regenerated by heating in an oven, are available from camera retailers and provide ongoing humidity control without replacement.

For transport, use a camera bag or case with adequate padding around the camera body and lens. Foam-padded dedicated camera bags protect against impact from drops and knocks. Avoid placing the camera in a general bag where it can shift around against hard objects. When travelling by air, carry the camera and lenses in a hand-carry bag rather than checked luggage — checked bags are subject to pressure changes, rough handling, and temperature extremes that can damage delicate equipment.

Cleaning the Camera Body

The camera body exterior can be cleaned with a soft, lint-free cloth — a microfibre cloth is ideal. For stubborn marks, lightly dampen the cloth with clean water. Never use solvents, alcohol, abrasive cloths, or cleaning sprays directly on the camera body, as these can damage the rubberised grip coating, the paint finish, or the LCD screen's anti-reflective coating.

The LCD screen should be cleaned with a dry or very lightly dampened microfibre cloth only. Do not press hard on the screen — the LCD panel beneath the protective glass is delicate and can be damaged by sustained pressure.

The lens contacts on the camera mount — the row of small gold electrical pins around the inner edge of the lens mount — should be kept clean and free of fingerprints. If the contacts become dirty or corroded, use a clean, dry cotton bud (cotton swab) to gently wipe the surface of each contact. Do not use any liquid on the contacts. Dirty contacts can cause communication errors between the camera and lens.

17.3 Battery Care

Understanding the LP-E17 Battery

The Canon EOS R10 uses the LP-E17 lithium-ion rechargeable battery. Lithium-ion batteries have specific characteristics that affect their performance and longevity — understanding these helps you get the best service life from your batteries and avoid situations where power failure interrupts a shoot.

A fully charged LP-E17 provides approximately 210 to 330 shots per charge under the CIPA measurement standard — the variation depends on conditions. Live view use, frequent autofocus operation, extended playback review, and Wi-Fi and Bluetooth activity all draw additional power beyond the basic shutter count. Cold weather significantly reduces available capacity. In practice, expect 200 to 250 shots per charge under normal mixed conditions, and plan accordingly.

Charging the Battery

Charge the LP-E17 using the included LC-E17 or LC-E17E charger, or via the camera's USB-C port using a compatible USB power adapter. The USB-C charging method charges the battery while it remains inside the camera — useful for topping up between sessions without removing the battery — but charges at a slower rate than the dedicated LC-E17 charger.

The LC-E17 charger fully charges a depleted LP-E17 in approximately two hours. The charge lamp glows orange during charging and turns green when fully charged. Remove the battery from the charger promptly when the lamp turns green — leaving it in the charger after full charge is complete is not damaging with modern lithium-ion batteries, but is an unnecessary habit.

Do not attempt to charge the LP-E17 with any charger other than the LC-E17, LC-E17E, or Canon-approved third-party chargers specifically rated for the LP-E17. Incorrect chargers may apply wrong voltage or current, causing overheating, swelling, or permanent capacity reduction.

Long-Term Storage of Batteries

Lithium-ion batteries should not be stored fully charged or fully depleted for extended periods. Both extremes stress the battery chemistry and reduce long-term capacity.

If you will not be using the Canon EOS R10 for more than a few weeks — during a holiday period, a change in photographic work, or seasonal storage — discharge the battery to approximately 40 to 60 percent charge before storing it. This is around the mid-range of the battery's state-of-charge indicator on the camera display. Store the battery in a dry environment at room temperature, away from direct sunlight and heat sources.

Check stored batteries every one to three months and recharge them briefly if they have self-discharged below approximately 30 percent. Lithium-ion batteries lose a small amount of charge through self-discharge even when not in use. Very deeply discharged lithium-ion batteries may become impossible to revive — if a stored battery is left depleted for months, it may no longer accept a charge and must be replaced.

Cold Weather Battery Performance

Lithium-ion battery capacity drops significantly in cold temperatures. At 0°C (32°F), an LP-E17 may deliver only 60 to 70 percent of its normal capacity. At minus 10°C (14°F), capacity can fall to 50 percent or below. This is not a permanent reduction — once the battery warms up, full capacity returns — but in the field on a cold day, you may find the battery indicator dropping much faster than expected.

14. Carry at least one spare LP-E17 whenever shooting in cold conditions. Warm it in an inside jacket pocket — close to your body — between uses. A warm battery placed in the camera immediately before shooting will have better initial capacity than one left exposed to the cold in a camera bag.
15. Keep the camera under your coat or in an insulated camera bag between shots when shooting in very cold conditions. The camera stays warmer and the battery drains more slowly.
16. If the battery indicator shows very low and the camera shuts down in cold conditions, remove the battery and warm it in your hands or pocket for a minute or two. Replacing it in the camera may give you additional shots from the recovered capacity — enough for the image you need.

Recognising and Replacing a Degraded Battery

Lithium-ion batteries have a finite number of charge cycles — each complete charge and discharge cycle reduces the battery's maximum capacity slightly. After several hundred cycles, the battery may hold only 70 or 80 percent of its original capacity, meaning noticeably fewer shots per charge than when new. This gradual degradation is normal and expected.

Signs that an LP-E17 needs replacement: the battery drains significantly faster than it used to under the same shooting conditions; the camera shuts down unexpectedly while the battery indicator shows more than one bar of charge remaining; the battery feels warm or hot during normal use (not just after a long charging session); or the battery has physically swollen — a swollen battery should be removed from use immediately and disposed of at a battery recycling point, as swelling indicates internal chemical breakdown.

Purchase replacement LP-E17 batteries from Canon directly or from authorised Canon retailers. Third-party LP-E17 compatible batteries vary widely in quality — some perform adequately but many have lower actual capacity than genuine Canon batteries, less reliable charge indicators, or quality control issues that can cause erratic camera behaviour or safety concerns. Canon genuine batteries are the reliable choice.

Important: *Do not attempt to disassemble, repair, short-circuit, or heat a lithium-ion battery. Damaged or improperly handled lithium-ion batteries can catch fire or explode. If a battery shows signs of damage — cracks, leaking electrolyte, severe swelling, or failure to charge after multiple attempts — dispose of it at a designated battery recycling facility and replace it with a new genuine LP-E17.*

17.4 Firmware Updates

What Firmware Updates Do

Firmware is the software that runs inside the Canon EOS R10's processor and controls every aspect of how the camera operates — the menu system, the autofocus algorithms, the shutter control, the image processing pipeline, the wireless connectivity, and the compatibility layer between camera and lenses. Canon periodically releases firmware updates that improve or extend these systems after the camera is released.

Firmware updates can add entirely new features to the camera — such as expanded subject detection capabilities, new autofocus modes, additional video recording formats, or improved compatibility with newly released lenses. They can improve the performance of existing features — faster autofocus response, better tracking behaviour, reduced hunting. They can fix bugs or errors that were present in previous firmware versions. And they can extend the camera's compatibility with new accessories, adapters, or communication protocols that did not exist when the camera was first released.

Keeping the R10's firmware up to date ensures you have access to the full current capability of the camera. Canon does not charge for firmware updates — they are free downloads from Canon's website.

Checking Your Current Firmware Version

17. Press MENU on the Canon EOS R10.
18. Rotate the Main Dial to navigate to the yellow Setup tab.
19. Scroll to the bottom of the Setup menu list. The last item is Firmware. Press SET to open it.

20. The current firmware version installed on the camera is displayed — for example, Version 1.1.0 or Version 2.0.0. Note this number.

21. To check whether a newer version is available, go to Canon's official website — canon.com — on a computer or smartphone, navigate to the support section, and search for EOS R10 firmware. The latest available firmware version for your region is listed on that page with its version number. If the listed version is higher than the version displayed on your camera, an update is available.

Downloading the Firmware File

22. On Canon's website, navigate to the EOS R10 support page and find the Firmware section.

23. Select the firmware download for your region (Americas, Europe, Asia, and so on — the firmware content is the same but the download pages are region-specific).

24. Download the firmware file to your computer. The file is typically named something like EOS_R10_FIRMWARE_X.X.X.FIR where X.X.X is the version number. Note where you save it.

25. Do not open, rename, or modify the downloaded file in any way. The camera reads the file by its exact name and format — any change prevents the update from being recognised.

Copying the Firmware to the SD Card

26. Insert a formatted SD card into your computer's card reader, or connect the Canon EOS R10 to the computer via USB and use the camera's card as a removable drive as described in Section 15.3.

27. Copy the firmware .FIR file directly to the root level of the SD card — not into any folder. The root level is the first level you see when you open the card in your file manager, before entering any sub-folders such as DCIM. The camera searches for the firmware file at the root level only and will not find it if it is inside a folder.

28. Safely eject the SD card from the computer and insert it into the Canon EOS R10.

Performing the Firmware Update

29. Ensure the Canon EOS R10 has a fully charged battery installed — a battery level of at least 50 percent is the minimum recommendation, but starting with a full charge is strongly preferred. If the battery runs out during a firmware update, the camera may be left in an unbootable

state requiring service to recover. Do not use USB power alone during a firmware update — the battery must be installed.

30. With the SD card containing the firmware file inserted, press MENU and navigate to the Firmware item in the Setup tab.
31. Press SET on Firmware. The camera detects the firmware file on the card and displays its version number alongside the currently installed version, confirming it has found the file.
32. Select Update and press SET. A confirmation screen asks whether to proceed with the update. Read the confirmation carefully, then select OK and press SET.
33. The camera begins the update process. A progress bar appears on screen. The process typically takes two to five minutes. Do not press any buttons, rotate any dials, remove the battery, remove the SD card, or allow the camera to be powered off during this time. Do not close the rubber port flaps, open the battery door, or touch the camera in any way while the update is in progress.
34. When the update completes successfully, the camera displays a completion message and restarts automatically. The camera powers off and back on as part of the restart sequence.
35. After the camera has restarted, press MENU → Setup tab → Firmware and confirm that the version number now shows the new version you installed. This confirms the update was applied successfully.

If the Update Fails

If the firmware update fails partway through — indicated by an error message on screen, the camera freezing, or the camera shutting off unexpectedly — do not panic. The camera has a recovery mode that allows a failed firmware update to be reattempted. Remove the battery, wait 30 seconds, reinsert it, and attempt the update again from the beginning. If the update fails repeatedly, check that the firmware file on the SD card is intact (re-download it from Canon's website and copy it again), that the SD card is not corrupted (try a different card), and that the battery is fully charged.

If the camera does not power on normally after a failed update, contact Canon's customer support or an authorised Canon service centre. Do not attempt to force the camera to operate or try alternative recovery methods — only Canon-trained technicians have access to the service tools needed to recover a camera from a failed firmware installation.

Important: *Never install firmware downloaded from any website other than Canon's official national or regional website (for example, canon.com, canon.co.uk, canon.com.au). Third-party firmware files are not authorised by Canon and can cause permanent damage to the camera's operating system. Canon does not provide unofficial or beta firmware for public download — any such file is either fraudulent or a risk.*

Note: *After a successful firmware update, Canon recommends performing a full Clear all camera settings from the Setup menu to ensure no legacy settings conflict with any new firmware features or changed menu structures. Make a note of your key settings — Custom Controls, My Menu items, Custom Functions, and shooting preferences — before clearing, so you can restore them promptly after the reset.*

Tip: *Subscribe to Canon's email newsletter or check the EOS R10 support page on Canon's website every few months to stay informed about new firmware releases. Significant updates — particularly those that improve autofocus performance or add new capabilities — are worth installing promptly. Minor bug-fix releases can be evaluated case by case depending on whether the fixed issue affected your shooting.*

PART 18 — Troubleshooting

Most problems you will encounter with the Canon EOS R10 have straightforward causes and equally straightforward solutions. This part works through the most common issues, their likely causes, and the steps to resolve each one — in the order you should try them. Work through the steps for your issue sequentially rather than jumping ahead, as earlier steps often resolve the problem before the later ones are needed.

18.1 Camera Will Not Turn On

When the Canon EOS R10 does not respond when you slide the ON/OFF switch to the ON position — no LCD activity, no EVF activation, no sound — work through the following checks in order.

Check the ON/OFF Switch Position

The ON/OFF switch is a rotating collar that surrounds the shutter button on the top of the camera. It has two positions: ON (rotated clockwise to the position away from you) and OFF (rotated counter-clockwise back toward you). It is easy to feel these positions without looking at the camera, but confirm visually that the switch is fully in the ON position and has not stopped partway. A switch that is between positions may not make the electrical contact needed to start the camera.

Check the Battery Charge and Insertion

1. Remove the battery from the camera by opening the battery compartment door on the base of the camera, pressing the orange release lever inside the compartment, and pulling the battery free.
2. Examine the battery. Check that the gold contact pins on the end of the battery are clean and unobstructed. If they are dirty or corroded, wipe them gently with a clean, dry cloth.
3. Check the battery charge indicator. Place the battery in the LC-E17 charger — if the charge lamp glows orange, the battery is partially or fully depleted and is charging. If the lamp glows green immediately, the battery is fully charged. If the lamp does not light at all, the battery may be faulty or completely exhausted beyond the charger's ability to recover it.

4. Allow a depleted battery to charge fully, then re-insert it into the camera. Slide the ON/OFF switch to ON and check whether the camera activates.

Try a Different Battery

If the camera still does not turn on after confirming the battery is fully charged and correctly inserted, try a different LP-E17 battery if one is available. If the camera turns on with the second battery, the original battery has failed and needs replacement. If the camera still does not turn on with a known-good battery, the issue is with the camera body itself.

Check for Automatic Power Off

If the camera was previously on and appears to have shut off by itself, the Auto power off timer may have activated. The camera shuts off automatically after a set idle period — by default one to three minutes depending on firmware version and settings. Half-press the shutter button to wake the camera from auto power-off. If it wakes, the camera is functioning normally and no further action is needed. Adjust the Auto power off timer in MENU → Setup tab → Power saving if the current timeout is too short for your workflow.

Inspect for Physical Damage

Examine the battery compartment contacts inside the camera — the small metal pins that touch the battery terminals. If these are bent, corroded, or visibly damaged, the camera cannot make electrical contact with the battery. This type of damage requires professional repair — do not attempt to straighten bent contacts yourself as this risks breaking them entirely. Contact an authorised Canon service centre.

Important: *If the Canon EOS R10 was recently exposed to moisture, condensation, or a liquid spill and will not turn on, do not attempt to force it on. Remove the battery immediately and leave the camera in a dry environment with the battery door open for at least 24 to 48 hours before attempting to power it on again. Attempting to operate a wet camera can short-circuit internal components and cause permanent damage. If moisture ingress is suspected, bring the camera to a Canon service centre for inspection before use.*

18.2 Images Are Blurry

Blurry images are the most common technical complaint in photography and have several distinct causes that produce different types of blur. Identifying which type of blur you are seeing points directly to the cause and the solution.

Overall Softness Across the Entire Frame — Camera Shake

If the entire image is soft and slightly smeared — not just one subject but everything including the background — the cause is almost certainly camera shake: the camera moved during the exposure. This is distinct from focus blur, where the subject is sharp but in the wrong place, or motion blur, where the subject itself has moved.

Camera shake occurs when the shutter speed is too slow for the focal length of the lens being used while handholding the camera. A commonly used rule of thumb is that the minimum safe handheld shutter speed equals 1 divided by the focal length in millimetres — at 50mm, 1/50 sec is the minimum; at 200mm, 1/200 sec is the minimum. With the Canon EOS R10's APS-C sensor multiplying the effective focal length by 1.6x, apply the rule to the effective focal length — a 50mm lens on the R10 behaves like an 80mm, so 1/80 sec (or 1/100 sec to be safe) is the minimum.

5. Check the shutter speed shown in the EXIF data of the blurry image — press the Playback button and then INFO to see the shooting data. Note the shutter speed that was used.
6. If the shutter speed was slower than 1 divided by your effective focal length, increase the shutter speed for the next shot. In Tv or M mode, rotate the Main Dial clockwise to a faster shutter speed. In P or Av mode, increase the ISO or open the aperture to allow the camera to select a faster shutter speed.
7. If image stabilisation is available on the attached lens, confirm it is enabled. The IS switch on the lens barrel should be in the IS ON position.
8. If the subject and scene permit, mount the camera on a tripod or support it against a stable surface — a wall, a fence post, a table. Any stable contact reduces camera shake significantly.
9. Use the 2-second self-timer (Section 11.2) for tripod shots to eliminate the shutter-press vibration.

Sharp Background, Blurry Subject — Motion Blur

If the background is sharp but the subject is blurred — appearing streaked or smeared in the direction of its movement — the subject was moving faster than the shutter speed could freeze it. The camera is working correctly and the focus may even be perfectly placed, but the subject moved during the exposure.

10. Increase the shutter speed to freeze the subject's motion. Switch to Tv mode and set a faster shutter speed — for walking subjects, 1/250 sec is usually sufficient; for running subjects or sports, 1/500 sec to 1/1000 sec; for very fast subjects such as birds in flight, 1/2000 sec or faster.
11. If increasing the shutter speed produces a correct exposure warning (the aperture value blinks), raise the ISO to compensate for the reduced light. Use the M-Fn button shortcut to adjust ISO quickly while staying in Tv mode.
12. Switch the drive mode to High-speed continuous and hold the shutter through the action — reviewing multiple frames gives you a higher chance that one frame was captured during a momentarily still phase of the subject's motion.

Blurry Subject, Sharp Background at Incorrect Distance — Focus Error

If the background at a different distance appears sharp while the intended subject is soft, the camera has focused on the wrong element of the scene. This is a focus placement error rather than a motion or shake problem.

13. During playback, press the Magnify button and use the joystick to inspect the area where the camera focused. Look for what is sharp — this reveals where focus actually landed. Use the AF point display (enable it in the Playback menu if not already active) to see which AF point was active when the shot was taken.
14. If the AF point was on the intended subject but the image is still soft, check whether depth of field was simply too shallow at the chosen aperture — at f/1.8 and close range, the depth of field may be only a few centimetres. Narrow the aperture (increase the f-number) to bring more of the subject within the depth of field.
15. If the AF point was on the wrong element of the scene, reposition the active AF point using the joystick or touch screen before the next shot so it is directly on the subject. Or switch to Whole-Area AF with People

or subject detection active to let the camera track the subject automatically.

16. If the lens has an AF/MF switch, confirm it is set to AF. If it is on MF, the autofocus system is disabled and the focus ring position determines focus — which may not be at the subject distance.

Blurry in One Corner or Edge — Lens Issue

If the centre of the image is sharp but one corner or edge is soft, the cause is likely optical — either the lens's natural softness at wide apertures toward the edges, or a lens alignment problem. Most lenses are softer at the extreme edges at wide apertures, improving as the aperture is narrowed. If the softness is severe and is present at all apertures in an asymmetric pattern (one corner much softer than the opposite corner), the lens may have a decentering fault. This requires professional lens servicing.

Consistently Soft Despite Correct Focus Confirmation — Lens Cleaning

If autofocus confirms with a green dot and a beep and the image still appears soft overall, check the front element of the lens for smudges, fingerprints, dust, or condensation. Hold the lens toward a light and examine the front glass surface. Even a light film of skin oil from a fingertip contact can reduce contrast and apparent sharpness significantly. Clean the front element with a lens cleaning cloth — breathe gently on the element to create a light moisture layer, then wipe in a circular motion from centre to edge with the cleaning cloth. Never use paper tissues, clothing, or abrasive materials on a lens element.

18.3 Camera Will Not Focus

When the Canon EOS R10 fails to achieve autofocus — the AF frame blinks orange, no green confirmation appears, the camera hunts back and forth without settling, or the image remains soft despite repeated half-presses — work through the following checks.

Confirm the Lens Is in AF Mode

17. Look at the lens barrel for a small switch labelled AF and MF. If the switch is in the MF position, autofocus is disabled at the lens level — slide it to AF.

18. If the lens has no AF/MF switch, confirm from the camera side: press MENU → Shooting Menu 6 → AF operation. If the mode shown is Manual Focus, change it to One-Shot AF, Servo AF, or AI Focus as appropriate for your subject.

Confirm the Lens Is Fully Attached

A lens that is not fully locked into the mount — one that did not click firmly into place — cannot communicate with the camera's autofocus system. Remove the lens by pressing the lens release button and rotating it counter-clockwise, then reattach it, aligning the red dots and rotating clockwise until you feel and hear the click of the lock engaging. Give the lens a gentle counter-clockwise tug to confirm it will not rotate — if it rotates freely, it is not locked and must be reattached.

Insufficient Light or Contrast

The Canon EOS R10's Dual Pixel CMOS AF requires visible contrast in the scene to calculate focus. In very low light or when pointed at a subject with very little contrast — a plain white wall, a clear blue sky, a uniformly coloured surface — the phase-detection system may be unable to find sufficient information to calculate the focus direction and distance.

19. In low light: check whether the AF-assist beam is active. The AF-assist beam is the small orange-red light on the front of the camera that emits a brief illumination pattern to help the camera find contrast on the subject. It activates automatically in One-Shot AF mode when the scene is too dark for unaided AF. If it is not firing, check MENU → Setup tab → that the beam has not been disabled by a prior setting change.
20. Point the AF point at a higher-contrast area of the subject — the edge where the subject meets its background, a visible texture on the subject surface, or any area with a visible tonal transition — and half-press to focus. Once focus is locked, recompose to your intended frame and shoot without releasing the half-press.
21. If the scene is simply too dark for autofocus to work reliably at any contrast area, switch to manual focus: set the lens to MF and enable MF peaking (MENU → Shooting Menu 6 → MF peaking settings → Enable). Rotate the focus ring while watching the coloured peaking highlights appear on in-focus edges. Use the Magnify button to zoom into the EVF or LCD for precise focus confirmation before shooting.

Subject Too Close for the Lens

Every lens has a minimum focusing distance — the closest distance at which it can achieve focus. If you are trying to focus on a subject closer than the lens's minimum focusing distance, the AF system will hunt without confirming focus because no focus position within the lens's range can form a sharp image at that distance. Check the minimum focusing distance of your lens (printed on the lens barrel as a distance marking) and ensure your subject is beyond that distance. Move back from the subject until it is within the focusable range.

Subject Behind Glass or a Net

If there is a glass surface, mesh, wire, or any semi-transparent barrier between the camera and the subject — shooting through a car windscreen, a zoo enclosure, a window, or a net curtain — the autofocus system will typically focus on the nearest surface (the glass or mesh) rather than the subject beyond it. This is normal behaviour and not a fault.

To focus on the subject beyond a barrier: switch to manual focus, use the MF magnification to zoom in on the subject through the barrier, and rotate the focus ring until the subject (not the barrier) appears sharp in the magnified view. Press the Magnify button to return to full frame and shoot.

18.4 Memory Card Error

Memory card errors on the Canon EOS R10 appear as on-screen warnings — messages such as Card error, Cannot access card, or No card, or icon warnings in the shooting display. Most card errors have simple causes and can be resolved without losing your images.

Card Not Recognised or Cannot Be Accessed

22. Open the SD card slot door on the right side of the camera and remove the card. Inspect the gold contact strip along the bottom edge of the card — if it is visibly dirty or smudged, clean it gently with a dry lint-free cloth.
23. Reinsert the card firmly with the label facing toward the back of the camera and the notched corner going in first. Push until you feel it click into place. A card that is only partially inserted will not make reliable electrical contact.

24. Power the camera off and back on with the card inserted. The camera re-reads the card on startup and may recognise it after the restart.
25. If the error persists, remove the card and try it in a card reader connected to a computer. If the computer also cannot read the card, the card itself is faulty and should be replaced. If the computer reads it correctly, the problem may be with the camera's card reader contacts — try cleaning the contacts inside the card slot with a clean, dry cotton bud and retry.

Card Is Full

If the shooting display shows a full card indicator or a zero remaining shots count, the SD card is full and cannot accept any new images. To continue shooting, either delete images directly on the camera to free space (Playback button → select image → Delete button), or swap to a fresh SD card. Alternatively, connect the camera to a computer via USB and transfer the images before deleting them from the card.

Reformatting a Problem Card

If the card is not full but the camera reports errors reading or writing to it — images fail to save, playback shows corrupted files, or error messages appear during normal operation — reformatting the card inside the camera often resolves the issue by rebuilding the file structure from scratch.

26. Before formatting, connect the camera to a computer and transfer any images you want to keep — formatting permanently erases all data on the card.
27. Insert the card into the camera. Press MENU → Setup tab → Format card → OK.
28. The camera formats the card and displays a completion message when done. Try shooting a test image to confirm the error is resolved.

Card Compatibility and Speed Requirements

The Canon EOS R10 requires SD, SDHC, or SDXC memory cards. Not all SD cards are fast enough to handle the R10's write demands, particularly during burst shooting and 4K video recording. Using a card that is too slow causes the camera to pause during bursts (waiting for the buffer to empty), may cause the camera to stop recording video mid-clip, and can produce write errors during high-data-rate operations.

For all video recording and continuous burst shooting, use a card rated UHS Speed Class 3 (marked U3 on the card label — a U with the number 3 inside it) or Video Speed Class 30 (marked V30). For general still photography without extended bursts, a UHS Speed Class 1 card (U1) is adequate. Cards without a UHS Speed Class rating — older or very inexpensive cards — may cause problems with the R10's higher write speeds.

> **Tip:** *Always buy SD cards from established retailers and recognised brands. Counterfeit or misrepresented cards — sold as high-speed cards but actually containing slow components — are surprisingly common online. A card that genuinely does not meet its stated speed rating will produce unpredictable behaviour in the camera. Test any new card's actual write speed with a computer speed test utility before relying on it for important shoots.*

18.5 Battery Drains Quickly

The Canon EOS R10's LP-E17 battery provides approximately 210 to 330 shots per full charge under standard conditions. If you are getting significantly fewer shots than expected — or the battery indicator drops from full to empty in a short session — several specific causes and their solutions are listed below.

Display Brightness Too High

The rear LCD screen and the electronic viewfinder are among the largest power consumers in the camera. Running them at maximum brightness significantly shortens battery life compared to running them at a lower, still-adequate brightness.

29. Press MENU → Setup tab → LCD brightness. Use the Main Dial to reduce the brightness from its current level. Reduce it to the lowest level at which the image and information remain comfortably visible in your current environment.
30. In bright outdoor conditions where maximum brightness may be needed to see the screen, consider using the EVF more and the LCD less — the EVF is more power-efficient than the LCD at high brightness and is easier to see in sunlight regardless.

Wi-Fi and Bluetooth Active When Not Needed

The Wi-Fi and Bluetooth radios in the Canon EOS R10 consume power continuously when enabled, even if no device is actively connected. Leaving them active throughout a long shooting session causes noticeable additional battery drain.

31. When wireless connectivity is not needed for the current session, disable both: press MENU → Setup tab → Wi-Fi settings → select Wi-Fi and set to Disable. Similarly, press MENU → Setup tab → Bluetooth settings → Bluetooth function → Disable.
32. Re-enable them only when you need to connect to Camera Connect or transfer images. The connection re-establishes quickly after re-enabling.

Enable Eco Mode

33. Press MENU → Setup tab → Eco mode → On.

Eco mode reduces battery consumption by dimming the LCD screen after a short idle period and applying an aggressive auto-power-off schedule. The screen wakes immediately when you half-press the shutter, so Eco mode does not impair shooting readiness — it only saves power during the intervals between shots when the camera is idle. For sessions with long gaps between shots — street photography, event waiting, travel — Eco mode can meaningfully extend battery life.

Shorten the Auto Power Off Timer

34. Press MENU → Setup tab → Power saving → Auto power off.
35. Set the timer to 1 minute. The camera shuts off automatically after one minute of inactivity and wakes immediately when you half-press the shutter. This single change can significantly extend total battery life over a long day of intermittent shooting, because the camera is not running its sensor, processor, and displays continuously during the many minutes between shots.

Continuous AF Drawing Power

When Continuous AF is enabled in Shooting Menu 6, the camera runs its autofocus system continuously in the background even before you half-press the shutter — constantly evaluating the scene and adjusting focus. This background operation uses the processor and the lens drive motor continuously, which draws additional power. If you are shooting stationary or slow-moving subjects where Continuous AF provides no practical benefit, disable it: press MENU → Shooting

Menu 6 → Continuous AF → Disable. The camera still focuses normally when you half-press the shutter — it simply does not evaluate focus before you initiate it.

Battery Age or Cold Conditions

If the above steps do not resolve the fast drain, the battery itself may be the cause. An LP-E17 that has been through several hundred charge cycles loses capacity gradually. If the battery is several years old and was used regularly, replacing it with a new genuine Canon LP-E17 will restore the original performance. In cold conditions, a battery that appears to drain quickly will recover capacity when warmed — this is normal lithium-ion behaviour, not a fault. Carry a spare battery and keep it warm in a jacket pocket. Section 17.3 covers battery care and replacement in full.

18.6 Wi-Fi Will Not Connect

Wireless connection problems between the Canon EOS R10 and a smartphone via Canon Camera Connect typically fall into a small set of common categories. Work through the following checks in order.

Confirm Wi-Fi Is Enabled on the Camera

36. Press MENU → Setup tab → Wi-Fi settings.
37. Check the Wi-Fi setting at the top of the list. If it shows Disable, press SET, select Enable, and press SET to confirm. The camera's wireless radio must be enabled before any connection can be initiated.

Confirm Bluetooth Is Enabled

Canon Camera Connect uses Bluetooth for the initial discovery and pairing handshake. If Bluetooth is disabled on the camera, the app cannot detect the camera even if Wi-Fi is enabled.

38. Press MENU → Setup tab → Bluetooth settings → Bluetooth function → Enable.
39. Ensure Bluetooth is also enabled in your phone's settings — in the phone's Settings app, confirm Bluetooth is switched on.

Confirm the Camera Connect App Is Running

The Camera Connect app must be open and active on the phone for the connection to complete. If the app is closed or if the phone's operating system has put it into a suspended background state — which some battery optimisation settings on Android phones do aggressively — the connection attempt from the camera will not find a recipient.

40. On the phone, open the Canon Camera Connect app fully. Do not rely on a background instance — close and reopen it.
41. On Android phones with battery optimisation enabled: go to the phone's Settings → Battery → Battery optimisation and set Camera Connect to Not optimised. This prevents the phone from suspending the app when the screen is off.

Initiate the Connection from the Camera

42. On the Canon EOS R10, press MENU → Setup tab → Wi-Fi/Bluetooth connection.
43. Select Connect to smartphone and press SET.
44. If a previously registered device is listed, select it. The camera initiates the Bluetooth handshake and then establishes the Wi-Fi connection. Watch the camera screen — a connecting indicator appears while the handshake is in progress. The Camera Connect app should respond within a few seconds and show the connection confirmation.
45. If no registered device is listed (or if you are connecting for the first time), select Add device to connect to. The full pairing procedure covered in Section 15.1 will be required.

Reset Wi-Fi Settings and Re-Pair

If the camera and phone were previously paired but the connection consistently fails despite both devices having Wi-Fi and Bluetooth enabled and Camera Connect open, the pairing data may be corrupted. A clean reset and re-pairing resolves this in most cases.

46. Press MENU → Setup tab → Wi-Fi settings → Clear settings → OK. This removes all saved pairings, access point data, and network configurations from the camera.
47. On the phone, open Camera Connect, locate the previously paired EOS R10 in the app's camera list, and remove or forget it.
48. Repeat the full first-time pairing procedure from Section 15.1 to establish a fresh connection.

Note: *If the camera appears to connect (the connection indicator appears on the camera screen) but the Camera Connect app does not respond or shows a connection error, the issue may be on the phone side. Check that the phone has not blocked Camera Connect's local network access in the phone's privacy or app permissions settings — particularly on iPhone with iOS 14 or later, which requires explicit permission for apps to access the local network.*

18.7 Common Error Codes

When the Canon EOS R10 encounters a problem it cannot resolve automatically, it displays an error code on the LCD screen. The code consists of the letters Err followed by a two-digit number. Each code indicates a specific category of problem. Here is what each code means and what to do when you see it.

Err 01 — Communication between the camera and the attached lens has failed. The camera cannot exchange data with the lens — it cannot read the lens type, focal length, aperture information, or AF drive commands. This prevents autofocus from operating and may prevent the camera from taking a photograph entirely.

What to do: Remove the lens by pressing the lens release button and rotating it counter-clockwise. Examine the electrical contacts on both the rear of the lens and the inside of the camera mount — a row of small gold pins visible on the camera side and matching contact pads on the lens side. Clean the contacts on both lens and camera using a clean, dry cotton bud, wiping gently across the surface of each contact to remove any oxidation, dust, or skin oil. Reattach the lens, aligning the red dots and rotating clockwise until the lock clicks firmly. Power the camera off and back on. If Err 01 persists after cleaning and reattaching, try a different lens — if the error disappears with another lens, the contacts on the original lens may be damaged and require professional repair. If the error occurs with all lenses, the camera's mount contacts require service.

Err 02 — The SD card cannot be read. The camera has detected a card in the slot but is unable to access its file system or data.

What to do: Remove the SD card and reinsert it firmly — a card that is slightly out of position may not make full electrical contact. If the error persists after reinsertion, try a different SD card. If the second card works correctly, the original card's file system is corrupted or the card itself has failed. To attempt recovery of the original card, connect it to a computer using a card reader and run the operating system's disk repair utility — Disk Utility on Mac, or CHKDSK in Windows Command Prompt. If the computer cannot read the card, the card has failed and should be discarded. If the computer reads the card successfully, transfer your images and then reformat the card inside the camera (MENU → Setup tab → Format card) before relying on it again.

Err 06 — The camera attempted to communicate with a connected printer but the communication failed. This error only appears during direct printing from the camera via USB or via a PictBridge-compatible wireless connection.

What to do: Check that the printer is powered on, is not in an error state, and has paper and ink loaded. Confirm the USB cable connecting the camera to the printer is securely plugged into both devices. Turn the printer off and back on, then turn the camera off and back on. If the error persists, check the printer's own display for any specific error message. If the problem is a wireless connection to a PictBridge printer, disconnect and reconnect the wireless session from the camera's wireless settings menu. If none of these steps resolve it, the printer may not be fully compatible with direct camera printing — connect the camera to a computer instead and print from there.

Err 20 — An internal hardware malfunction has been detected. This is a mechanical or electrical fault within the camera body.

What to do: Remove the battery and leave the camera without power for at least one minute. This clears the temporary electrical state that may have triggered the error. Reinsert the battery and power the camera on. If the error does not reappear, continue using the camera and monitor for recurrence. If Err 20 appears again — particularly repeatedly or under specific circumstances such as during high-speed burst shooting — the camera requires professional diagnosis. Contact Canon's customer service or an authorised Canon service centre.

Err 30 — Shutter malfunction. The camera has detected an error in the shutter mechanism during a shooting operation.

What to do: Remove the battery, wait one minute, reinsert the battery, and attempt to take a photograph. If the error reappears immediately, the shutter mechanism has a fault that cannot be resolved by the user. Do not attempt to operate the shutter repeatedly if Err 30 keeps appearing — repeated triggering of a faulty shutter can worsen the mechanical failure. Bring the camera to an authorised Canon service centre. Shutter mechanism repair or replacement is a standard service operation.

Err 40 — Power source malfunction. The camera has detected an issue with the power supply.

What to do: Remove the battery and inspect it for any physical damage — cracks, swelling, leaking electrolyte, or damaged contact surfaces. If the battery appears physically damaged, do not reinsert it. Replace it with a known-good genuine Canon LP-E17. If the error occurs with multiple different batteries including a new one, the power management circuitry inside the camera has a fault that requires professional service.

Err 50 — Malfunction in the electronic control systems. An error has been detected in one of the camera's internal control circuits.

What to do: Remove the battery, wait one minute, and reinsert it. Power the camera on and test its normal functions. If Err 50 appears again or if the camera behaves abnormally after the reset, professional service is required. This error indicates an internal electronic fault that cannot be resolved through settings changes or user intervention.

Err 60 — Malfunction in the image sensor or image processor. An error has been detected in the sensor readout or image data processing pipeline.

What to do: Remove the battery, wait one minute, and reinsert it. If the error persists after resetting, the sensor or processor hardware has developed a fault. This requires professional service — bring the camera to an authorised Canon service centre for diagnosis.

Err 70 — Write error to the SD card or internal memory. The camera was unable to write image or video data to the card during recording.

What to do: Check the SD card. Ensure it is properly inserted and is not full. Try a faster card — if the card's write speed is insufficient for the current image format or burst rate, write errors can occur. Use a UHS Speed Class 3 (U3) or Video Speed Class 30 (V30) card for demanding operations. If the error occurs with a fast, known-good card, reformat the card inside the camera. If the error persists across multiple cards after formatting, the camera's card writing hardware may have a fault requiring service.

For any error code that reappears after the camera battery has been removed and reinserted, or any error that is accompanied by abnormal camera behaviour — buttons not responding, the shutter not firing, the LCD displaying garbled information, the camera making unusual sounds — do not attempt further field repairs. Power off the camera, remove the battery and card, and bring it to an authorised Canon service centre or contact Canon's customer support for your region. Continuing to operate a camera displaying persistent error codes risks worsening any underlying fault and may result in unrecoverable damage.

> **Note:** *Canon's authorised service centre network is listed on Canon's official website by country and region. For warranty service, bring the camera with the original purchase receipt or proof of purchase. For cameras still within the warranty period, repair of manufacturing defects is typically covered at no charge. Physical damage from drops, moisture, or user error is generally not covered by the standard warranty regardless of the camera's age.*

www.ingramcontent.com/pod-product-compliance
Lightning Source LLC
LaVergne TN
LVHW020539100826
845148LV00010B/1530

* 9 7 9 8 8 9 0 3 6 2 5 7 5 *